C000064583

World Cinema

1: POLAND

World Cinema series

General editor and publisher:
Matthew Stevens

The **World Cinema** series aims to give historical and appreciative surveys of the cinema of various countries. The first two titles are published as follows:

1: Poland
Frank Bren
ISBN 0 948911 46 8 (Hardback)

2: Sweden
Brian McIlroy
ISBN 0 948911 48 4 (Hardback)

Further titles are in preparation.

World Cinema

1: POLAND

Frank Bren

flicks books

British Library Cataloguing in Publication Data

Bren, Frank
 World cinema 1: Poland.
 – (World cinema, ISSN 0269-2600; 1)
 1. Moving-pictures – Poland – History
 I. Title II. Series
 791.43'09438 PN 1993.5.P55

 ISBN 0-948911-46-8

cover still shows Tadeusz Janczar and Teresa
Izewska from Andrzej Wajda's *Kanal/They
Loved Life* (1957).

cover design: Barry Walsh

First published in 1986 by
Flicks Books
9-11 Kensington High Street
London W8 5NP

Phototypset in 10 on 11 point Palatino by
Thomas/Weintroub Associates
Printed and bound in Great Britain by
the Bath Press

Contents

Introduction

When originally commissioned to write a history of Poland's cinema, I had a general passion for movies, some of them sub-titled, a few of them Polish. This book is the result of detective work: viewing features and shorts, and interviewing a span of directors, actors and actresses, technicians, writers and theoreticians, in and out of Poland. Oddly, no British or American publisher has produced a history of Polish film. There are some English translations – for example, Fuksiewicz's book: see bibliography – which are good primers but they are brief and skirt over important areas, such as the pre-war industry. There are studies on directors such as Wajda and compendiums on Eastern European cinema, but no whole book.

So why is an Australian actor/writer investigating Polish movies? Often in conversational midstream I was hit with "How come *you're* writing this book?" to which I could only hold up my accreditation and mutter "detective" or "*someone's* got to do it". My contact with Poland began in 1973 with a visit to Cracow's international film festival, following an earlier enthusiasm for the stories of Slawomir Mrozek, two of whose translated plays I had staged in Melbourne. As a first impression there could be no more beautiful city than Cracow and it inspired rapid return visits to Poland, each one enlarging a circle of friends.

Large parts of this book deal with films which were impossible to see – particularly from the Yiddish and pre-war cinema. I thank Stefan Themerson, an avant-garde film maker from Warsaw, for initiating my long trail of contacts and sources, and *L'Avant Scène du Cinéma* for their wonderful "pamphlet", issued in November 1983, letting me know that Themerson still lives in London.

In a book of this size some names and films will be missing but there comes a stage where you either produce a directory or go for a much larger work such as the Finnish *Maisema Taistelun Jaikeen*, a 365-page book on *contemporary* Polish cinema published in 1980 by the late Markku Tuuli, said to have been "a walking encyclopaedia of old and new Polish cinema". Often, a written chronicle is the only remains of a particular film, out of all those huge resources that went into its construction. Stanislaw Wohl vividly reminds us that his entire life's work, negatives and all, went up in smoke with "the first German shell from the West" at the beginning of the Occupation in 1939.

Polish names have been anglicised, with accents omitted. For example Łódź is Lodz and pronounced 'Woodzh'. Thus the pun, 'Hollywoodzh', loses something as 'HollyLodz'. In Polish accented letters are *different* letters of the alphabet; the language has more than twenty-six characters. In the text, therefore, 'ż' is merged with 'z', 'ą' with 'a', 'ł' with 'l', and so on. For errors beyond this shorthand, my apologies.

There is no such pill to make the profusion of -owski's, -ewska's, -icki's and -owicz's any simpler to memorize, or swallow. (Wajda was wise in choosing parents with a catchy name.) Annie Daubenton, in her book, *La Pologne: un pays dans la tête*, cut up interviews with seventeen prominent Poles. She had a chart of their names and descriptions for ready reference in case readers attri-buted statements by Andrzejewski to Kloczowski, or to Strzelecki, or vice versa. Such an operation is impossible here.

Frank Bren
August 1986

Acknowledgements

I have many people to thank and the following have my deepest gratitude.

TRANSLATION AND INTERPRETATION

The assistance of translators and interpreters has been crucial:

In England

- Lucyna Zajcer-Zacharska for translations of interviews with actors and with Stanislaw Bareja.
- Aleksander Nowak for a whole range of translations, including extracts from *The Tenth Muse* and tributes to Cybulski, and especially for reading the complete text for any inaccuracies in the spelling of Polish names.

In Poland

- Maria Malinowska for *weeks* of interpretation and translation
- Maria Zurawska-Denus for translating and interpreting interviews with Andrzej Wajda and Zbigniew Zapasiewicz
- Margaret Grabinska
- Joanna Schoen (Yiddish cinema)
- Jolante Szawiel

INTERVIEWS AND GUIDANCE

Lindsay Anderson, Stanislaw Bareja, Jerzy Bereda, Walerian Borowczyk, Jerzy Bossak, Ernest Bryll, Ryszard Bugajski, Leslie Caron, Ewa Dalkowska, Feliks Falk, Maciej Falkowski, Agnieszka Holland, Krystyna Janda, Krzysztof Kieslowski, Miroslaw Kijowicz, Andrzej Klimowski, Krzysztof Klopotowski, Henryk Kluba, Maja Komorowska, Antoni Krauze, Jerzy Kucia, Jan Lenica, Marcel Lozinski, Juliusz Machulski, Wojciech Marczewski, Andrzej Mellin, Boleslaw Michalek, Tadek and Bozena Palka, Jacek Petrycki, Radoslaw Piwowarski, Marek Piwowski, Tomasz Pobog-Malinowski, Roman Polanski, Wieslaw Saniewski, Tadek Sobolowski, Witold Stok, Jerzy Stuhr, Boleslaw Sulik, Grazyna Szapolowska, Daniel Szczechura, Piotr Szulkin, Jerzy Toeplitz, Andrzej Wajda, Danny Webb, Andrzej Werner, Janusz Wisniewski, Stanislaw Wohl; Krzysztof Zanussi, Janusz Zaorski, Zbigniew Zapasiewicz.

Nothing was possible without the assistance of Film Polski, particularly Grazyna Ramatowska who generously arranged an avalanche of screenings for me on two sites and a supply of extraordinary posters and most of the stills that illustrate this book. Special thanks should go to Jerzy Bereda, Secretary of the Film Makers' Association, who gave me plenty of his well-booked time and numerous contacts and addresses, as well as arranging my visit to the 1985 Gdansk Feature Film Festival. Thanks also to the animation studios at Se-Ma-For in Lodz and in Cracow, the Filmoteka in Warsaw for archive information and photographs, the Documentary Film Studio in Warsaw, the Lodz Studios, Falkowski and others from the Irzykowski Studio, the 1985 Gdansk Feature Film Festival organisation, Henryk Zietek at the Polish Cultural Institute in London, Phil Casoar in Paris and Hugh Gordon Ltd.

in memory of Margaret Grabińska (née Targowska)

1 : Zero, the beginning, no studio

Poland: a brief history

"The action takes place in Poland... that is to say, Nowhere." (*Ubu Roi*: Alfred Jarry).

The target of Jarry's black 'Polish joke' was a nation which was just a state of mind and which in 1795 had vanished into Prussian, Russian and Austrian zones under the rites of the Third Partition.

Not only was 'Poland' non-existent but the most brilliant and original phase of her culture, from 1831 to 1863, emanated from a community in France. Between two abortive insurrections against Moscow, emigres in Paris produced a body of writing that was Shakesperian in quality and scope. They were also active in the struggle for the freedom of their country: of particular note are Adam Mickiewicz, Juliusz Slowacki and Zygmunt Krasinski. Their plays and poems and Frederic Chopin's music were appeals to Poles of current and future generations.

The effects of this branch of Romanticism led to the "January Uprising" and a guerilla war against Russia during 1863/64, drawing patriots from all the partitioned zones. The underground 'dictator', Romauld Traugutt, was captured in Warsaw and then publicly hanged, effectively stalling insurrectionary activity for the next forty years.

Throughout the 19h century, the tone of culture, and especially literature, went from rebellious Romanticism to patient 'Positivism' (ie working for *attainable* gains, readying the nation for power when the time was right. The *constant element* of culture was the maintenance of national identity, which is normally achieved by a State or by the defined outlines of a map. The identity of Poland was sustained by the poems of the Romantics and by Henryk Sienkiewicz's popular historical novels, with their reminders of an aspiring past.

By 1905 hopes for restoring the state were consciously linked to the inevitable Great War (1914-1918). Though it forced Poles into opposing camps (and fratricide) their nation was finally disgorged from the guts of a defeated Germany, a Russia in civil war and an Austrian empire in ruins. She reappeared on the map, legally supported by the Versailles Treaty and by an artist who became her first prime minister: the celebrated pianist-statesman, Ignacy Paderewski.

The 'Polish Film School' (roughly 1956-1961) defines the Golden Age of Polish cinema which not only produced its finest movies but also provided a distanced view of that vile parody of the Partitions: World War Two. The 'Polish Film School' and the 'Cinema of Moral Anxiety' (1976-1981) describe the two homogeneous 'movements' of the Polish cinema though such waves are partly illusory and are usually defined by outsider critics and historians. The 'Polish School' flourished when in 1956, a radical change in administration returned decision-making to the artists. The 'Polish Film School' is dispersed throughout various chapters of this book. The films and the characters of its two giants, the Andrzej's, Munk and Wajda, could not, for example, be welded into a thematic Siamese twin. The School brackets a fertile five years in the history of Polish film. Its concerns are mainly the war of 1939-45. Wajda's *Lotna* looks at the September Campaign and the fate of a white horse which was not just a symbol of freedom but a major form of military locomotion pitted against German tanks, twenty years on from the nation's rebirth – a tragedy that is obliquely expressed in Jerzy Kucia's wonderful cartoon, *Refleksy*.

Lights Out Over Europe

Herbert Kline, the American

documentarist, had gone to London in August 1939 with an assignment to film the expected attack on the 'Polish Corridor' (Gdansk, Pomerania). President Roosevelt advised his ambassador in Warsaw to offer every assistance to Kline, and *Lights Out Over Europe* was the result - the only filmed record of the invasion and proof against Hitler's lie that the Poles had attacked first. Kline's crew was in the thick of the first invasion, freezing flat along with the soldiers under the first German air bombardments and strafing. Two Polish cameramen were killed but most of the team, including cameraman Douglas Slocombe, escaped at considerable risk through Riga in Latvia. Author James Hilton collaborated with Kline on the final script and Fredric March narrated this acclaimed and widely distributed *first film document* of World War Two.

On September 18 the country was pincered by a second attack: the Soviet army moved in from the east, in spite of a non-aggression pact, and once again the country was partitioned by its two traditional enemies.

In the inter-war years the film making world regarded Polish cinema as a backwater that produced inept, technically poor imitations of the worst Hollywood plots, with local variations. At the start of the war, Poland became a two-fold prisoner-of-war camp at the hands of both Hitler and Stalin. The national cinema was wiped out. Most of the film makers were dispersed in Russia, France or England but some remained and even survived the nightmare. Antoni Bohdziewicz, who would later found the Film Institute at Cracow (the kernel of the Lodz Film School) survived in Warsaw where he ran an underground teach-in for all those interested in film. Together with his colleagues he shot scenes of the Occupation and the notorious Warsaw Uprising – footage that was to be used in countless post-war films and as evidence in war crime trials. Film makers, with rare exceptions, refused to collaborate with the Nazis for there *was* an industry as such. Theatres and cinemas were powerful channels of Nazi propaganda but, as a whole, the locals boycotted them.

That Polish cinema burst upon the world with so few films and so many prizes between 1946 and 1950 is the result of decisions taken in 1945 when practically nothing existed in terms of equipment, cinema halls or old Polish movies.

Stanislaw Wohl

"I made many, many films, a lot of shorts – sixty or seventy, I've lost count," said Wohl who acted as cameraman on films by colleagues from the Co-operative of Film Authors, formed in 1937. "We started feature film production with a film whose title was *Strachy*. 'Strach' is 'fear' and 'strachy' is 'fears' plural. It was a success and we started to make more feature films but the war started in 1939. I took all the prints or negatives of picture and sound out of the laboratories where they were stored and put all of that in my apartment to preserve them...it was nitrate you know...and the first shell, coming from the west of Warsaw (the windows were facing west) fell in my apartment, and the whole lot exploded, like a bomb...I was stupid enough to do such a thing."

Stanislaw Wohl scowled at the memory of his (then) life's work going up in flames. He was twenty-seven, a vigorous director-cameraman. Wohl recalled: "At the end of 1939 I went to Russia; I worked there in the cinema and had the opportunity to know such people as Pudovkin, Dovshenko, Eisenstein and many others. In 1941, when the war started with the Germans, I was evacuated with the studio to

Turkmeniya . . . that's 'town of love'. From May 1943 I went to the Polish Army and was a war correspondent – with a camera – at the front, all the way from Russia to Berlin."

In June 1945 only two hundred cinemas were still intact out of approximately eight hundred before the war. There were no studios left and practically no technical equipment. To make matters worse, there was a shortage of trained personnel; many had been killed during the war. In such a condition of chaos the Polish government began to rebuild the film industry.

Film Polski

Fortunately there was a well-known dictum of Lenin's – that cinema is the most important of all arts – which aided the task of Film Polski in its mandate as a mono-producer. Film was tailor-made as a propaganda tool – after all the state was footing the bills – but the first features had the best of both worlds: a hundred per cent subsidy and remarkable individuality. Furthermore, the films were identifiably 'Polish' in gaining their wide appeal. Film Polski was set up in November 1945, administered by film makers and with Aleksander Ford at its helm. It embraced every section of the trade, including the manufacture of raw stock as well as scientific research. The government made an appeal to anyone with technical expertise and qualifications

By the end of 1945 it was reported that 235 halls had been constructed and a laboratory was opening in Warsaw with the "most modern multiplex Debrie equipment". Lodz, relatively intact and close to Warsaw, was a logical site for the first new studios and a system of payment by artistic results was worked out for stars and technicians in the newly-born industry. The first feature had yet to be made.

Whereas the pre-war industry was miraculously sustained by entrepreneurs who rarely outlasted two or three films, the new, one-and-only producer, backed by the will of the state, would rapidly erect far more cinemas than existed before the war. There were foreign films to fill these halls but for local production a technical base was needed. Wohl was asked quite simply to equip a national industry:

"After the war I went to Berlin and a task was given to me to gather as much equipment as possible. All the big studios were already occupied by Soviet troops. So I took a telephone book of Berlin and found all the small film companies. I had a car and a Studebaker truck and I went from one place to another and found here a camera, there a cutting table, here something else . . . so I brought back to Poland a lot of equipment – calculated at around two million pre-war dollars. I had some luck . . . by accident I found a warehouse of film and photography belonging to the Luftwaffe . . . and I took from this store thirteen new Arriflexes – brand new! – two Schlechter cameras, two Askania cameras and magnetophones and much other equipment. On the whole I brought back everything that was needed because in Poland there was only one developing machine which was transported from Warsaw to Cracow, and which I found in Cracow. Otherwise, there was practically nothing.

"I made an arrangement with an American film officer in Berlin – he gave me permission to go into the American occupation zone and look for equipment there. I had to give him 50% of everything I found . . . of course I didn't give him anything. I brought a lot of things from the American zone because I knew some Germans who, for a bottle of vodka or a little piece of bacon, gave me all of the addresses where equipment was buried undergound. Yes, I found cameras, lenses, everything you want! In 1946 our cinematography was ready to produce feature films, documentary films, everything!"

Jerzy Bossak

Some intuitive decisions were made. After the practical need for equipment was the impulse, says Jerzy Bossak, to make documentaries "about the present time, 1944/45, how it was, the Polish situation, and to mobilize the nation to start reconstruction, since everything was destroyed. The second thing was to organize the film school because for a state without experts, without a good tradition in film, it was necessary. The third was how to organize a partnership between the producers and film makers. The partnership in capitalism is a normal one: as a film maker you are looking for a producer and you want to propose a project which is good to make as a film and which will make you a lot of money. That is the normal way. It is not the same in Socialism; you must find another direction. A 'normal' way is to have the idea, to make a film which would be important from your point of view, for your political leaning. This is the primitive way. In my opinion it was necessary to organize the milieu, the film group, the film makers . . . it was the germ of the idea to create film units. A film unit is something like a theatre . . . a group of film makers having confidence in the chief, the artistic supervisor, and him having confidence in the younger film makers. They are organized something like a theatre . . . And it was for me the best way – to be a partner of the state, of the producer."

Lenin

Jerzy Toeplitz commented on the opening years and on Lenin's belief in film as a powerful art: "Certainly at the beginning it was very difficult but there was a lot of enthusiasm and goodwill – help certainly from the government which considered the film situation very important. Lenin's formula that film is the most important of all the arts probably had a very beneficial effect. He was especially interested in the educational aspects and the newsreel but I doubt - this is my personal opinion – whether he was really speaking of the *art* of the cinema. In any case he disliked Majakowski; he wasn't a great friend of all the new trends, the experimental art, and he was certainly never aware of the possibilities of the cinema art . . . but still, this quote remains and is a great help in all Eastern countries to the film makers because when we are being criticised and are told – you cannot spend so much money on film – we always say: 'Well . . . remember what Lenin said' (*laughs*)."

Early inventions

As with many nations, Poland produced her share of inventors who were keen to animate the new art of photography. Most have been forgotten or swamped by the worldwide dominance of Edison and the Lumière brothers, but they have a place in the history of Polish film.

Piotr Lebiedzinski

The beginnings of Polish cinema – the breakthrough in animating photography – can be dated at around 1893. An engineer, Piotr Lebiedzinski, belonged to a young generation of Warsaw photographers. He became widely known in international journals as a designer and producer of all sorts of photographic equipment, principally for paper of a high quality. Lebiedzinski was actively interested in all 'problems' relating to photography and in 1893 he showed off his own 'solution' to the puzzle of illusory movement.

In constructing his apparatus – a combined camera and projector – he rejected celluloid film as at that time it gave poor results: under action of the chemical bath, the film degenerated and twisted. During projection all the emulsion faults were magnified on-screen: these defects naturally disqualified celluloid film for Lebiedzinski.

His 'cinematograph' – a word rather owned by the Lumières – was in two parts: one for taking shots and the other for projection. The first comprised a magazine for loading a hundred plates, each encased in metal. On each plate were five successive shots, and so each magazine allowed for five hundred shots. Since the shooting rate was fourteen shots per second, a scene lasted just half a minute. But by loading the magazine with cassettes which contained more plates, in theory one could shoot indefinitely. The plate was displaced five times in front of the lens during one third of a second and, after exposing all of its sections, fell to the back of the apparatus with the aid of a special device.

The projection part had two lenses and the transparent images passed alternately, first by the left, then by the right. The lenses opened successively with the help of a blinking disc, rotating automatically. According to contemporary witnesses, the use of a double lens completely eliminated the 'flickers'.

Naturally the machine had its drawbacks: the use of plates instead of film was a fundamental mistake. They added enormously to the weight of an already heavy machine and often broke when crashing into the storage part at the back: it was not for slim cameramen! To shoot, the handle was cranked with great effort. As for the projector, the problem was having to adjust both lenses to direct them to the very same point – otherwise even a misalignment of 1/15th of a millimetre gave a defective image.

Josef Poplawski

One of Lebiedzinski's collaborators, Josef Poplawski, built an 'amateur' machine of a different type called a 'universal zooscope'. It looked like an ordinary 18 x 24cm camera but Poplawski installed a very luminous, microscopic lens which gave results good enough for a commercial studio. The unusual, rounded glass plate had on its circumference three series each of ninety-six shots. Fifteen 1 x 1.75cm shots were taken every second. They were, according to one, "so clear and plastic that all who saw them were full of admiration". Again, one cranked a handle to shoot. After developing the image in a special tank, it was projected with light from a bright petrol lamp. Its size was limited by the qualities of the emulsion on the plates and the maximum image size was roughly one metre^2.

These two early devices never went beyond the laboratory stage. Lebiedzinski cursed his backers for refusing that 'little extra' to exploit the machines commercially. Nevertheless, he was frequently called upon as a technical consultant when Polish cinema took its first tentative steps. He directed some essays in trick film in 1901 using the rescue service as his subject; but filming – or cinematography – was always the secondary interest. Finally, in 1919, Lebiedzinski collaborated on making a special projector for use in schools.

Proszynski's pleograph

Another inventor who was associated with Lebiedzinski came up with a better apparatus. Kazimierz Proszynski (1875-1945) was inspired by a photographic demonstration in 1891 to tackle 'animated pictures' and cinematography. His recollection is a clear picture of the 'idea' of cinematography flashing worldwide through the brains of those engaged in optics or photography:

"It struck me right away that one could use a light strip of celluloid. It also meant finding a device to move the strip rapidly, without damage. I developed a system of claws and teeth which, moving carefully, inserted themselves in holes in the strip and moved it rapidly forward. The mechanism was the result of mounting tiny levers and handles working without friction or shock. That was the fundamental based of the 'pleograph'". The machine combined a single lens camera and a double lens projector. Proszynski was no dreamer: "an idea is not yet an invention. A complete elaboration from detailed drawings is a step in the right direction, but only the building – not of a single model but many – will permit the inventor and his team to tell themselves that here is something worthy of the name invention".

Proszynski completed his studies in engineering at the Liège Polytechnic and in 1895-86 he applied his energies to the development of a commercial 'dispatcher' which wrapped and addressed newspapers. The first model of his pleograph appeared, but with his energies stretched on other projects, the first working model left much to be desired. When the pleograph went back to the drawing-board, along came two other machines by Lumière and Edison.

Actually getting his hands on the celluloid strips presented a major problem for Proszynski. Max and Emil Skladanowsky, the 'German Lumières', prepared their own strips because Eastman sold them only in lots of 1000 km minimum length. There is no evidence that Proszynski solved this problem at the time of his first model pleograph which was certainly not commercially promoted.

Animated photographs

The first public screenings of animated photographs began as late as the second half of 1896 when various entrepreneurs organised nationwide tours with ticket-entry screenings. They used a mixture of apparatus. Earlier in the year the Warsaw press ran news items on the cinematograph, date-lined Vienna and Berlin. The newspaper *Kuryer Warszawski* commented: "the cinematograph that the French took from an idea of Edison's . . . made them 400 or 500 roubles a day". Edison's apparatus had already been on display during the winter of 1895/96 at two locations in Warsaw.

In July 1896 the Theatre of Animated Photographs screened its movies at the Proprietors' Circle, 65 Krakowskie Przedmiescie, then (as today) one of the busiest thoroughfares in Warsaw. The clips comprised some busy street scenes, a duel, cats at play and firemen saving people from a burning house. One critic gave it a "so what?" shrug and bemoaned the quality of projection. A different demonstration took place in Lwow, probably of an Edison apparatus; one writer graphically sketched the performance:

"The public sits on benches facing the screen . . . the light goes down. On-screen a circular image appears – very indistinct through enlargement . . . then all at once, it moves, it flickers and blinks. And with that all the fissures, ruptures, specks and bubbles, which occur during the preparation of the strip (on which the negatives of all images were fixed), appear ten times bigger on the screen, so that the tableau does not present an impression of scenes from life but a debilitating hallucination of a madman . . . Furthermore, everything is so imprecise that yesterday we saw spectators totally misreading the action.

They took 'boxers' to be 'fencers'; an 'ocean liner' for 'the boulevards'; a scene in the lunatic asylum for Scottish dancing."

Finally the Lumière apparatus arrived. It was the real cinematograph, with a repertoire of shorts, including the famous *Arrival of a Train* and *The Waterer Watered*. Several demonstrations took place from November 1896 at the Municipal Theatre in Cracow. There were still complaints about the projection but the films attracted a big public. Spectators were reportedly astonished by the foaming waves crashing against rocks on a screen stretched across the curtains.

The coincident Lumière invention put paid to Proszynski's form of success. It edged his activities and his name into near oblivion. However, he had improved and patented the pleograph and with his collaborator, Puszkin, shot some fifteen films over 1902 and 1903 – mostly short comedies which were a big success with the public. Film production was, however, a side-line and the Pleograph company later dissolved. The machine became a museum piece, but the quality of the films it produced more than matched those of the 'true cinematograph'. Moreover, these films mark the first commercial film production in Poland.

Boleslaw Matuszewski

The early activities of Boleslaw Matuszewski remain a little unclear. His pioneering work in two areas of cinematography, however, is confirmed: medical films and film archives. He lived for a time in Paris where he picked up considerable skill as a photographer. He is thought to have worked as an operator for the Lumières since three of his own films coincided with those produced by them in 1896/97. They appear in the Lumière catalogue: the coronation of Czar Nicholas

II in 1896; the jubilee of Queen Victoria and the visit by President Faure of France to St. Petersburg – both of the latter in 1897. In this year also, Matuszewski filmed two official visits by the Czar – taking advantage of a six-month appointment as photographer to the Czar's court.

Matuszewski and his brother had opened a photographic shop at 111 Marszalkowska in Warsaw and as soon as he severed contact with the Lumières he began to concentrate on cinematography – not just as an operator, but also in screenings, publicity and the formulation of theory. In 1898, Matuszewski on his own initiative pioneered medical cinematography, filming (under available lighting) important operations in St. Petersburg and Warsaw: leg amputations, complicated childbirths and epileptic fits. However, his projection equipment continued to be unstable and it was impossible to appreciate the results. He went to Paris to seek help; some technicians produced a projector which gave a fixity to the image and Matuszewski was encouraged to write to several physicians. He finally in April and May 1898 persuaded French doctors and surgeons to let him film their cases; much of the genesis of medical cinematography is contained in these films.

A young surgeon then employed cinematographer Clement Maurice to film his operations. The publicity for Maurice's work regrettably overshadowed his debt to Matuszewski who returned to Warsaw to screen his own assorted medical material. *The Morning Courier (Kuryer Poranny)* wrote that if cinematography was not so expensive, it could play an important role in teaching whereby students could see operations by celebrated surgeons.

In a celebrated case in France, Matuszewski increased his fame. After President Faure's stay in St Petersburg in

1897 Prince Bismarck slandered the French premier by saying that he had betrayed his ignorance of military protocol. In bestowing honours on the regiment of Cossacks on parade the president was accused of having raised his hand instead of removing his hat. Matuszewski projected his film of President Faure's trip at the invitation of the Elysée Palace. The screening in January 1898 proved that the President had adhered strictly to the ceremonial. The screening was repeated about sixty times for soldiers of the Parisian garrison and safeguarded the honour of the President.

Matuszewski worked freely between Paris and Warsaw and made numerous short films depicting all classes of Polish society. He made a notable film on a horse-racing event at the Mokotow Field in Warsaw – a subject that offered an intelligent operator enormous opportunities of showing the city population. It was said that the aristocracy, officers and Russian bourgeoisie arranged a generous display of their mistresses to provoke their rivals' envy. The film was described, but not titled as 'Horses, Muscovites and Tarts', and *Tygodnik Ilustrowany (Illustrated Weekly)* wrote that "Mr Matuszewski has a surprise in store for us ethnographers; he sends his specialists around the country and photographs balls, manners and customs of our people".

Film archives

In Paris in March 1898 Matuszewski was the first to outline his beliefs in the need for film archives. In a French language brochure, *La Nouvelle Source de l'Histoire*, he called for the creation of a cinemathèque in Paris and a cinema museum to which films of historical interest would be sent from all over the world. Though he was aware that sudden events could not always be recorded, their symptoms could be by the aware cinematographer. While also praising the infallibility of the camera, he predicted the disquieting character of the new breed of cameramen and women:

"The cinematic photographer is indiscreet by profession, on the lookout for any occasion; his instinct will allow him to sniff out (very often) the whereabouts of some happening which will become a historical cause; there will be more a case for preventing excessive zeal than deploring his timidity. By and by the natural curiosity of the human spirit and the lure of gain – two sentiments which are natural allies – will make him more inventive, more daring . . . he will leave no stone unturned, without authorisation, to weave his way into others' affairs and will know more often than not how to find the occasions and places which will prove to be tomorrow's history . . ."

Together with his Warsaw colleagues, Lebiedzinski and Proszynski, Matuszewski developed Polish cinema – albeit somewhat restrictedly – parallel to the development of film in Western Europe. These men disappeared from view and their position and efforts took some decades to be recognised and restored to public knowledge within the history of world cinema. Jerzy Toeplitz – a historian and ex-president of the International Federation of Film Archives – lays great stress on film archives as repositories of human experience:

"each country claims to have the inventor of cinema, which is partly true and untrue . . . Matuszewski, on the contrary, is considered now the father of the film archive. And it was really a kind of tremendous discovery in those days to write that it's the film history – as a historical document – that must be preserved – two years after the first projections of Lumière!"

2 : The silent and inter-war cinema

Aleksander Hertz's Sezonowa mitosc

The first 'Polish' film is acknowledged to be the short feature, *Anthony in the Capital (Antos po raz Pierwszy w Warszawie)*, directed by cameraman Jozef Meyer of Pathé in 1908. It should be remembered that visiting French film makers had excited the interest of the Warsaw population with documentaries about life in the city. Aleksander Hertz was eager to become the Polish Pathé and in 1914, when Sfinks absorbed Kosmofilm, he began to dominate the scene. An authentic national cinema started to grow while nationhood was still a dream.

Hertz was joined by the directors Edward Puchalski and Ryszard Ordynski.

Ordynski was a consummate man of the theatre and an assistant to the great Max Reinhardt in Berlin. Hertz's *Pani Walewska* appeared in 1913 starring Stefan Jaracz and Maria Bulebianka. In the same year Puchalski adapted *Halka*, Moniuszko's classic Polish opera; it was to be one of several films remade in the coming decades. Sienkiewicz's book *The Deluge (Potop)* had its first screen adaptation in 1915 under the direction of Tchardynine. It was shot partly in Poland but the Czarist censors in Warsaw considered it dangerously patriotic; oddly, it had to be finished in Russia. The film stars Jaracz, Bulebianka and Aleksander Zelwerowicz.

Pola Negri

In 1914, a stage dancer and actress, Apolonia Chalupiec, was discovered by Hertz and became Poland's first real film star. Apolonia or 'Pola' adopted the surname Negri from her favourite Italian poetess, Ada Negri. When told that 'Negri' didn't sound Polish, she replied: "Does 'Bernhardt' sound French?" There are differing accounts of her early life, including the year of her birth and her parentage – she was supposedly the daughter of a gypsy violinist who died exiled in Siberia. Her autobiographical book *Memoirs of a Star*, describes her first encounter with Hertz and his offering her the star role in *Slave of Sin/Love and Passion* (*Niewolnica Zmyslow*, 1914) which was an enormous success and marked her screen début. (One filmography co-credits Negri and Jan Pawlowski with the direction.)

In accordance with her contract Negri made seven further films for Sfinks, all in quick succession and all directed by Hertz: *Beast* (*Bestia*, 1915); *Yellow Passport* (*Zolty Paszport*, 1915 – remade two years later in Germany as *Yellow Ticket*); *Room No. 13* (*Pokoj Nr. 13*, 1915); *Arabella* (1916); *His Last Deed* (*Jego Ostatni Czyn*, 1916); *Students* (*Studenci*, 1916) and *Wife* (*Zona*, 1916) Negri recalls *Yellow Passport* as her final film in Poland before leaving for a career in Berlin in 1917 – initially at Reinhardt's invitation. Whatever the chronology, the film is notable for evoking life in the Warsaw ghetto. The film is about a young Jewish student (Negri) whose yellow card is her 'passport' to and from her home and school; the film combines a love-story with a picture of Czarist oppression.

A Nazi link

In *Memoirs of a Star* Negri also recalls meeting Hermann Goering at a party in

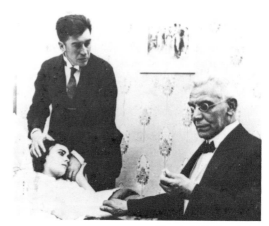

Hertz's 1916 film, Wife

Berlin during her film stint there in the 1930s. Goering insidiously praised her 'convincing' portrait of a Jewess in *Yellow Passport*; she was soon banned from working in Berlin by Goebbels because of her 'non-Aryanism'. She was forced to produce documents to prove otherwise and was reinstated on Hitler's personal intervention – the cause of some gutter-press gossip about an affair between them.

The war years

In 1914 Warsaw was ruled by the Russians but was soon occupied by the Germans; there were few moral traumas regarding collaboration since Poles were drafted into fighting both oppressors! In the middle of this great European war, with Pole fighting Pole, the cinema flourished.

Richard Ordynski contributed *Kosciuszko* (*Kosciuszko Pod Raclawicami*, 1914), starring Edmund Rygier and Maria Jurandowna. Puchalski produced the trilogy *Antichrist/King Hero/Judas of the Crown* (*Antychryst/Krol Bohater/Judasz w Koronie*, 1914/15) and in 1915 the highly contemporary *Death of a Millionaire Aboard the Lusitania* (*Smierc Miliardera Amerykanskiego Na Luzytanii*), which dramatises the death of Vanderbilt on the great British ship (it was sunk by a German submarine in the same year).

Wiktor Bieganski

In 1916 a talented actor named Wiktor Bieganski made an impression with his production *The Secrets of the Warsaw Police (Ochrana Warszawska i tej Tajemnice)*. Excited by the new medium he apprenticed himself to the studios in Berlin and then returned to his base in Cracow, hoping to rival Hertz. Less prolific than the latter he nevertheless set up a few projects and during the 1920s was acknowledged for his inventive and more purely cinematic style. He was not tied to any one company and more or less made the films he wanted in his own individual way.

During these war years – as seen by the career of Negri – the industry won audiences and established a commercial base in addition to its group of stars. Following Negri there were Lya Mara (who also left for Berlin), Jozef Wegrzyn, Kazimierza Junosza-Stepowski, Halina Bruczowna and Aleksander Zelwerowicz. There was also Antoni Fertner who established himself as a popular comedian throughout the Russian Empire. One of the best of the war-year films was *The Czar's Favourite (Carska Faworyta)*, with Jozef Wegrzyn and Halina Ostoja, showing Czar Nicholas II's love-affair with the dancer, Mathilde Drzenska.

At the end of the war in 1918, production abruptly ceased but quickly resumed at the end of that year with the arrival of other directors such as Eugeniusz Modzelewski, Wladyslaw Lenczewski and Zygmunt Wesolowski.

Richard Boleslawski

With support from the new Polish state, production boomed to twenty-two features in the first year of independence, 1919. Warsaw became the film capital and well into the 1920s produced a blizzard of 'grudge' movies settling scores with their old oppressors, Czarist Russia. Typical titles were *The Criminals, For You, Poland, The Mystery of the Warsaw Citadel, Heroism of a Polish Boy Scout* and *Miracle of the Vistula (Cud Nad Wisla*, 1920) directed by thirty-one-year-old Boleslaw Srednicki, later to be famous as Richard Boleslawski.

Like the animator Wladyslaw Starewicz, Boleslawski's professional

Ryszard Boleslawski

formation was in Moscow where he directed for the Second Studio of the Moscow Art Theatre, then hailed as "the world's first playhouse". His book, *Acting: the first six lessons,* became a primer for young actors worldwide. Boleslawski's career in Poland was brief and amounted to two productions for the National Theatre of Warsaw and some short film comedies starring Antoni Fertner. He then went to Germany and was noted for a role in Carl Dreyer's film, *Malediction,* before emigrating to the United States and employment in Hollywood where he directed star-studded pot-boilers for MGM until his death in 1937. His *Rasputin,* produced by Irving Thalberg, united the three famous Barrymores for the only time on-screen.

From 1919 the state's chief priority lay in protecting its new frontiers and it narrowly averted a disaster in the Polish-Bolshevik war (1920). Its interest in the cinema rapidly declined except that it imposed taxes which took more than 40% of ticket revenue. Occasionally it would assist a project and offer resources – such as the army – but only for overtly patriotic films.

Early film criticism

Film journals were already popular in 1910 though they were mainly of an intimate gossip type. Serious criticism and writing rose to a high standard over the next decade and, in artistic circles at least, aroused an awareness of the special possibilities of the new art form. At the same time it underlined the shortcomings of the contemporary cinema in practice, particularly the adaptations of literature, such as *Pan Twardowski* by Bieganski in 1920, *The Peasants (Chlopi,* by later Nobel prize-winner, Wladyslaw Reymont) by Modzelewski in 1921, and the classic Mickiewicz poem, *Pan Tadeusz,* by

Ordynski in 1928. The latter was panned for its over-illustrative acting in the depiction of Pan Tadeusz, Pani Sophie and General Dabrowski.

Karol Irzykowski

Eminent literary critic and novelist Karol Irzykowski contributed many articles on the cinema from 1913, culminating in his book, *The Tenth Muse (Dziesiata Muza),* published in 1924. He recognized films as something more than photography with movement or an amusement arcade or a weak offshoot of any of the higher arts. He was particularly keen on the films of Chaplin and Paul Wegener and on the detective-thriller genre. Irzykowski defined cinema as 'the visible contact between man and matter'. Writing in the silent era he naturally emphasized optics and its ability to re-examine reality – the wildest gags of Chaplin did just that.

Irzykowski's ideas, which are discussed in chapter 11, penetrated the sound era too – in that they remained modern – and found resonance among a co-operative of young film makers who formed the Irzykowski studio in 1979. He was less concerned with the argument for social reality – the line later pushed by START – but he similarly aimed at encouraging a cinema of originality and quality. He ceased his flow of articles in 1925, disappointed by the consistently low standard and derivative nature of most of his country's movies.

Other theoretical works covering the general development of film art were contributed by Tadeusz Peiper and Leon Trystan in publications over the years 1924 to 1926. Trystan took the unusual step from critic to film maker and practised what he wrote in his feature, *The Revolt of Blood and Iron (Bunt Krwi i Zelaza,* 1927), with Halina Labiendzka – an adaptation of two works by the novelist Gustaw Danilowski. It was compared not unflatteringly by French critics to Abel Gance's *La Roue* and was one of the few works to date that avoided theatrical conventions in its staging and acting.

In the same year Trystan shot *Szamota's Mistress (Kochanka Szamota)*, starring Helena Makowska and Igo Sym. It confirmed his talent for interesting montage but from then on Trystan was sadly neglected by the commercial producers.

A typical 'patriotic' film was *Love Through Fire and Blood (Milosc Przez Ogien i Krew:* director uncredited) which featured, as characters, Marshal Pilsudski, General Haller and President of the National Council, Witos. But a 1928 production *The Commandant (Komendant)*, glorifying Pilsudski (played by Antoni Bekarski), was banned by the Marshal's entourage. This was two years after his coup d'état and the great soldier was now dictating behind a facade of ministers. But there were more films to come in homage to the man and his legionnaires.

Among the few anti-German grudge-movies one should note *The Caravan of Drzynala* about a hero from Poznan who, when hunted from his land by the Germans, survives among gypsies. Puchalski then made *Bartek the Victor (Bartek Zwyciezca),* adapted from Sienkiewicz. Conversely, a German, Franz Porton, was hired to direct the anti-Russian *Under the Yoke of the Tyrants (Pod Jarzmem Tyranow)* in the early 1920s. Immediately after the war there was a substantial import of German and Austrian movies as a by-product of old trade ties, but they were soon overshadowed by the Americans who eventually cornered two thirds of the Polish market.

Hertz and Sfinks

Hertz continued to foster stars and his greatest discovery was the actress Jadwiga Smosarska, who first shone in *The Shot (Strzal)* in 1922. She reached her peak in 1926 and remained the major screen actress of the 1930s. Others introduced by Hertz were the actors Mieczyslaw Frenkiel and Theodore Roland, the dancer Feliks Parnell, and the actresses Maria Malicka and Maria Chaveau. His company produced the country's most technically proficient films, aided in 1922 by the establishment of Falanga, the second of the three main film companies between the wars. Falanga continued to provide good studios and up-to-date equipment until 1939.

The Sfinks films unfortunately continued their reliance on melodrama and a certain theatricality. They were accused of trivialising and distorting the intentions of the writers whose books they frequently plundered.

A good idea of their style can be gleaned from the title, *When a Wife Cuckolds Her Husband (Kobieta Ktora Grzechu Pragnie)*, a 1927 film that introduced the opera-singer Kazimiera Niewiarowska in her first and only film; she was tragically burned alive later that year in the course of a

Lalnzy spojrzenia, 1922

theatre tour at Wilno. Hertz's sixtieth production was *Land of Promise (Ziema Obiecana)* from the book by Wladyslaw Reymont. Its background is a slice of the industrial revolution in Lodz which would be lavishly remade by Andrzej Wajda in the 1970s. Hertz had the assistance of Puchalski and Stanislaw Szebego as directors and the popular actress Jadwiga Smosarska as star but the film was a disappointment.

Hertz also produced two films from the novels of Gabriela Zapolska: *That Which Is Unspeakable (O Czym Sie Nie Mowi)* and *That Which Is Unthinkable (O Czym Sie Nie Mysli)*. The latter was described as a mediocre production in "bad taste", dealing with the struggle against VD and stars Maria Modzelewska with Igo Sym.

Bieganski

Wiktor Bieganski continued his productions in Cracow. Together with Hertz he strove for popular films but in a more cinematic way. Like everyone in Poland he shot movies on scanty capital: he turned out *The Idol (Bozyszcze)* in 1922 and went to the Tatra mountains south of Cracow to make *The Abyss of Repentance (Otchlan Pokuty)* in 1923. It was the first of his films to attract good reviews for its technique.

In 1925 he undertook his most ambitious project, *The Vampires of Warsaw (Wampiry Warszawa)*. The film underlined Bieganski's talent for direction and his rare sense of montage and rhythm. One of the

The Vampires of Warsaw, 1925

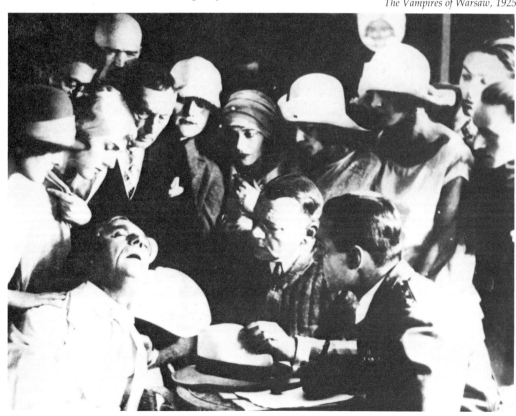

scenes is often cited as a daring narrative innovation: two drunken revellers – one of them actually dead and killed in the past by the other – huddle together in a long taxi ride under the curious gaze of the driver. The ex-assassin, who may or may not have recognised his victim (now a vampire) tries to free himself of his companion. This long sequence is expertly played by Lech Owron, who had a long and impressive career in the silent era, and Igo Sym, who had returned from the Viennese studios where he was under contract to Count Kollovrath.

Owron gives another superb portrait as the bandit Janosik in Bieganski's *The Young Eagle (Orle,* 1926) which also stars the aviator Boleslaw Orlinski, a hero of the Warsaw/Tokyo raid.

Smosarska

Smosarska continued to charm both critics and the public with her films, despite the clichéd plots and technical deficiencies. She appears in *The Tramway Stop (Tajemnica Przystanku Tramwajego,* 1922), *Iwonka* (1925), and *The Leper (Tredowata,* 1926), considered by some to be Hertz's best film and where Smosarska reached her peak. She continued winning good reviews well into the 1930s – from the *New York Times* amongst others. Sadly Hertz died in 1928 before realising a favourite project called *Prince Poniatowski.*

Leo Forbert

Hertz's main rival was the cameraman Leo Forbert who formed Leofilm in 1926, the only company besides Sfinks and Falanga to continue vigorously into the sound era.

Technically, Forbert's first efforts matched those of Sfinks and comprised two detective stories: *The Twilight Men* and *Son of Satan (Syn Szatana)* as well as two

Aleksander Hertz in his Sfinks studio

Jewish-theme films whose directors would be key figures in the Polish-Yiddish cinema of the 1930s: *The Oath/The Vow (Tkijes Khaf,* 1926) from Yiddish actor-director Sigmund Turkow and *One of the 36, (Jeden z 36/Der Lamedvovnik,* 1926), the début of Henryk Szaro. Chief cameraman for Leofilm was Seweryn Steinwerzel who directed his own comedy, *The Rivals (Rywale),* from a gag-filled scenario by caricaturist Henryk Tom. It is played with great panache by Antoni Fertner, Eugeniusz Bodo and Elna Gistedt. Szaro's much-praised *Red Clown (Czerwony Blazen,* 1926) like *One of the 36,* depicts the life of Jews in Poland before the Great War.

Hurricane

Shortly after Hertz's death there was a genuine international success and perhaps the best of the silent films – *Hurricane*

(*Huragan*, 1928) directed by Josef Lejtes. He later confirmed his remarkable début as the most consistent director of quality films between the wars.

Hurricane stars Zelwerowicz and newcomer Zbyszko Sawan and its visual compositions are based on the tableaux of Artur Grottger, the famous historical painter. A Polish/Austrian co-production with a screenplay by Jerzy Braun, its setting is the 1863 Uprising against the Czar. It avoids being simply anti-Russian and was a popular film in France where it was praised for its scenes of grandeur. Austria provided cameramen Hans Theier and Julius Mars and the art director Hans Rouc.

By 1928 companies in the United States were busy handling recorders and microphones and making silents obsolescent. But there was still a little time left in Europe and more still in Poland whose cinemas were painfully slow in converting to sound.

Outside Warsaw, apart from Bieganski little activity emerged in the commercial cinema. A Cracow company, Ornak, had an office by Wawel Castle but was noted only for one feature, *The Peasants* (*Chlopi*, 1921), from the book by Nobel laureate, Wladyslaw Reymont. In Lodz local

Przestepcy

theatre director Jozef Maszycki declared himself a producer but burned his fingers on a disastrous film called *The Evening Bells* (*Dzwony Wieczorne*), using actors from the Municipal Theatre. These aside, Lodz caricaturist Stanislaw Dobrzynski produced some notable animation.

Lejtes's next project deals with the 1920 Polono-Bolshevik war. Taken from the book of the same name, *One Day to the Day After Next* (*Z Dnia na Dzien*) by Frederic Goetel, it stars Irena Gawecka and Adam Brodzisz. Goetel's cinematic style of writing was naturally attractive for adaptors. Lejtes's film was praised for its bravura passages and established his position as one of the country's top directors. Goetel had already adapted the Ordynski version of Mickiewicz's poem, *Pan Tadeusz*.

Other débuts

Other important débuts were by Leon Buczkowski – whose film, *The Madmen* (*Szalency*), an epic about Pilsudski's legionnaires, stars Marian Czauski and Jerzy Kobusz – and by Michal Waszynski, the most prolific 30s director who shot the risqué *Cult of the Flesh* (*Kult Ciala*, 1929) from the book by Mieczyslaw Srokowski. He used foreign actors and once again the Austrian cameraman Hans Theier. The film won first prize at Nizza and could be called Poland's first sound film since a track was recorded on gramophone. However, there were no sound theatres in Poland at this time.

Henryk Szaro's next film was *The Strong Man* (*Mocny Czlowiek*, 1929) starring the Russian comedian Gregory Chmara, who was something of a disappointment. The photography by the Italian Giovanni Vitrotti, however, was outstanding and the story (about a talentless writer who steals a manuscript from a dying comrade) looked promising at least.

Jules Gardan

Szaro's assistant, Jules Gardan, showed promise with *The Dot Over The 'I'* (*Kropka nad 'I'*, 1928), followed by two high-class features: *Police Chief Tagueieff* (*Policmajster Tagiejew*, 1929), with a powerful performance by Samborski, and *The Beauty of Life* (*Uroda zycia*, 1930) from a well-known book by Zeromski. The work is considered faithful to the author's original and a remarkable film in its own right. It has first-rate performances by Adam Brodzisz, Eugeniusz Bodo, and Irena Dalma, an actress tragically killed some years later by a tram in Milan, just one day before starting work on a Polish production, *Ballerina*.

An offbeat début in the 1920s was by Count Ireneusz Plater Zyberk – an author-actor-director born without any arms. His one exploitation picture, *The Man Without Arms* (*Czlowiek bez Rak*), is an adventure yarn starring, naturally, himself.

Several other one-off projects on a variety of topics found their way onto the screens as adaptations or original ideas. For example, Michal Machwicz arranged his own finance in a Viennese co-production for a story called *The Man with a Soul of Azure* (*Czlowiek o Blekitnej Duszy*), starring Eugeniusz Bodo, Dolores Orsini and Zbyszko Sawan. Once again it involved Viennese cameraman Julius Mars and art director Hans Rouc.

Ford and Cekalski

Finally, there are two 'talkie' directors who began with silent shorts. Aleksander Ford made *At Dawn* (*Nad Ranem* 1929), *The Pulse of the Polish Manchester* (*Tetno Polskiego Manchesteru*) in 1930, and *Birth of a Paper* (*Narodziny Gazety*, 1930). His first feature, in the same year – *Mascot* – was a disappointment. Eugeniusz Cekalski, a film theoretician and instructor, made

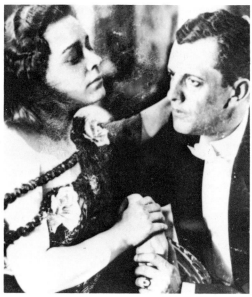

Melodie Duszy, 1918

several avant-garde shorts over 1929 and 1930, including *Gatekeeper No. 24* (*Droznik Nr. 24*) with the actor Stefan Jaracz, *The Making of a Film* (*Jak Powstaje Film*) and *Dawn, Day and Night in Warsaw* (*Swit, Dzien i Noc Warszawy*).

If this chapter is a catalogue of works now mainly forgotten, it also illustrates a diversity of ambitions unfortunately hampered by an absence of courageous investors and by a generally indifferent state.

But by the end of the 1920s there were a handful of directors who had discovered film language and who were prepared to tackle contemporary life as well as ambitious classics. Unfortunately sound interfered and wiped out the markets for the kind of film they had so painstakingly learned to produce. The technology switch coincided with a worldwide economic collapse which hit developing nations, such as Poland, particularly hard. It remained to see whether its rich theatrical tradition would be a positive advantage in the demand for the new 'talking pictures'.

3 : Yiddish cinema

Yiddish and Hebrew theatre flourished in Poland and Russia from the end of the 19th century and only just predates the mass migration of Jews to South Africa and the Americas in the 1880s. Actors, playwrights and a hunger for entertainment went with them. Large European cities maintained professional Jewish theatres – for example, the Vilna troupe (Wilno was part of Poland until 1945), the Warsaw Art Theatre and most famous of all, the Habimah troupe formed in Moscow in 1922, much under the influence of Stanislavsky. Many troupes were eventually established in New York.

The Sila company

These companies – and the family melodramas, musical comedies and mystical historical plays that formed their repertoire – were the roots of the Yiddish cinema which can be said to have begun in Poland with the Sila company, established in 1908. This was the year that Pathé's Jozef Meyer made *Anthony in the Capital*, "the first Polish film". Sila filmed Yiddish stage-productions in Warsaw, beginning with the Kaminski troupe, founded by Avram Izhak Kaminski. His wife, Ester Kaminska, was known throughout the empire as the 'Jewish Duse', a reputation earned by extensive touring throughout Russia and Poland. Their daughter, Ida Kaminska, would be nominated for the best actress Oscar in 1966 for her role in the Czech film, *The Shop on Main Street*.

Sila's first film was *The Cruel Father (Der Vilder Fater/Okrutny Ojciec*, 1911), directed by Aleksander Marten, with a screenplay credit to Jacob Gordin. Many of Gordin's plays would be filmed in this way. The cameraman was Stanislaw Sebel who directed Sila's next film. The company went bankrupt in 1912 and its activities were taken over by Kosmofilm, which

itself would be absorbed by Sfinks in 1914.

Sebel then directed, for Kosmofilm, all seven of its films made with the Kaminski troupe. These were in the Film d'Art tradition introduced by film makers from France – that of filming eminent stage-actors in classics. These silent films were important to scattered Jewish communities around the world to whom professional Jewish companies toured at best intermittently, at worst not at all. Even without sound, those filmed stage performances drew full houses night after night whenever they played in a large transplanted community. The Kaminski troupe made one last film, *His Wife's Husband (Zaja Wajbsman)*, in 1916 and it was the last Yiddish film for a decade.

In Poland some three and a half million Jews formed a handsome market but it was not until 1936, under the stimulus of a Lodz-born American, Joseph Green, that a series of Yiddish films began to be systematically made in Poland principally for the American market. Otherwise, in spite of repressions, Jewish culture had flourished. Before the Great War it had been unsafe to wander outside the tight little ghettoes and while the new Poland publicly declared equality for all, and barred public office to no-one, there were still problems. Several pogroms took place as a by-product of the Polono/Russian war in 1920/21 when the Jews' neutrality infuriated both sides.

In 1926 Ida Kaminska and her husband Sigmund Turkow formed the Yiddish Art Theatre of Warsaw. Turkow worked for the newly formed Leofilm which began with a trilogy of films on Jewish themes. He took over direction of the first, *The Vow (Tkijes Khaf)* in 1926. Seweryn Steinwurzel, cameraman on the film, then directed the second, *One of the 36 (Jeden z 36/Der Lamedvovnik)*, starring another Turkow, Jonas, who directed the third, *In the Polish Woods (w Lasach Polskich)*.

Judith Goldberg's wonderful study, *Laughter through Tears*, published in 1983, deals with Yiddish cinema worldwide, and is drawn from a rich variety of sources; the anecdotes, particularly about Joseph Green, make entertaining reading.

Joseph Green

Born in Lodz, Joseph Green arrived in the United States as an actor with the touring Vilna troupe. He remained in the States and had a bit-part career in films. He 'stars' in a film called *Joseph in the Land of Egypt*, an Italian silent redubbed with new and edited scenes. Turkow's silent version of *The Vow* was similarly released in the States as a 'talkie'.

When Green returned to Poland in the early 1930s he saw an opportunity to make quality productions on the best available equipment for about a quarter of its American cost.

Yiddle with his Fiddle

From 1936, Green spent half the year in Warsaw with his company Green-Film, and the other half in a rented space at the Paramount offices in New York – his company there was called Sphinx. He prepared his first film with a maximum budget of US $ 50 000 and persuaded Molly Picon, the American-Jewish comedienne, to star in the film which was given a spur-of-the-moment title: *Yiddle with his Fiddle* (*Yiddle mit'n Fiddle*, 1937). He then hired American composer Abe Ellstein to write the music. Green's collaborator was Jan Nowina-Przybilski who directed the technical side while Green worked with the actors. The classic mogul of Yiddish cinema, Green brought together Hollywood production know-how, American-Jewish stars and composers, and American publicity techniques.

Yiddle, a musical comedy, has Molly Picon dressed as a boy fiddler in a band of musicians who tour the country, playing at weddings and other events. She eventually falls in love with a man and is forced to unmask. Goldberg relates in her book that Norman Jewison studied *Yiddle* in preparation for his 1971 film of the Broadway hit, *Fiddler on the Roof* – itself an adaptation of short-stories by Sholom Aleichem. Konrad Tom scripted *Yiddle* and among the stars are Max Bozyk, S Landau and Leon Leibgold. The film was a success at home and abroad, and made a handsome profit from its showings in Paris, Vienna, London, Belgium, Holland, Australia, Palestine (in Hebrew) and South Africa.

The Jester

Green then staged *The Jester* (*Der Purimspieler*, 1937) with Sigmund Turkow as the 'spieler' (jester), a role written for the larger comic talents of Josef Bulof. Nicholas Brodsky, a non-Jew, scored the music and although the film was critically well received, it lacked the magic ingredient of *Yiddle*. Purim is a joyous festival in the Jewish calender and a festival provides the expected happy ending to this music-filled melodrama. Set in Galicia, it involves a cobbler's daughter (Miriam Kressyn), Getzel, the purim jester, and a circus performer, Dick (Hymie Jacobson). When a cobbler becomes unexpectedly wealthy he tries to have his daughter married into a prominent family. But she falls in love with a circus performer. During the purim festival the jester breaks up the impending unhappy marriage by insulting prominent members of the groom's family. The purim festival, with its performances by small groups and individuals, was the kernel of true Jewish and Yiddish theatre.

A Little Letter to Mama

In 1938 Green shot two films almost side by side. He delayed his first project, *A Little Letter to Mama (A Brivele der Mamen)* (for which he brought Lucy and Mischa Gehrman from the United States) in order to accommodate Molly Picon in a film of her stage success, *Mamele (Little Mother*, 1938). Picon was forty but managed to bring off a performance as a twelve-year-old for some scenes. Abe Ellstein composed the music.

A Little Letter to Mama has many traditional elements of Jewish melodrama – heart-breaking family separations and coincidental reunions many years later. The story introduces a Jewish family before the Great War. The jobless father goes to America and finally makes enough money to send for the young son – the older boy having died in battle. After the war the mother finds that her husband has died and that the young son is missing; she goes to America and eventually finds her son in a joyful reunion.

Green collected the negatives for both films and took them back to America early in 1939. He declared that if there was no war in September or October he would probably come back to Poland soon after. He never got the chance.

Green also introduced publicity splashes for his films and the Yiddish cinema became a prominent part of the Polish film scene. In America, where most Yiddish films were made, they were hardly noticed but in Poland mainstream directors and actors gave their services to the Yiddish cinema. Aleksander Ford shot his 1933 film, *Sabra/Chalutzim*, in Hebrew using actors from the famous Habimah theatre in Palestine; he also made a documentary for the other Yiddish specialists, *Sektor*. Henryk Szaro directed *The Vow* (1938) in conjunction with the Warsaw Art Theatre.

The Dybbuk

Two directors renowned for their Polish comedies, Nowina-Przybilski and Michal Waszynski, also contributed. Waszynski's *The Dybbuk* (1938) is regarded as his best film and as the classic of all Yiddish films. The stage-play was written by a Russian Jew, Shlomo An-Ski, in Russian in the hope of collaborating with Stanislavsky at the Moscow Art Theatre. The script was handed to the radical theatre director Vakhtangov who adopted it enthusiastically. His 'Expressionist' production was the founding of the Hebrew-speaking Habimah theatre in 1922.

The story is a Romeo and Juliet tragedy with mystical overtones. Two men pledge their unborn children to marry. One of the men dies; his friend becomes a rich merchant, ambitious to make a suitable marriage for his daughter despite the solemn pledge. When Chanan, the poor student son of the dead man, turns up he falls in love with the daughter, Leah (Lili Liliana), but learns of her betrothal. Heart-broken, he dies and his spirit enters Leah's body on the wedding-night. She too was in love with Chanan. There follows a struggle by the rabbinical elders to exorcise the 'dybbuk' from her body, during which the original marriage pledge is revealed. The dybbuk is driven out but Leah dies and is reunited with her lover in death. It is impossible to look at this film, shown in 1938, without wondering which of those 'ghosts' moving on-screen ultimately perished in the holocaust.

The Vow

Szaro's *The Vow* (1938), a remake of the 1926 film by Turkow (who also plays in this version with Dina Halpern and M Bozyk), also concerns a pledge of marriage by the parents of unborn children. However, in spite of tear-filled trials and tribulations, the lovers fulfill their destinies and marry. It is a reflection on life, not death as in *The Dybbuk*. The script was by H Bojm.

Dzigan and Schumacher

Joseph Green encouraged the efforts of others and the laboratory owners Yitzak and Shaul Goskind teamed up with satirists Shamon Dzigan and Israel Schumacher to form a co-operative of Jewish actors and artists. Dzigan and Schumacher generally played comic relief. Two of their productions in 1938 were Aleksander Marten's *Without a Home (Ahn a Heim)* and L Freannik's *Jolly Paupers (Die Fraileche Kaptzunim)*. *Without a Home* stars Ida Kaminska in a family break-up melodrama about a poor family from a fishing village who move to New York. *Jolly Paupers* features Dzigan and Schumacher along with Max Bozyk and Menasha Oppenheim. Its plot concerns a promoter planting oil in an old farm and duping the local tailor who in turn brings in investors from all over the country – until the bubble bursts.

Goskind, Schumacher and Dzigan survived the war and made a semi-documentary, *Our Children (Unzere Kinder, 1949)*, starring the two comedians as actors who make a show about the Warsaw ghetto which painfully affects a group of orphans who survived the war. The film was banned by the new Polish government. Goskind went to Israel in 1952. So did Schumacher and Dzigan and with them the remnants of a once-promising ethnic industry.

Wyrok zycia (1933) *directed by Nowina-Przybylskiego*

4 : The sound era

People of the Vistula

START

The arrival of sound coincided with the formation of an influential group of film makers and theorists – START (Stowarzyszenie Milosnikow Filmu Artystycznego: Society of the Devotees of the Artistic Film). This collective – labelled 'avant-garde' in some circles – was formed by several key figures and it eventually numbered over three hundred.

Formed in 1929-30 by Stanislaw Wohl, Eugeniusz Cekalski, Wanda Jakubowska, Jerzy Zarzycki, Aleksander Ford, Jerzy Bossak, Jerzy Toeplitz and others, START attacked the dullness of the national cinema and also its technical poverty. Its aim was to raise standards, to root Polish films in reality and to change the attitude of the state, who preferred to tax the industry to the limit, rather than regard it as an asset. START's credo in 1932 was "Fight for films for the public good".

START prefigured the French film critics who became La Nouvelle Vague (the New Wave) and the British Free Cinema movement – both in the 1950s. All these groups promoted their unashamed insistence on Art and on a certain social bias. START failed in its aim of creating an alternative cinema movement; some of its members made shorts and Ford made full-length films but generally these were outside the collective. These films did, however, reflect START's aims: they were superior to many of those slung into the cinemas in their artistic ambitions and generally better photography. *Three Studies* (*Trzy Etiudy Chopina*), made by Wohl and Cekalski in 1937, won an award at the Venice Film Festival; others also gained prizes abroad.

START's dissolution

The group was dissolved in 1935 due to a so-called "internal crisis". Although nothing very tangible emerged during the group's short existence, its credo and surviving members would become the new Polish cinema of the post-war years. The true genesis of Polish cinema may have been in 1945, but the student enthusiasts in 1930 provided the direction and inspiration. In Jerzy Bossak's words:

"START was the beginning because the programme of START was also the programme of Polish film makers and critics after the war in 1945 . . . the time when it was zero, the beginning, no studio. Everything was destroyed in Warsaw and there were no professional film makers – some were in the West, some dead - and frankly before the war the Polish film industry was a small one, a very poor one . . . The idea of START first of all was to find a way to make it connected with art . . . above all a social art. The second point was that the state should give support in this direction, to launch a school. Before the war there was a school for the theatre and actors, but not for film. The third was to make film directors not only employees of the industry, but also to give them influence, to organize the cinema in a new way."

The Co-operative of Film Authors

Although START was dissolved in 1935 it resurfaced in 1937 as the Co-operative of Film Authors (Spoldzielna Autorow Filmowych), comprising Wohl, Ford, Zarzycki, Cekalski and - among others - the experimentalists, Stefan and Franciszka Themerson, who are still active in London. The Themersons' surreal comedy, *Day in the Life of a Citizen*, had two men, forever carrying a wardrobe on an erratic odyssey through the city and out into the country. It was 'remade' by Polanski, perhaps unconsciously, in his *Two Men and a Wardrobe* in 1959.

Cekalski's Fears

The co-operative produced *Fears* (*Strachy*, 1938) directed by Cekalski, as its first full-length feature. Its next two films – Wanda Jakubowska's *On the Niemen* (*Nad Niemen*, 1939) and Zarzycki's *The Soldier of the Queen of Madagascar* (*Zolnierz Krolowej Madagaskaru*, 1939) were not released in time before the onslaught of the Second World War.

The 'talking cinema' arrives

Talkies came at a bad time for producers in Poland. Seven hundred or so theatres had to be wired for sound, and anyone determined to stick with the 'purity' of the silents would soon be out of the market. Silents now were strictly for the avant-garde.

Talkies also made the movies more parochial for silents could play practically anywhere in the world, given a little re-editing for intertitles which, in the current state of the art, were kept to a minimum. Assuming you could read, films were truly universal, on a level, say, with music; dialogue films were for the nation, though dubbing was done for particular markets abroad. The headaches of adaptation were resolved only slowly and by 1938 there were still twenty-four unwired theatres in Poland.

German was an acceptable language for almost a third of the inhabitants, mainly to the west. However, the Polish government placed an import ban on German-language films as a so-called gesture of support for the industry whose output dipped to around half the 1929 level. German films were the main rivals to the Americans who continued to dominate the market.

Neither the ban nor the 'support' lasted and the industry continued on a low plateau until 1936 when the Central Council of the Polish Film Industry – a lobbying unit started in 1934 – began to exert some weight with the government and things started to improve. However, there never would be any subsidy or willingness to write off loans in the manner, for example, of Canada and Australia in the 1970s. Eventually a revised tax system encouraged the exhibition of domestic films and production rose sharply in the three years before the war.

Richard Ordynski

Producers faced competition not only from abroad but also from 'Polish version' films produced by the urbane Richard Ordynski at Paramount studios in Joinville-le-Pont near Paris. Productions at these studios, using Polish talent, were chosen for their convertibility into any language (Ordynski spoke many) and if the films attempted to be everything to everyone they were not a success in Poland. Ordynski directed the first of these features, *The Doctor's Secret* and announced it as "the first Polish talkie", but it was preceded by Waszynski's *Cult of the Flesh* (*Kult Ciala*, 1929), produced in Vienna, with sound recorded on gramophone.

The first authentic Polish sound films were Henryk Szaro's *Towards Siberia* (*Na Sybir*), starring Jadwiga Smosarska and Adam Brodzisz, and Michal Waszynski's *A Dangerous Romance* (*Niebezpieczny Kochanek*), both completed in 1930 and released the following year. Somewhat more reputable were the first sound films by Jozef Lejtes and Aleksander Ford, shot in 1931 – respectively *Wild Fields* (*Dzikie Pola*) and *The Street Legion/Legion of the Streets* (*Legion Ulicy*).

The Street Legion

Historians differ in their preferences for the classic Polish film of the 1930s. There were not many contenders and Ford's *Legion Ulicy* always figures highly though a certain 'HTS' was unimpressed when he attended its New York première in 1933. He refers to the film as a silent motion picture with Polish and English titles:

" . . . it is unfortunate that the technique of this fairly interesting offering is so poor . . . . the director evidently thought that plenty of street noises and fast action could compensate for its many defects . . ." (*New York Times*, January 27 1933). Presumably a butchered print was released for American audiences at the Fifth Avenue Playhouse which specialised in foreign movies.

The Street Legion

Produced by Leofilm and starring Tadeusz Fijewski and Stefan Rogulski, it won praise at home for its rare blend of social critique and realistic locations (the streets of Warsaw). It was the most popular film of 1932, winning the gold medal in a poll conducted by the film weekly, *Kino*. This was at a time when, in Poland as everywhere during the depression, people wanted farces, musical comedies and melodramas, anything but a mirror held up to their daily grind.

Serious literary adaptations continued and producers chopped up the novels of Sienkiewicz, Gabriela Zapolska, Eliza Orzeszkowa and Stefan Zeromski. The scripts, particularly from books by Zeromski, aroused vehement protests over distortions of the author's themes and the patchy technique of the films themselves. Other notable films in 1931 were *Wind from the Sea* (*Wiatr od Morza*) by Kazimierz Szynski, with Adam Brodzisz and Maria Malicka; *The Well* by Leonard Buczkowski; and *Anonymous Heroes* (*Bezimienni Bohaterowie*), Waszynski's tribute to the Polish police, starring Brodzisz, Maria Bogda, Eugeniusz Bodo, and Wiktor Bieganski, working once more as an actor.

1932-1934

There was a rise in the number of features in 1932, among them *Brushwood* (*Wrzos*) by Ryszard Fiske, *Voice of the Desert* (*Glos Pustyni*) by the prolific and eclectic Waszynski, who moved his crew out to Morocco along with Brodzisz, Bodo, Bogda and Nora Ney, and a historical film, *The Duchess of Lowicz*, (*Ksiezna Lowicka*), directed by Mieczyslaw Krawicz and Janusz Warnecki with Wegrzyn, Jaracz and Smosarska. Lejtes's *Wild Fields* (*Dzikie Pola*, 1932) deals with roving bands of Polish soldiers caught between firing lines in the First World War. It attempts to give an authentic portrait of rural life and was shot in the steppes and swamps of Polesie.

The outstanding productions of 1933 were Adam Krzeptowski's *The White Track* (*Bialy Slad*) with Andrzej Krzeptowski and Jeanne Fischer; *Lost Treasure* from Dal-Atan and Augustynowicz; and Waszynski's comedy, *The Twelve Chairs* (*Dwanascie Krzesel*), a Polono-Czech co-production starring Adolf Dymsza, Zula Pogorzelska and the Czech Vlasta Burian. One offbeat entry was a sporting comedy, *100 Metres of Love*, exploiting the Olympic champions, Kusocinski, Weissowna and Heliasz.

In the same year Ford went to Palestine to make the semi-documentary film, *Chalutzim (Sabra)* with an original version in Hebrew, but it failed to top his success with *Legion Ulicy*. The setting is Palestine in 1918 and the film dramatises the hardships endured by the Jewish pioneers. Its cast of unknowns came from the celebrated Habimah theatre.

In 1934 Edward Puchalski made *Father Kordecki* about the Polish-Swedish war of 1655: the conquest of Polish liberty was always a favourite topic. Znamirowski directed *Attack Against Skallon* about the struggle for national independence. Josef Lejtes reinforced his reputation with *The Young Forest (Mlody Las)* and it was a choice for best film of the decade. Starring Mieczyslaw Cybulski, Brodzisz, Boguslaw Samborski and Michal Znicz, the film

The Young Forest

dramatises the revolt of high school students against their Russian masters in 1905 when a near-revolution in Moscow emboldened Polish groups to political and terrorist action – for the first time in forty years.

Ford's Awakening

Ford's next film was a setback to his career due to the scissor-work of the censors who rendered his film, *Awakening* (*Przedbudzenie*, 1934) into a meaningless and poor movie. Its premise was the 'awakening' of three high-school girls whose independence in the matter of their careers and lives flies in the face of social and family pressures. It is about an actual problem for women, at least at the time.

Critic Jacek Fuksiewicz writes that Ford's left-wing politics, explicit in the credo of START, went against his artistic temperament, which shows its style in the films made after the Second World War as "expressive, with images inspired by romantic painting, impressionist chiaroscuro, abrupt dramatic effects and psychological shocks". *Awakening* stars Igo Sym, Zofia Nakoneczna and Bazyli Sikiewicz. Also in 1934 the important Central Council of the Polish Film Industry was founded. Ryszard Ordynski was elected as its president and the following were represented: – The Polish Association of Film Producers – The Polish Association of Film Industrialists – The Association of Short Film Producers – The Association of Polish Motion Picture Theatre Unions – The Association of Warsaw Motion Picture Theatre Proprietors.

1935-1936

In 1935 there was still a turnover of only a dozen features and forty to fifty shorts – hardly any great advance during the industry's five years of sound. Two features worth noting are *The Young Sailor*, directed by Aleksander Lowicz and starring Michal Znicz, and *The Black Pearl* (*Czarna Perla*) which introduced an 'American' star called "Reri", (who actually played 'foreigners' in support roles in Hollywood).

Aleksander Ford

Tax measures

By 1936 a series of tax and import measures were introduced to favour Polish films or those with a Polish theme. For the commercial exhibition of foreign films a high tax was levied: from 60% of the admission price in Warsaw (population 1 260 000 at the end of 1937) down to 15% for cinemas in cities of 10 to 25 000. Cinemas were entitled to a rebate provided that a minimum 10% of screen playing-time was taken up by domestic features. Then the Warsaw rate dropped to 37½% of the ticket price. Taxes plunged when a film was Polish or of 'Polish theme', lowering the Warsaw tax to only 5%. Provided that a domestic film was on a level with the average import, there was a vast improvement in the profit margin for exhibitors.

Boycott of Germany

Since 1933 Germany had been effectively shut out of the market. Poland was an important outlet for their films and likewise for the Americans. Most exhibitors and distributors were Jews who effectively boycotted German films in retaliation against Nazi policies. For a while there was a private committee to ensure that the boycott was kept and when it was publicly banned, the committee continued its work in secret. For those who broke the boycott the consequences were unpleasant. The *Motion Picture Herald* in March 1936 reported that the exhibition of a German-made film brought stink bombs thrown by "unknown persons" and handbills describing the exhibitor as a "renegade dead to the Jewish nation". The film was quickly withdrawn.

Meanwhile German studios were busy making 'Polish theme' films, hiring recognised Polish actors in an attempt to break down hostility and gain an inroad into the market.

Film import quotas

From 1936/37 feature film import quotas were imposed worldwide on the basis of the average imports per country over the past three years. For example, within a maximum of three hundred films (approximately what the market could bear) France was allowed twenty-five, Great Britain thirteen and the USA 190 - or 63% of the total. A separate agreement with Germany signed in February 1937 allowed the latter to sell fifty features per year without any obligation to take Polish films in return. The agreement was renounced by the Poles in October and in December they obtained a more equitable deal which reduced the quota to twenty-seven. When the sales figure reached fifteen, each additional four had to be covered by buying one Polish film. Further exports were negotiable but the Germans would have to maintain the one-in-four ratio. Work was channelled into the local laboratories by imposing stiff duties on positives. Importers and distributors were therefore obliged to have extra prints made locally.

Production

At the end of 1937 there were seventeen companies in business, six of them permanently. Eleven ran their own rental and film sale bureaux. The only production company at that time to have its own studio and laboratory was Sfinks. The only other two studios were also in Warsaw, namely Polska Akustyka who used British Acoustic recording apparatus, and, the best equipped of all, Falanga, who possessed two studios wired with Eurocord Klangfilm, Super-Parvo Debrie and Camereclair Radio systems. British Acoustics was also used by Sfinks in conjunction with Super-Parvo Debrie.

Polska Agencja Telegraficzna – PAT

The Polish government was also a producer through its news agency, Polska Agencja Telegraficzna – better known as PAT. Foreign news items had to be edited into PAT's own newsreels and could not be exhibited separately. PAT went in for cultural and propaganda shorts but they also made features – the best of which was *Genius of the Stage (Geniusz Sceny*, 1938), a record of the life and work of the eighty-year-old actor Ludwik Solski, who was then still working and who lived to be a hundred. The film was mentioned at the festival in Venice in 1938, though without enthusiasm, and directed by Romuald Gantkowski.

Using 1937 as a basis, the cost of features was on average 150 000 zloties. This compares with an export price per film (the German agreement) of 6-10 000 zloties. The top price for the best seat in Warsaw was 2.5 zloties and the lowest, in the rural area, 0.25 zl.

According to an American study from which these figures are drawn, Polish audiences favoured 'star' films and showed little interest in problem plays or cultural themes. They were demonstrative and "frequently applauded American shorts or good scenes within American full-length films". Total box-office receipts came to 40-42 million zloties, 12 million being taken in the capital. There were 769 theatres of which twenty-four remained 'silent'. Out of twenty-five features, ten were comedies, eleven dramas, two melodramas, one musical comedy, and one other.

In general production companies were financially weak and completing a project was a gradual affair. Of the 150 000 zl. budget, about two-thirds would be covered by advances from bookers (theatres and rental bureaux), plus the producers' own money and credit extended by the studios, laboratories and sellers of raw stock. The remaining third covered other deferred costs to be gradually paid off from rental receipts after deducting the credits and advances.

There were five laboratories in the country, two each owned by Falanga and Sfinks, but none was equipped to print colour positives of features - though there was one small studio able to print colour shorts. Dubbing foreign films was encouraged by reducing the gross entertainment tax by 50%. For exclusively short film theatres the maximum tax against tickets was 20% in Warsaw and lower for the smaller cities, without any further rebates.

The quotas for foreign countries were still on trial in 1938. Germany absorbed Austria and the Sudenten of Czechoslovakia adding 1100 extra cinemas into the Third Reich. In spite of a large population and the importance assigned to its market by the United States and Germany among others, Poland's 745 cinemas compared to 721 in tiny New Zealand, 1245 in neighbouring Czechoslovakia or 5300 in England. Internationally, Polish films did not attract much attention. At the Venice Film Festival in 1935 Josef Lejtes' *Day of the Great Adventure (Dzien Wielkiej Przygody*, 1935) was awarded a prize, as was the documentary, *Polesie*, in 1936. Lejtes' *Barbara Radziwillowna* was mentioned by the jury in 1937 and received with some warmth there by the public.

Waszynski and Szaro

Michal Waszynski and Henryk Szaro, as leading commercial film makers, were comparable to good contract directors of a Hollywood studio. Given any script they could turn in a professional job with no discernible political line or consistent point of view. Waszynski in particular was prolific and directed around forty films before 1939. *The Dybbuk*, his one excursion into Yiddish, was regarded as his best Polish film.

Waszynski had a better fate than that of the unfortunate Szaro. He fled Warsaw just before the arrival of the Germans; when General Anders came to Moscow in

1941 to form the Polish Army Waszynski volunteered. With the rank of corporal he immediately drafted cameramen Seweryn Steinwerzel and Stanislaw Lipinski into his army film unit.

Disbanded in Rome after the war, Waszynski directed some films in Italy, assumed royal blood as 'Prince Michal' Waszynski and became an active member of the jet set. He was casting director for the Hollywood epic, *Quo Vadis*, and then became Vice-President of production at Samuel Bronston Productions in Madrid where he died at the age of sixty-one in 1965. Like many directors, Waszynski was a former actor and began his apprenticeship in Berlin as an assistant to Murnau on features such as *Faust* and *The Last Laugh* (with the actor Emil Jannings). He was half-Polish and half-Russian by birth.

Waszynski turned many bestsellers into films but a French critic cited his *The Vagabonds of Leopol* (1938) as one of the most original and ingenious Polish films before the war. The scenario was based on a famous Radio-Lwow broadcast. Few details remain of this film.

Szaro's sound career was as varied as Waszynski's. In 1933 he shot *The Story of Sin (Dzieje Grzechu)* from Stefan Zeromski's novel starring Karolina Lubienska, Boguslaw Samborski and Kazimierz Justian. The story had already been shot 'silent' and would be remade in the 1970s by Walerian Borowczyk. In 1936 he made *Pan Twardowski* from a script by Anatol Stern based on old national legends, with Francis Brodniewicz and Maria Bogda among the cast.

This is a Polish *Doctor Faustus* with a twist, set in the Middle Ages when Poland was a powerful kingdom. The twist is that the devil fails to gain the soul of Twardowski (Brodniewicz) who is condemned instead to spend eternity as the man in the moon. According to our friend 'H.T.S.' this seemed "a big price to pay for a few merry months with the beautiful, but faithless, Neta, who married him for his satanic gold, and for the selfless love of pretty Kasia, the country girl who loses her life trying to save Twardowski's body and soul . . . " (*New York Times*, September 25 1937).

In 1942 Szaro – like Waszynski a Jew – was cornered by the Gestapo in a Warsaw street and shot.

poster for the 1938 film, Pawel i Gawel

Jules Gardan

Regarded as a more 'personal' director, Jules Gardan made the much-praised *Halka* in 1937 from the classic 19th century Polish folk opera by Moniuszko. Gardan collaborated with renowned stage director, Leon Schiller, whose name is included in the full title of the Lodz Film School. The production company Rex Films initiated the project as a possible Polish-British co-production. That deal fell through and the purely Polish version was a tremendous success starring Jan Kiepura's brother, Wladislaw Ladis-Kiepura, in his only screen role. A lead tenor with the Hamburg Opera, he came to Warsaw to make the film with Ewa Brandrowska-Turska as Halka. It was judged one of the most satisfying Polish screen adaptations of a literary or stage work at that time.

Lejtes

One of Jozef Lejtes's best works, *Barbara Radziwillowna*, is a lavishly mounted spectacle made in 1936 with Jadwiga Smosarska triumphing in the title role. The story is a faithful and dramatic account of the wife of King Sigismund Augustus, the last Jagiellonian king, played by Witold Zacharewicz. This romantic tragedy depicts the king's mother, Queen Bona Sforza, as a "domestic tyrant and political intriguer, quite capable of poisoning an unwanted daughter-in-law". The acting, the exciting dramatic incidents and a script full of humour are elements that gave the picture considerable appeal, both abroad and in Poland; it was produced by the Star company. Several other epics appeared at that time.

In 1938 Lejtes won the City of Warsaw Grand Prix for *The Young Ladies of Nowolipki Street* (*Dziewczeta z Nowolipek*), adapted from the book by Pola Gojawiczynska. It stars Elzbieta Barszczewska, considered one of the great beauties of the Polish screen in the 1930s.

Ordynski's The Life of J Pilsudski

Ryszard Ordynski made films from time to time but his presidency of the Council curtailed this activity. Perhaps his best film is the drama, *Ten from Pawiaki Prison*

(*Dziesieciu z Pawiaka*, 1931), with Wegrzyn, Brodzisz, Samborski and Karolina Lubienska: an action/love-story about ten Polish revolutionaries who blow up the carriage of the Russian Governor General in 1906.

In 1935 Ordynski directed a 'film record' feature entitled *The Life of J Pilsudski* (*Zycie J Pilsudskiego*), completed shortly before the marshal's death. Ordynski weaves old news clips with shots of historic sites of Pilsudski's actions and recent newsreels. It takes the audience through Pilsudski's young days as a member of the PPS (Socialist Party) through to his involvement in the attempted revolution of 1905, the formation of his mounted legions in 1911, the Great War, his imprisonment at Magdeburg by the Kaiser, the formation of independent Poland, and his heroic repulsion of the Bolshevik invasion in 1920.

Stanislaw Wohl

The film is fortunate in having good shots of the funeral, taken by Stanislaw Wohl who worked for Fox Movietone News as a Warsaw correspondent. Wohl described it as his greatest newsreel success. The event was important and several heads of state – Hitler included – were present. A German cameraman was sent from Fox Movietone's head office in Berlin to supervise the shoot.

Wohl was instructed to set his heavy camera on a balcony in Krakowskie Przedmiescie – one of the two 'high streets' in Warsaw – to take long overhead shots of the procession, then to go directly to the airport, from where the body of Pilsudski was to be transported to its burial place. With his able assistant and a first-class newsreel camera, Wohl resented being stuck out of the action under a German's orders:

"I wanted to show him that I am better than he thinks. Knowing Warsaw very well I hired a taxi driver who put me down on the corners of various streets where I could get close-ups of all the personalities. At the last corner it was impossible to go by taxi. My assistant got lost in the crowd and when I got to the airfield by foot the military parade had started. On the other side of the parade was my assistant with the tripod and battery! It was impossible to get through. Then there was a gap and I crossed and had the camera on the tripod. The German cameraman's equipment was out of order. He didn't get a single shot! And he was *crazy* and wanted to take my camera away, but I refused . . . At the end the only shots of the whole of Pilsudski's funeral were mine."

November Night

The famous Wyspianski drama, *November Night (Noc Listopadowa)* – on the surface a poetic drama strictly for Poles – was directed by J Warnecki in 1932 and enthusiastically received in New York. In fact it lacked English titles but the *New York Times* applauded the action as "so well directed that Americans at all familiar with the dramatic events leading up to the temporarily successful uprising of the Poles against their Russian oppressors in November 1830 will have little difficulty in following, and enjoying, the story".

It has a superior cast in Smosarska, Wegrzyn, Aleksander Zelwerowicz, and Jaracz as the Grand Duke Konstantin, a role made famous in the 1970s by Jan Nowicki in Wajda's acclaimed production at the Cracow Stary Theatre. The Wajda television film of this play is certainly not as accessible to non-Poles as the reviewer claimed *this* version to be. Furthermore, he declared that Polish film makers had "at last attained the technical level of their foreign confrères" and had proved that

"scenario writers can turn out highly interesting historical films without doing damage to the facts".

Comedy – The Apartment Above

Some of the best known comedians in this period were Eugeniusz Bodo, and Adolf Dymsza – a great favourite with Polish audiences. Dymsza's most famous persona was Dodek, a Chaplinesque figure often involved in complicated scrapes. Directors best known in this field were Mieczyslaw Krawicz, Jan Nowina-Przybilski and Michal Waszynski, both of the latter contributing works to the 'Yiddish cinema'. This genre embraces Hebrew as well and includes Leon Trystan's *The Apartment Above (Pietro Wyzej*, 1938).

This film was a great comedy success with songs contributed by Henry Wars, one of the most important film composers of the decade. The script was by Joseph Turkel and played by a classy cast comprising Bodo, Helena Grossowna and Josef Torwid. The plot has two men named H Pompek, one living above the other in an apartment block. The older Pompek has a passion for classical music while the younger – a radio-announcer upstairs – has an equal passion for swing. The two are always feuding and several complications arise because of their same name. The elder Pompek's niece (Grossowna) comes to visit but she goes to the wrong Pompek and an exceedingly complicated love-affair follows.

The Apartment Above was described as "an imitation of American musicals" but enjoyed favourable criticism in New York and is listed a little inaccurately as a "Yiddish" film. In fact it was redubbed as a sales pitch to Jewish audiences in New York, inspired by the example of Joseph Green, the American entrepreneur who set up offices in Warsaw to produce Yiddish films for New York.

The war years

The murder of Henryk Szaro by the Gestapo in 1942 was one of many. Not long afterwards a former screen idol walked into a similar trap and the surrounding soldiers slew the terrified actor without remorse. The killers, however, were not Germans, but Poles and they were fellow comedians. It was no mistake – Igo Sym was not just a scared collaborator, he had been in the pay of Goebbels since 1933.

The rollcall of screen personalities who, along with most of their films, perished during the Occupation is a long and melancholic list of those whose careers can only be gleaned from archive articles and reviews. Among them, the actresses, Stanislawa Wysocka and Lili Zielinska; the actors, Eugeniusz Bodo, Tadeusz Frenkiel, Stefan Jaracz, Witold Zacharewicz, Kazimierza Junosza-Stepowski, Francis Brodniewicz and Antoni Piekarski; the directors, Juliusz Gardan and Leon Trystan. Luckily, Jozef Lejtes, perhaps the finest inter-war director, escaped to Palestine and eventually made his way to the United States. In 1958 he surfaced as a respected television director (*Alfred Hitchcock Presents, Bonanza, Dick Powell Theatre*). Michal Waszynski, the most prolific film maker of the 30s and an important personality in the short-lived world of Yiddish cinema, was also fortunate. He resurfaced during the 50s in Italy as an assistant to Orson Welles.

By the time of the Nazi invasion in September 1939, the year looked set for a record output of features. Of the nineteen to date, five were completed after the October occupation and cleansed by the 'gouvernement générale', an organism set up by the Germans to regulate the lives of Poles, including their entertainment. Cinemas remained open – as essential relaxation for the soldiers, and to seed propaganda to the natives.

Following their conquest of France, the Nazis attained a base of support through the Vichy administration but it was impossible in Poland where there were too few collaborators to sustain a puppet government. A film industry functioned in France under the Vichy umbrella and even gave us a masterpiece in Carné's *Les Enfants du Paradis*. But in Warsaw film making was banned outright except to a film and propaganda body (FIP) which made Polish editions of Hitlerite newsreels and shorts. For example, there was *The Fight Against Typhus*, which attributed the dangers of an epidemic to the "filth" and habits of the Jews.

All the best cinemas were annexed as 'Soldaten Kinos'. The rest were available to the citizens but eighty per cent of the fare was in subtitled German, the rest in Italian, Franco-Spanish or carefully edited Polish from the pre-war production. The resistance discouraged attendance with pamphlets ("Only pigs go to the cinema") and stink bombs, which were hurled into halls during projection.

Heimkehr

Igo Sym collaborated as an actor in the German production, *Heimkehr (Return to the Country*, 1941), produced by Wienfilm and directed by Gustav Ucicky in Vienna. The film is set in the West of Poland just after the outbreak of war – an 'adventure' film in which the German First Stukas liberate a group of their countrymen who are condemned to death by the Poles. The latter are characterised as beasts and torturers eager to commit genocide against German minorities. The French historian Georges Sadoul described the film as a strong incitement to "massacre the Poles in showing them to be butchers of German priests from Volhynie". To lend authenticity, Polish actors were sought to portray the nasties and the producers induced two prominent stars in Sym and Boguslaw Samborski.

By all accounts the film was well made and was awarded a prize in Berlin and at the Venice Festival in 1941. It buttressed one of Hitler's excuses for the Polish invasion, namely to protect the German minorities. In all of these regions – Little Poland (Galicia), Poznan, Silesia and Pomerania – the people had been Germanised by a century and a half of Austro-German domination and it was impossible to define many of them as either Polish or German. Certainly German was a good second language which explains why an import ban on films from Berlin and Vienna during the first days of the talkies was impractical. Even the Jews preferred 'German' to French well into the 30s, for when Nazi films were proscribed, Austrian films were not.

The Spy

Apart from Sym, most of the actors survived and faced trials for collaboration after the war. Samborski faced eight years in prison. Ironically, he and Sym star in the 1934 film, *The Spy* (*Szpieg*). It has a formula plot about the ingenious invention of an old Polish engineer which is incapable of protecting Poland from invasion and of putting an end to all wars. Two foreign spies – a villain (Samborski) and his blonde girlfriend (Hanka Ordonowna) – set about stealing the blueprints to this amazing invention. But she falls in love with the engineer's young assistant (Sym) and is reluctant to go ahead with the snatch. The action, scenography and performances were highly praised.

A vast amount of pre-war production was destroyed in the Warsaw Uprising. It has since been said that a second-rate industry existed between the wars and that few worthy films were issued. But in a nation of thirty-five million, there were fewer than eight hundred cinemas, a small urban population, few willing investors and little state encouragement until the tax laws of 1936, which gave exhibitors the incentive to buy local features and shorts. It was an industry for madmen and mavericks; nothing else can explain how the films got produced at all. The principal madman was Aleksander Hertz who formed Sfinks in Warsaw in 1911, thus gaining his own independence from the Russians.

Even during the depression, films could be good business but banks here were unwilling to invest and the moneymen who did expected an immediate return. It is small wonder that against the tide of big money products from the States, Germany or France, few Polish movies were sold abroad except to ethnic populations in, say, Chicago and New York. With its inadequate technical resources the industry lagged years behind in its adaptation to sound, in eschewing the theatricality of its staging and acting and in developing the techniques which are the specific domain of the cinema. However, a film market was slowly developed and the early directors forged a star system that aroused the keen appetite of the public who went to see their idols whatever the standard (consistently low) of their movies. There was also the national literature which film makers plundered as hungrily as those in the 50s and 60s. This epoch is readily forgettable because there are few tangible remains – the films, sadly, are simply not there.

5 : Kanal and the frozen years : 1949-54

Tadeusz Janczar trapped at the end of A Generation

In 1945 the social structure of Poland was unfixed. A provisional government was set up in Lublin in 1944 under the thumb of the Red Army which was then overruning the Germans and recapturing the west of Poland before its ultimate assault on the capital. The Soviets, with Polish divisions, retook the city in January 1945, months after the Home Army, the 'Armia Krajowa' (the main Polish underground), had been decimated in the Warsaw Uprising. The Home Army was drawn from diverse fighting units of all political shades – except red – and was subject to a national command. It was no more a state organism than the army under Jan Sobieski which had routed the Turks in Vienna over two centuries before. It was the core of a national resistance, not only to the Germans but also to Russian-imposed power.

The Home Army in action was portrayed with great sympathy in Wajda's hallucinatory *Kanal* (1956) but only after the thaw had allowed a measure of reinstatement for these post-war political 'criminals'. Above all, the 1944 Uprising had been timed to pre-empt the Red Army's 'liberation' and to retain control for the exiled government in London and its 'legal' prime minister, Mikolajczyk. Not only did the Uprising fail but pockets of maverick Home Army units would perish in the forests in their civil resistance to the

Reds. Immediately after the war, leaders of the resistance were invited to Moscow by the Molotov Commission to discuss a reorganisation of the Polish government; they were promptly arrested and put on trial for 'war crimes', a policy that was echoed in Warsaw as the Communists increased their power.

In June 1945, Molotov's international commission (himself and the United States' and British ambassadors) announced the formation of a 'Polish Government of National Unity', which consisted of two London Poles (including Micolajczyk), sixteen Communist supporters and some homeland Poles of other colours. The PUWP (Polish United Workers' Party – the Communists) held vital temporary posts: President of the National Council – Bierut (therefore Head of State); First Vice-Premier – Gomulka (the Second being Micolajczyk); Minister of Public Security – Radkiewicz (chief of the Secret Police), and Under-Secretary – Jakub Berman (later, feared Head of the Interior). However, pending eventual elections there was certainly a non-Communist opposition in the Peasant Party under Mikolajczyk.

Whatever the truth about the Communists' behaviour in the January 1947 elections – they were accused of vote-rigging and terrorising electors – the party rode into power on the results. This formalised Bierut's position and issued a licence for the repression of all non-Communist opposition – which naturally included adherents to the Armia Krajowa. One of the charges against the Home Army was the enormous loss of life in the Warsaw Uprising: it stood accused of futile heroics and of an unforgiveable attempt to reinstall those 'Fascists' from London.

Kanal

Kanal depicts this futility and shows one of the final days in the Uprising. A squadron of Polish soldiers tries to regroup with its command and works its way through the sewers to another part of the city. They have practically no ammunition and it is well past the time when the sheer audacity of the Uprising caused serious German reversals. Futility is written into the narration which accompanies the long opening shot, tracking over ruined Mokotow and introducing the doom-ridden squadron (in effect, a collective hero): "... these are the tragic heroes ... watch them closely in the remaining hours of their lives". Apart from the group of soldiers there is a composer who manages to phone his wife in the centre, only to have the line cut off – presumably by the Gestapo. Amidst all the destruction such things actually happened. There are two love stories – two women accompany the men when the group receives orders to descend to the sewers to try to regroup in the centre.

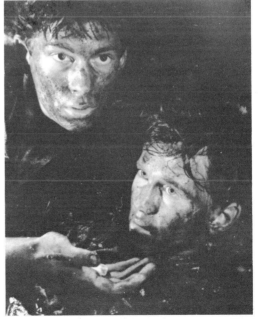

Kanal

What may have looked, in the script, like an acceptable view of the resistance was transformed on-screen into a romantic lament for the inevitable deaths. If the futility amounted to criticism on paper, on film it is elevated to the dimensions of a modern Greek tragedy: the end is given away at the beginning but the death throes and disintegration of these people are compelling to watch in their dark odyssey through the sewers. Most of the film takes place underground – the set was built in Lodz – but beyond this earthy setting there is an enormous dreamlike beauty in the images.

Kanal

At the beginning, young officer-cadet Korab (Tadeusz Janczar), shaving in an upstairs room of the skeleton brick structure (the squadron's temporary base), rejects the embrace of his girlfriend Daisy (Teresa Izewska). He accuses her of promiscuity and of stinking from the sewers. Later, supporting the dying Korab in the sewerage, Daisy finds the exit she has been looking for but it is barred. Korab has tried to apologise and before her discovery of the exit they embrace in a screen kiss which may lack a clean background but nothing in terms of romance. She allows Korab to die in her arms believing that they have found an exit.

Film Polski

On November 13 1945 the film industry was nationalised by decree, with the National Board of Polish Film (Film Polski) in control. Aleksander Ford became Chief of Film Polski from 1945 to 1947 and one of his jobs was to encourage and develop film making talent. He was assisted by his two ex-START colleagues, Stanislaw Wohl, and Jerzy Bossak who was effectively director of production. And so, on a small scale, initiative remained with the film makers.

Forbidden Songs

Important as the first post-war feature, *Forbidden Songs* (*Zakazane piosenki*, 1947), was filmed by Leon Buczkowski from a script by Ludwik Starski, known for his comedy writing in the 1930s. It was intended as a short but the material was expanded into the first full-length film for the new Polish cinema. The film was a big hit, and up to the mid-1950s it had been seen by more people in Poland than any other feature. The count to 1963 was over ten million admissions. The film is flexibly plotted: in a street in the occupied capital a group of Conservatoire musicians play the

Forbidden Songs

ditty *The Girl from Warsaw*. The tune is taken up by various groups and adapted to humorous lyrics which satirise the invaders. The idea catches on: other songs spring up, salted with coarse local humour which attacks the Nazis and raises general morale. The Germans declare war on the songs but cannot control such weapons; the songs become hymns to the Uprising.

The Last Stage

Wanda Jakubowska, born in 1907 and a co-founder of START, made documentaries and a feature before the war. She was interned in the prisoner camps of Auschwitz and Ravensbruck and later claimed that her survival was due to a capacity for regarding the horrors as documentary material, for she was determined to put the experiences on record.

Auschwitz, the most notorious of the camps, is a short train ride from Cracow. It sits by the small town of Oswiecim (ie Auschwitz) between Cracow and Katowice. The region is part of Galicia which was ruled by the Austro-Hungarians before reversion to Polish control. A military barracks was built near Oswiecim as the base of a cavalry regiment (as a boy the director Andrzej Wajda lived with such a regiment). It was well built though extremely austere and eventually it was abandoned. When Hitler's armies arrived the structures were still intact, but rife with vermin and unfit for human habitation – exactly right for a concentration camp which on April 27 1940 Heinrich Himmler ordered to be established on the site. In June of the same year, the first internees arrived.

The Last Stage (*Ostatni Etap*) may be called Jakubowska's 'one' film, though she was a film maker before these experiences and during the forty years since. In 1985 she

The Last Stage

had booked Lodz studios for a remake of the project and the new film would incorporate some of the sequences from *The Last Stage*. Her film was shot in 1947, screened throughout 1948, and was the first full-length film to bring international attention to the existence of Polish cinema. It concerns mainly women deportees to the camp at Oswiecim and presents their appalling existence. It suggests rather than depicts the cruelties of the Nazis; it shows trains and lorries disgorging the deportees, the cruelties of the 'kapos' (prisoner prefects), and the selection processes for the crematorium. The strength of the film lies in its refusal to make a spectacle of death and in the low-key acting. Wohl, who often worked with her, affirmed: "It is still a very good film today … her 'one' film". It is an affirmation of the courage of women known to the director and of their dignity compared to the captors' barbarity. In addition, many of the performers and participants had shared her fate at the camp. The story ends with the escape of some of the inmates.

Solving a costume problem

An interesting footnote to the production (related by a studio head in Lodz where much of the film was shot) concerns the well-known lack of resources available to Film Polski at the time – a factor in some measure repeating itself today – and a solution to a costume problem by means of 'Polish know-how'. One scene in the script shows the arrival of Hungarian Jews. It was well-known that they were better dressed than the Poles, and so it presented a costume problem. Good clothing, like practically everything else, was scarce. Several Poles from the West, however, had returned to look for their relatives and a special tour was arranged in Cracow for one group. It was normal for relatively well-dressed tourists to be taken around in any large vehicle and in this case they were 'sealed up' in a lorry for a special mystery tour: straight to Oswiecim, to the entrance of the former camp. Auschwitz was now a film set; it was alive with uniformed prisoners and Gestapo officers with machine-guns. When the back of the lorry was opened, there was the convincing death camp before the appalled gaze of the tourists. Their reactions were filmed and a costume problem was solved.

The Last Stage had a tremendous impact: it won the Grand Prix at the International Festival of Marianske Lazne in 1948, first prize at the Workers' Festival in Gottwaldowo in the same year, and Jakubowska herself was awarded the International Peace Prize in 1951. It was the first feature to be exported by Film

The Last Stage

Polski and was sold to many countries, including the USSR, France, USA, Great Britain, Palestine, Bulgaria and Holland. It was shot by the Soviet cameraman Borys Monastyraki, though Wohl did some uncredited shots during his colleague's absence. The cast includes two French and two Soviet actresses and introduced the Polish actress Alexandra Slaska, who subsequently starred in *The Young Chopin* and *Five Boys from Barska Street*.

That Others May Live/ Border Street

With the shortage of studio space, the Barrandov studios (near Prague) were obtained for Aleksander Ford's Polish/Czech co-production – *That Others May Live/Border Street* (*Ulica Graniczna*, 1948). It deals with the partition of Warsaw by which residents of Jewish origin were deported by the Nazis to a ghetto in the Old Town and forced to build the dividing wall. Some Jews were denounced to the Nazis by opportunist Poles, anxious to obtain the vacated flats, but the film also stresses the courage of those who smuggled in bread to the ghetto. The acting is superb, particularly by the youngsters.

Ten-year-old David, son of a tailor, is bullied by his anti-semitic 'chums' and is ashamed of his Jewish ways. As the film progresses, David and his family are deported beyond the wall. The theme of lost childhood has never been better portrayed than in the switch from this cry-baby kid into a decision-making adult in the ghetto. He becomes involved in smuggling and other life-and-death choices and the transformation is effected without any physical change (the boy is played by J Zlotnicki). It is a concentrated example of a whole generation of youth

Border Street

Border Street

which is forced to mature abruptly. The story takes place from 1939 to the razing of the Warsaw ghetto in 1943 in response to the Jewish uprising. It has a documentary feel and concentrates on two families, one of which is divided by the wall. Ludwik Starski, Ford and Jan Fethke collaborated

on the script and it was filmed by the Czech J Tuzar . According to Toeplitz, the wall part of the set (which is seen in its various stages in the film) remained on the Barrandov lot for many years after. *Border Street* received the Gold Medal – a special award – at the 1948 International Film Festival in Venice.

The Lonely House

Taken from a story by the celebrated novelist J Iwaszkiewicz, who also wrote the script, *The Lonely House* (*Dom na pustkowiu*, 1950) deals with a resistance fighter who flees to a house on the outskirts of Warsaw where two women have managed to ignore the Occupation. The younger woman (Alexandra Slaska) falls in love with the intruder and the ensuing events cause them all to cease their isolation from moral and social issues and to become involved with the work of the partisans – the Communist resistance – numerically tiny compared with the Home Army.

The chief interest in the film, directed by Jan Rybkowski, who was assistant director to Jakubowska on *The Last Stage*, is that it was one of the first to be sent back

for recutting according to the dictates of
'socialist-realism'. The 1949 Conference of
Film Makers at Wisla defined the 'norm' of
movies for the next six years: that is,
socialist-realist in form with quality taking
precedence over quantity. In Rybkowski's
case his film lost its edge as a personal
drama and his point, which was clear
enough, was reinforced with the sledge-
hammer blows of propaganda for social
responsiblity. The photography was by
Stanislaw Wohl.

Unvanquished City

As with *The Lonely House* this film was
completed and taken back for surgery. It
was directed by Jerzy Zarzycki, who was
born in 1911. He participated in START
and made his feature début in 1937, co-
directing *People of the Vistula (Ludzie Wisly)*
with Ford. During the Warsaw Uprising
he shot several films on the fighting and
the final destruction, parts of which were
incorporated into this first solo film, *The
Warsaw Robinson Crusoe*, which was to
become (via the censor) *Unvanquished
City (Miasto niepokonane, 1949)*. Like
Jakubowska, he was determined at some
later date to record his experiences in a
dramatic film and he was struck by the
idea of a single man living in the ruins of
Warsaw after its forced evacuation by the
Germans: there were such cases. Zarzycki
felt he could show more about the effects
of the insurrection by focusing on one man
rather than by showing the destruction as
a whole. 'Robinson's' island was the
abandoned and empty city.

The script for the film was a
collaboration between the well-known
writer, Jerzy Andrzejewski (who wrote
Ashes and Diamonds), and the director
Zarzycki. The scenario presents some
tableaux of the city in the process of rapid
destruction following the failure of the
Uprising. Sporadic groups of partisans

and snipers still do battle with the Nazis.
One man manages to adapt his mode of
living amongst the desert of city ruins.
'Man Friday' comes in the form of a Jewish
girl who has escaped from a group
machine-gunned by the Nazis; Robinson
saves her life. The script takes their story
up to the point of liberation.

Unvanquished City

The Central Office demanded
sequences spelling out positive roles
played by the fraternal Red Army and the
Polish Communists. According to Wajda
(see interview on page 172), the original
print, though never released as *The Warsaw
Robinson Crusoe*, remains intact in Warsaw
and is something of a psychological
masterpiece. The film, as released and
altered against Zarzycki's will, still
remains impressive enough for the author
to consider it his best. It was shot by the
French cameraman Jean Isnard assisted by
fellow Frenchman J Klein. V Spiri-
Mercanton, also French, was responsible
for the editing.

The Treasure / Skarb

A comedy from the team who worked on
Forbidden Songs – scriptwriter Ludwik
Starski and director Leon Buczkowski –

this film was shot in 1949. By Wohl's account it is the best comedy of this period, starring the experienced comedian Adolf Dymsza who had many comedy vehicles between the wars. The film's subject is the search for a flat by a newly married couple. With this social background (an accommodation crisis) the story unfolds in the basement of a sinister building where the young couple expect to obtain lodgings only to discover that an assortment of other characters have similar ideas. To get rid of them the groom invents a story of treasure buried elsewhere in the building. Farcical events build up to the discovery of an unexploded bomb.

The Young Chopin

Ford's second post-war feature, *The Young Chopin (Mlodosc Chopina)*, made in 1951, avoids the bland formulas imposed by the Wisla Conference by going back to history. However, it departs from the Hollywood bio-pic in that instead of showing the story of a genius, misunderstood in his time and fighting amorous battles in between bouts of 'inspiration', the film tries to uncover the seeds of Chopin's genius.

The story takes place over a few years pre- and post-1830 – a time of great revolutionary ferment in Europe, particularly in Paris – which took in the 1831 Warsaw Uprising. In 1830 Chopin is a brilliant student in the Warsaw Conservatoire. The capital is under the heel of the Czar, police make arbitrary arrests and acts of repression occur daily. Chopin meets and falls in love with a young woman with whom he becomes lost in a wood. He encounters a country wedding and joins in the celebrations which are accompanied by country musicians; this music proves to be a profound influence on Chopin. Other dramatic incidents lead to his first

The Young Chopin

understanding of the problems and difficulties in the lives of country people. Attending a concert by Paganini he realises the immense scope of the piano which will be worth more to him than any orchestra. He travels abroad and enjoys a concert success in Vienna where he learns of the Warsaw Insurrection. Illness prevents him from rejoining his comrades but he meets some of the survivors later in Paris and they act in solidarity with French citizens behind the barricades.

Chopin was played with considerable success by the actor C Wollejko. Music is used to illustrate the organic growth of his genius. It does not entirely avoid cliché – such as the moments when Chopin is 'seized' with inspiration. The scenario was written by Ford and he collaborated once more with the Czech cameraman J Tuzar.

Five Boys from Barska Street

Ford's next film, *Piatka z ulicy Barskiej*, shot in 1953, is his first in colour and again shot by Tuzar. It deals with delinquents in the post-war malaise of Poland's instability. The youths are arrested for theft but the court guardian gives them a sense of direction by finding them regular work. They revolt and attempt to sabotage a new highway project. Finally, the boys re-embrace society which tries to educate, not reject them. It was awarded a prize at Cannes in 1954 but was criticised for some of its two-dimensional typecasting. Ford adapted the script with K Kozniewski from the latter's novel. The film stars Tadeusz Lomnicki, and Tadeusz Janczar – a kind of Polish Dirk Bogarde in the 1950s. Ford's assistant was a young man named Andrzej Wajda who was shortly to make his début featuring the same two actors.

Five Boys from Barska Street

A Night of Remembrance and Under the Phrygian Star

This double feature, made in 1954 under the direction of Kawalerowicz, is a two-part adaptation of I Newerly's novel, *A Night of Remembrance*. The second part, *Under the Phrygian Star (Pod Gwiazda Frygijska)*, won an award at the Karlovy-Vary Festival in 1954.

It is an epic story. The first part, *A Night of Remembrance (Celuloza)*, deals with the formation of a young man, Szczesny, as a Communist. Set in the countryside before the war, the story starts with Szczesny's father who moves to the city to find work. He finds a job but almost at once is asked by strikers not to blackleg. He thus loses his job and Szczesny learns something about the fortuitness of capitalist economics. He becomes an apprentice but is dissatisfied and makes trouble at work instead of being grateful . After military service he becomes a social security agent, turning in cheating employers. He meets a young girl and begins telling her his life-story. This clarifies his confusions and he begins to see where his future lies. The odyssey followed by Szczesny to his own illumination gives the viewer a panoramic view of pre-war Poland from the hunger of the countryside to the misery of shanty town workers and the contemporary social and political conflicts.

The second part is less documentary and more romantic in tone, and is the more dynamic of the two: Szczesny becomes active in a decision to join the Communists rather than passively absorbing experiences. He organises a strike and falls in love with a girl called Madzia whom he discovers to be a party militant. She rejects happiness with Szczesny as something that would weaken her militancy but eventually they do marry. Tension mounts in the city when the authorities move in against the strikers. Barricades are erected against the gendarmes, and peasants from the surrounding villages support the workers with bread. Disappointed by failure with

A Night of Remembrance

the strikes, Szczesny leaves for Spain to join the struggle against Fascism in the ranks of the International Brigade. Little of ordinary daily life is seen in *Under the Phrygian Star*: it concentrates on political battles and Szczesny's personal 'fight' to win Madzia. The film is described as one of the first romantic works of the new cinema in which the heroes faced and were overcome by uneven odds or by the unpredictable movements of history.

Andrzej Wajda

By 1954 Andrzej Wajda had dropped out of painting at the Academy of Fine Arts in Cracow and had completed his course at the Lodz Film School, having made four short films and worked as Ford's assistant on *Five Boys from Barska Street*. Whatever his technical skills, the training in Cracow and his desire to paint were undoubtedly useful in transferring his ambition to the cinema. Ford's film was criticised for making 'heroes' of semi-criminals but the character developments were positive – delinquents returning to the fold and growing up to realise their responsibilities. In essence it resembles a Hollywood pic

about redeemable hoodlums and was a marginal diversion from the film making rules of the Wisla Conference. It was also regarded as Ford's update of his 1932 movie *The Street Legion*.

A Generation

Wajda later recalled that he and his colleagues in 1954 wanted to depart from the cardboard people and dialogue prominent in Polish films of the time. *A Generation (Pokolenie)* was adapted for the screen by Bohdan Czeszko from his own novel. It was Wajda's début and Ford therefore was his 'Master'. (Such supervision is done today by the artistic head of the unit to which a débutant belongs). The connection between *Five Boys* and *A Generation* goes further. Wajda cast two of the actors from the former film and *A Generation* also features the 'growth' of a delinquent boy, Stach. The film opens with him looting coal from a German train and ends with him ready to train a younger generation to work for a Communist cause – in this case, anti-Nazi resistance.

Stach and two chums jump on a passing train ferrying coal for the Germans. One of Stach's pals is shot: Stach too is wounded but escapes across the fields. He turns up at a bar just before curfew; the barmaid and owner panic when they see the wound, but the boy is befriended by a middle-aged worker, Sekula, who offers him a job at the local joinery owned by the Berg Brothers and run under Nazi supervision. One of the Bergs stores weapons on behalf of the non-Communist partisans.

On his first day at work, Stach (Tadeusz Lomnicki) meets the outgoing apprentice Jasio (Tadeusz Janczar) whom he is to succeed. Stach makes some errors and is bawled out by Ziarno, the nasty foreman (a member of the non-

Communist underground), but is helped by Sekula. The latter encourages the boy to continue studying at school and delivers a lecture on capitalist economics (ie the system of the Bergs): "There was once a wise, bearded man by the name of Karl Marx ...". Naturally the line gets hoots when the film is screened today but the speech is intelligently delivered by Paluszkiewicz (as Sekula) and is quickly put out of the way. It is probably the first and last time when such 'obligatory' dialogues were inserted in a Wajda film. It was also the same year in which the policy of 'dictated' films was taken to task by Toeplitz and others at a September conference of theatre and film artists in Warsaw.

A young Communist worker, Dorota, visits Stach's school and agitates for youth volunteers to join Communist cells against the Nazis. She distributes leaflets by hurling them in the air, and disappears. Stach is fascinated, half in love with a girl he has never seen before. He learns that she is a partisan and begs Sekula to help

him join the same organisation. Sekula finally agrees and arranges a street meeting between the two youngsters a day or two later; she invites him to visit her 'cell' that evening. Stach becomes involved in the Communist underground – drawn in by love – and he in turn encourages others. Dorota suggests that he form his own cell. Stach tries to persuade Jasio who holds back, saying that his old father has just been sacked (by the Bergs) and has to be cared for. But in self-defence he mutters, "I'm a Communist too." "A Communist!" retorts Stach, "You're a fool. Communists fight!" Jasio ponders continuously over joining or rejecting the 'People's Guard'. Finally he joins, and as proof of his conversion murders a German commandant who had earlier beaten Stach with a whip.

Dorota is furious over the killing, not for the fate of the German but for the misuse of the gun and ammunition which is scarce and belongs to the movement. Jasio, who is a sort of anti-hero through vacillations between cowardice and

Tadeusz Janczar in A Generation

Tadeusz Lomnicki

bravado, is a secondary but more developed character than Stach who, nevertheless, dominates the screen as played by the excellent Lomnicki. When bawled out on the shooting, Jasio quits the movement.

The ghetto rises up. Sekula bids farewell to Stach and his friends and goes off to help the Jews. Stach tries to persuade Jasio to join him for 'work' in the ghetto. Jasio backs out and later, at home, he turns away Abram, a Jewish friend who is fleeing from reprisals in the ghetto. Jasio sees Abram killed and in a fit of remorse he rejoins Stach and his friends who help ghetto fighters escape through sewer man-holes. Germans arrive but Jasio draws them away in a chase through back-alleys. Jasio holds back his pursuers by hurling his last grenade. He runs into an

apartment block and up its central stairway, then finds himself cornered against a barred window, leading to the roof. He is wounded but defiantly leaps to his death down the middle of the stairway.

Stach faces trouble from the non-Communist underground. The foreman, Ziarno, accompanied by another ruffian, visits Stach and his mother at their home and accuse Stach of having stolen one of their pistols. Stach refuses to return the gun and rouses his neighbours who force the two Home Army 'villians' to leave. Stach visits Dorota and says that he must move away from his mother since he expects further trouble from Ziarno. Dorota invites him to move in but explains that she too must move out due to a recent round of arrests. She formally appoints Stach a platoon leader and arranges for him to meet a group of young trainees the following day. Curfew descends and it is impossible for Stach to leave. He spends a night of love with Dorota. In the morning an extremely happy Stach goes to buy some food at the shop, and then returns to see Dorota being taken away by the Gestapo. He hides in the shadows recognizing the futility of open resistance. Next day he waits in a field for the new recruits; two keen-eyed youngsters appear and give him the password. Stach, wiping away a tear, straightens up and goes to meet his new trainees.

The film is full of incidents and attitudes which adhere to the acceptable rules of that era but these are less important than the love-story which develops convincingly as the real motor for Stach's growth; dialogue and information are minimised. However 'correct' the scenario may have looked, it is well undermined by strong visuals and fine acting, particularly from Lomnicki and from Urszula Modrzynska as Dorota. As with Andrzej Wajda it was her feature film début.

6 : Zespol

Between 1947 and 1954 some twenty-four features were made. In 1947 the Polish United Workers' Party (PUWP) – the Communist logo – became the national government following the first general elections. Stanislaw Mikolajczyk, who had led the Polish government in London, was now in opposition as head of the Peasant Party. He fled the country in October 1947 and in 1949 the Stalin wing of the PUWP took over – an end to the 'Polish road to Socialism'.

Wladyslaw Gomulka

Mikolajczyk's opponent, Wladyslaw Gomulka, had remained in Poland during the war. He was a Communist with a local power base and he served in the new government as deputy to the Soviet-groomed leader, Boleslaw Bierut. But under Stalin's 'internationalist' pressure, Moscow became a Mecca for the ruling regimes of several neighbouring states – Hungary, Bulgaria, Czechoslovakia, Rumania and Poland. Gomulka, who supported the 'Polish road', was expelled and ultimately imprisoned. Unlike some of its neighbours, however, Poland was less catholic than the Pope and so show trials and public executions were mercifully more absent. However, the era had its share of extracted confessions and public penance, victimisation, the settling of scores and prisoner-torture. It would form an obsessional backdrop for film makers of a different generation, pre- and post-Solidarity. There are few today without any relatives or friends in some way scarred by that era. Its first review would emerge spectacularly in Wajda's *Man of Marble* in 1976, on its release one of the biggest-ever box office hits among Polish films. Its lead, Krystyna Janda, would also star in the most emotional of these films, Ryszard Bugajski's *The Interrogation*, completed just prior to the 1981 coup d'état.

Socialist-realism

Stalinist philosophy regarding the arts bore the crisp title 'socialist-realism' but its interpretation was entirely another matter. Moreover, the official guidelines would shift under varying winds from Moscow and it was a quicksand base for even the most avid party-line hack. But broadly speaking, in cinematic terms, positive heroes were in order, and works were required to support an economic or ideological struggle for the ultimate Socialist triumph. There were lists of sanctioned topics. For example, in painting, permissible themes included the alliance between peasants and workers, Polish-Soviet friendship, the bond between the city and the countryside, and electrification. In the cinema some films of quality emerged but no-one was interested in state melodramas. The box-office was aided by distribution of tickets to factories which were obliged to buy them for their workers.

The political winds of change were not evident in Poland, as with its neighbours, until more than a year after Stalin's death in 1953. For the Poles they culminated in October 1956 when Gomulka was installed as Head of the PUWP and leader of the nation. His popularity and the people's support were genuine and could even compare with the national euphoria over Pope John Paul II in later years. Unlike many of the deposed leaders of neighbouring states, Gomulka's rehabilitation was not posthumous. He was inconveniently alive and his accession to power was opposed by the Soviet leaders. Krushchev and Mikoyan bullied and threatened the liberal wing in charge of the PUWP, but Gomulka held firm. The risks of intervention – and war – were real but the Soviet leaders returned with Gomulka's assurance that the Polish road would harmonise with their wishes and that their economic links would be strengthened.

Krushchev, however, was still gambling for ultimate power in the USSR. He had already taken the initiative at the 20th Party Congress to denounce the "personality cult" of his late comrade Stalin along with a catalogue of his crimes; the system itself was not attacked but it was bound to have an impact well beyond Soviet borders. Bierut from Poland was in Moscow for the Congress and shortly after Krushchev's demythification he had a heart seizure and died. It can be seen as a sincere and clear indication that it was impossible to be a good Communist in one shade of red, at least for more than a few years at a stretch. This point is wonderfully made in an Andrzej Munk film, *Bad Luck (Zezowate Szczescie)*, a story, spanning the 1930s through to contemporary times, of a conformist who tries to be politically in tune only to find the mood swinging in the opposite direction once he's jumped on the bandwagon. The film is discussed later on in the book.

Gomulka, on the contrary, was consistent: he had suffered for his convictions, fought it out with Krushchev, freed political prisoners and dismantled the secret police. The nation stood behind him. Times were indeed changing: discussions and criticisms were practically uncensored. There had been signs, however, well before the 'October Spring'. Film makers were certainly grumbling about a system that kept output to just four or five features per year and denied any initiative to the artists. It was obvious that the passion and will to make movies could not simply be commandeered. A rigid central authority determined the required themes such as "works of women in factories" or "new agricultural policies", and reckoned on quality more than quantity. The problem (with noted exceptions) was that too much care was taken to ensure that films were all-embracing and packed with information. The educational process had to be crammed into too few movies with the result that, as Jerzy Toeplitz complained in a celebrated attack, film makers had "killed the visual aspect of film" with over-verbosity and hard-sell propaganda. Documentaries were "narrations accompanied by photographs" and the idea of "social content in national form" had become mere "folkloric exhibitions" or regional costuming ad nauseam.

The first public airing of film makers' feelings was in Warsaw in September 1954, at the Congress of the Polish Association of Theatre and Film Artists. This assembly was held in spite of opposition by cultural and political conservatives who were undoubtedly the mainstream force: there were few signs of the political liberalisation to come but here there were virulent arguments over the state of the arts and attacks on conformism in any shape. The thrust of Toeplitz's attack was that directors had "misinterpreted" socialist-realism, that their misuse of the medium was counter-productive, so much so that not even the exceptional efforts of Ford and Kawalerowicz would be picked out by the public from the dross. The need was for a much bigger output of films, more personal, and free to deal with individual problems, all of which would enhance the dramatic, emotive and visual power of the nation's cinema. Throughout the 1954-56 period, the desired changes took place – the state surrendered part of its power to a group of autonomous film makers, who were the nearest thing in a nationalised cinema to independent production companies. The gamble was unique and it was an unprecedented move in the Socialist bloc. And so, *zespoly* (literally, 'film teams') were formed.

Zespoly

It is generally believed that the zespoly were strictly brainchildren of the 'thaw'. This is not historically true: the first three groups were actually started in 1948, directed respectively by Leon Buczkowski and Ludwik Starski, Aleksander Ford and Wanda Jakubowska. They constituted a sort of production organisation whose main function was to assure worthwhile literary material for film production. A further development arose with the creation of literary groups set up exclusively to prepare scenarios. These were later replaced by a centralised Bureau of Scenarios which commissioned and adapted outlines for assignment to a film making team. Thus, until 1949, the Polish cinema sought ways of effective organisation, and lively debates took place with a view to improving the way in which the state gave support. Jerzy Bossak, who would head one of the 1956 units, is adamant that the idea had been aired much earlier:

"I first proposed it in 1948; it was not accepted ... By 1950 I was unable to pursue any activity in film. It was my waiting time until the end of Mr Stalin ... Afterwards it was a new beginning for me, tied in with my suggestion to organise the groups. It was my own proposition ... My own unit was *Kamera* , associated with some very good people like Polanski, Skolimowski, Wajda, Wojciech Has, Janusz Majewski, who is now Chairman of the Film Makers' Association, Jerzy Hoffman ... there were a lot of people, good, better, not very good; still it was a very important unit, part of the history of Polish post-war film."

These eight units each comprised an artistic chief (usually an eminent director), a literary chief (who commissioned and selected scenarios) and a production manager. There could be about thirty associates in the group which would attract colleagues with a similar outlook on film making. The groups therefore had characteristics usually stemming from the personality of the artistic head. The above roles of course would be taken by others for individual films produced within the unit. An inner council of its members would have a say on films accepted and on general matters affecting the group. A federal council made up of representatives of all units would decide larger matters, such as the division of film making funds and whether there were not too many films on similar themes. The relationship between state bodies, the units, the federation of units, the studios, and so on is fairly detailed. This system was adapted to some extent by the USSR, Hungary and other nationalised cinemas. The model was revolutionary and is largely unaltered today.

The eight units were as follows:

Kadr (Artistic Director: Jerzy Kawalerowicz · Literary Chief: Tadeusz Konwicki)
Studio (Aleksander Ford · H Hubert)
Rytm (Jan Rybkowski · A Scibor-Rilski)
Start (Wanda Jakubowska · J Putrament)
Kamera (Jerzy Bossak · Jerzy Stawinski)
Iluzjon (Ludwik Starski · Z Skowronski)
Droga (Antoni Bohdziewicz · A Braun)
Syrena (Jerzy Zarzycki · J Pomianowski)

The 'Black' documentaries: Paragraph Zero

Until Gomulka's return any changes were tentative and experimental, but the new atmosphere was already evident in 1955 when the first of the so-called 'Black' documentaries appeared.

The term 'Black series' bracketed those films which attacked problems that were not supposed to exist. One of the films, *Paragraph Zero* (*Paragraf Zero*), was directed by Wl. Borowik in 1957. It opens with a staged set-piece: hooker enticing man under a lamplight. Borowik's camera accompanies police on an authentic round-up of prostitutes in Warsaw; the spectator is taken into alleys and basements were women are caught (in the act!) with their clients. A large part of the film is shot in an office where several repentant hookers are interviewed and reprimanded by various police officers. The most nerve-wracking aspect of the film is the little black box, inserted into the footage by a lab to mask identities. It assumed that it is impossible to recognise anyone in sun-glasses since this is the size of the oblong box which leaps back and forth over the frame, only just covering the area of the eyes. Around about dawn after a night of lectures, the women are released.

Other 'Black' documentaries

Borowik's short was one of the last in the series which began with *Watch Out! Thugs!* (*Uwaga Chuligani*) in 1955. This film was made by Jerzy Hoffman and Edward Skorzewski, graduates from Moscow's All-Soviet State Cinematographic Institute. It deals with the growing problem of Poland's juvenile delinquency. The pair then made *The Children Accuse (Dzieci Oskarzaja)*, a shocking report on adult misbehaviour directly attributable to alcoholism. In the same year Jerzy Bossak and J Brzozowski made *Warsaw 56*. After opening shots sweeping the capital's new buildings, the film moves to the fringes of the city centre and to the ruins where a great many people live in crude conditions. As in many of these interesting shorts, the directors stage some action to reinforce a point. A family squats in a high-up floor of a partly bombed-out block; there is a baby, secured by a leash

onto some item of furniture. It gets loose and explores the floor dangerously close to the edge: a precipice with a sheer drop. After some effective suspense shots, the baby is swept up in the nick of time by its parent.

The documentaries reject the idea that you phototgraph reality on the move. They show that film making is a subjective thing. It may have seemed odd that documentaries had to prove the point but what, after all, were documentaries? If Robert Flaherty in *Nanook of the North* could pull an Eskimo from a reservation, dress him in an Eskimo suit and 'document' a way of life that Nanook had abandoned in the North some time before – was *that* a documentary? Yes it was – and in Poland the distinctions between fiction and documentary were blurred. Many celebrated directors who came from documentaries simply enlarged their horizons: fiction proved to be a more elastic and satisfying method and it was no less 'true' as a document. Munk is a case in point; so – twenty years later – is Kieslowski. It is arguable that, for some, the grounding in documentaries made their fictional characters ring true and thus strengthened the link between artist and spectator. But not for others: neither Wajda nor Polanski, for example, needed an approach through documentaries.

There are other films in this series that should be noted. *The Old City of Lublin* (*Lubelska Starowka*, 1956), directed by Jerzy Dmowski and Bohdan Kosinski, is a sort of cousin to *Warsaw 56*, and shows the dilapidated ruins behind new facades. In the same year *The Little City (Miasteczko)* by Jerzy Ziarnik deals with second-class citizenship and the decay of less important provincial cities. *Rocky Earth (Skalna Ziemia*, 1956) by Wl. Borowik is a portrait of a country doctor, faced with the prejudices and conservatism of people in a small village. Finally, Kazimierz Karabasz and

Wl. Slesicki made two fine films about delinquency: *Where the Devil Says Goodnight (Gdzie Diabel Mowi Dobranoc)* made in 1956 and *Men from the Desert Zone (Ludzie z pustego obszaru)* a year later. The latter had startling impressions of gangs of city youths, unemployed and angling for trouble. Here too some scenes were staged – rock 'n' roll jiving in a café, for instance.

The 'Black' films made the public more aware of the documentary genre. It soon became more than a filler before a long movie, and began to excite discussion in cine-clubs and journals on a par with full-length films.

The working of the zespoly system

A review of the zespoly system in 1959 showed it to be working well. The change from centralised direction to the autonomies of several units – the film makers themselves – saw the annual output of films rise to nineteen, the cost per film fall, and international awards in abundance. The world was talking about Polish cinema and, for many, it 'peaked' around 1961/62. By 1960 the system had a capacity production of some twenty features per annum, something like the pre-war figure but with nothing like its uncertainties. Looking back on that 'jungle' of pre-war film making, we see that out of 147 companies set up between 1918 and 1939, ninety (more than 60%) folded after only one film; thirty-two others produced two films, and only twenty-five produced three or more films.

The industry is overseen by the Central Office of Polish Cinematography, directly under the eye of the state through its Ministry of Arts and Culture. The Office makes an overall plan of production, distribution of funds, control of budgets and the import and export of films.

Various commissions or councils meet in the Office and are made up mainly by representatives of the profession – directors, critics, technicians, designers, and so on. The spirit of the 1956 reforms was to establish the individuality of the creators and give them autonomy. The groups would form in a natural way via creators who were united through personal affinity.

The self-management also carries with it some financial autonomy. A council within the unit examines projects and once a script or outline is approved, a budget is drawn up and submitted to the economic department of the Central Office. A commission assesses its artistic value; its decision is also affected by the overall scheme for the industry – for example, quotas are allotted to different genres as part of the marketing scheme. While the Office favours films of artistic value, it also accepts, say, an average comedy that has its own public, which in turn is a marketing factor.

Financial accounting for the units is centralised in their own federation, Zespoly Filmowe, whose council is drawn from the artistic directors and production managers of each unit. The council may transfer funds from one group to another, having reference to the actual films made and the actual expenses – both of which may differ from the plans. The total budget handled by the federation is guaranteed by a Film Fund which is not a public donation; it takes income from the box-office. A financial success at home or abroad can enlarge this fund. Films are generally expected to bring in a profit, though on the bottom line the state is the guarantor.

The film makers receive, according to their qualifications, minimum guarantees to live on if they are not engaged on a film. For each film a director usually picks his own collaborators, especially the chief technicians and the musician. But team members may be assigned from other units depending on available manpower or the requirement of some skill not available in the group. The team members sign contracts for the film and at the end of shooting receive a variable bonus, based on a mixture of artistic and economic success. Generally, upon completion of the film, a commission assesses its artistic worth. Full marks gets the team (being the chief technicians, director, production manager, scenarist and musician) a top bonus; those with smaller credits are paid the going rate for their labour on the project. If the film is considered artistically poor they receive very little; if it does well at the box-office the 'economic' bonus comes into effect.

The Office may suggest a particular film to a unit to help fulfill some overall plan but it is no longer a commandment and the units can accept or reject such proposals. Since the national product is a fraction of the total, the Office can establish a balance between genres through selectivity in its import of foreign films.

Zespoly Filmowe

Literally meaning 'film units' this federation of the units is housed in Pulawska Street in Warsaw, where the Filmoteka archive and some individual units are based. It represents the organisational, juridicial and economic framework for all units making features. It also offers technical and production services to foreign companies. The technical bases – labs, equipment, scenery, props – are provided at three main studios – the Documentary Film Studio in Warsaw and the feature studios in Lodz and Wroclaw. The Documentary Film Studio produces mainly shorts but has studio space for features.

The council of Zespoly Filmowe determines the distribution of funds according to the creative potential of each unit, the present state of films in the course of realisation, and to the number of scenarios accepted for production (there are sometimes independent directors who do not work under any unit and they are also taken into account). It co-ordinates the works in progress and arbitrates disputes arising between the collectives; it gives advice on propositions received by the units for the débuts of young directors and it assesses results after the realisation of these films; it considers proposals for new units or the dissolution of those that have fallen short. The units are voted a life of three years, after which film makers may want to transfer from one to another; certainly, eight units should offer sufficient alternatives and contrasting styles of work.

For a long time the flood of graduates from Lodz Film School was safely absorbed by the industry. Since many of the directors teach in the school at one time or another or continually on a part-time basis and since most of them are also ex-students, a graduate will often head for the unit of his favourite ex-teacher. Some with exceptional talent may be taken on at once, but even the most talented, say, of the director-graduates often have to wait for years before making their début. He or she will normally work as an assistant until offered the chance with a suitable script. The rules are sometimes bent in the case of a determined personality, (Skolimowski: see page 66) but often directors are hitting thirty at the time of their débuts – one reason for the overall level of maturity.

Once a film gets the go-ahead the unit signs a contract with the author who begins elaborating the scenario. Then a production team is assembled, usually on the initiative of the director. The council assesses the bank credit needed and oversees all stages of pre-production. The unit is free to cast and to select the location or studios. All members may see and comment on the rushes.

After the editing and dubbing, a print of the film, numbered 'zero', is presented to the kolaudacja, a special commission under the auspices of the Director of Cinematography. This broad-ranging commission comprises artistic and literary directors from all units, eminent film theoreticians, critics, representatives from all professional branches of the industry and personalities from the cultural world. It assesses the artistic and ideological merits of the work, its technical qualities and the competence of its producer. It is on the artistic and economic appreciation of this commission that the rate of supplementary payments to the principals depends.

The relationship between the film's director and production manager and the equivalent two heads of the unit are variable and depend in practice on the authority, experience and character of the people concerned. Sometimes the artistic chief intervenes in crucial decisions, but more often interference is kept to informal suggestions and freely exchanged discussion; the individuals are often close friends.

Once the film has been handed to the state distribution body, the unit chief obtains re-imbursement for the expenses of the production and this money is repaid to the bank. When the film comes in under-budget the unit can pocket the difference and if over-budget it naturally bears the loss. The same system of finance applies to both shorts and features. The unit chief is expected to assist the distributor in promoting the film. The Film Fund is expected to make a loss against production costs on the internal market because, unlike the USSR, the United States and India for example, the number of theatres and seats is inadequate, particularly when seats are deliberately sold low. However, individual films do make profits and if exports cover some purchases of foreign movies, then the distribution of the profits brings in further receipts to the Fund.

The units were born in the brief period before and after Gomulka's return. The system remained whilst other organs of free expression – such as the journal *Po Prostu* – were suppressed within a year and a half of the October Spring. Film censorship and controls existed of course, but outside approval of the script and of the 'zero' print, there was a long engagement on the work, free from the constraints suffered by their literary colleagues. Boleslaw Michalek concludes:

"In my experience the most important period of creating is when you're shooting; once you have the script . . . My experience is that, in that time, the film makers feel absolutely free and give no thought to censorship. This is important for the actual process of the film. Of course, once it's ready, there are sometimes arguments from the censor . . . one scene is damned as too daring but it's at the moment when the thing is *done*. So there is no stress in the making. You know, even in Western production this is not really the case because the producer is with you, watching you and supervising everything . . . not in this system, I mean at the *crucial* time".

7 : Munk and the second wave

Kobiela in Munk's Bad Luck

Andrzej Munk

Andrzej Munk was born in Cracow in 1921. Jewish in origin, he spent the Occupation years in Warsaw as an underground freedom fighter. At eighteen he was a cultural 'animateur'; after the war he studied architecture and then attended the Lodz Film School, graduating in 1950 as director and cameraman.

Munk was a considerable influence on young directors such as Polanski who was his assistant on his last complete feature, *Bad Luck (Zezowate Szczescie,* 1960). Like the 1970s school of documentarists – Kieslowski, Lozinski and Piwowski, who in a way are his heirs, Munk approached 'real life' with an open mind, since all documentaries stem from choices made by the film maker and his editor. Munk reconstructed 'reality' by organising, for example, miners in their real-life roles, within a prepared script or scenario.

His first notable medium-length films were fiction documentaries: *The Stars Must Shine (Gwiazdy musza plonac,* 1954) and *Men of the Blue Cross (Blekitny Krzyz,* 1955), a recreation of ambulance drivers at work during the last war, using 'Blue Cross' employees. In an early interview Munk pondered his own influences: the experience as a documentary cameraman and the Soviet cinema in its great period – for Munk the first major film movement to show man "in his true nature; man in his behaviour and not at play, the man not the actor".

Man on the Track

Munk's first feature, *Man on the Track (Czlowiek na torze,* 1957) was also the début of co-scenarist Jerzy Stawinski, who would later write *Kanal* for Wajda, and *Eroica* and *Bad Luck* for Munk. *Man on the Track* integrates Munk's documentary experiences (which he consciously stored for later use in his features) and a so-called neo-realism, though he did not accept the new Italian cinema as an influence.

Man on the Track

The film deals with an old mechanic, Orzechowski (played by Kazimierz Opalinski), an anti-social man forced into early retirement. He sacrifices his life by jumping onto a railway track and prevents a train from heading into certain disaster. Then the film gives four different witness reports to determine who is responsible for Orzechowski's death, which may well have been suicide. It was completed just prior to the new political conditions of October 1956 and released in 1957, winning the Polish Critics' Prize and Best Director award at Karlovy-Vary that year.

The neo-realism was due partly to Munk's use, as a sound-track, of natural sounds and effects instead of music. The flashbacks and the four 'versions' of Orzechowski, far from being different realities in the manner, for example, of *Rashomon*, each form a complete picture or 'reality' of the man: a saboteur hoping to derail the train; a hero sacrificing his own life to save the passengers from a catastrophe; a suicide victim; and so on. The witnesses dredge up facts about Orzechowski to support their own case. (This method of arriving at the truth by fragments was echoed by Kieslowski in the 1970s.) The 'truth' about Orzechowski is, by Munk's intention, enriched from our receiving four biased points of view.

Eroica

Eroica (1958) was originally intended as a trilogy of stories but finished up as a two-part feature. The first part has Dzidzius, a con man 'anti-hero', who in spite of being quick to act for his own survival, nevertheless crosses and recrosses the enemy lines to and from Warsaw during the 1944 Insurrection. Finally he goes back to Warsaw to join the partisans in what he knows to be a lost cause, and which he deserted in the first place to look after 'number one'.

It is the details which make the story anti-heroic. Without forcing the comedy, the loose, amoral expression of the central character, Dzidzius, 'blasphemes' against the accepted Polish image of heroism. In 1958 there still seemed little room for ordinary human psychology when dealing with soldiers in the war.

The film opens with partisans being drilled by their commander on open ground somewhere in Warsaw during the 1944 Insurrection. Dzidzius's face looms into frame as he marches to camera, stops and marches back. It is a *real*, funny face, without a spark of idealism, unilluminated by any passion for throwing off the oppressors – a thoroughly pissed-off face. Here the business of liberation is not merely dangerous but a routine drag. So busy is the commander sharpening his recruits and so intent are they on being moulded into fighters, that only Dzidzius notices a plane above, about to swoop and riddle them all with bullets! He is the only man with a healthy sense of the obvious, and without a heroic self-image. An ordinary man but an extraordinary celluloid man.

Dzidzius escapes from Warsaw – and from probable death in the hands of the absurd commander – to visit his wife, Zosia (Barbara Polemska), who has teamed up with a Hungarian, Kolya (Leon

Niemczyk), technically on the side of the Germans. Dzidzius is persuaded that Kolya will throw his army in with the Underground and is obliged to make two trips through enemy lines to set up the deal. A funny scene during his last trip has Dzidzius drinking himself into a stupor on a grass bank. A huge German tank sneaks up behind him; the shock sobers him but the German tankmen (never visible) laugh, reverse their machine and drive off like some inquisitive space robot or a fading monster from Dzidzius's delirious mind.

Munk always expressed his love of music but used it in film strictly as a functional element and occasionally avoided it altogether. Perhaps for him the rhythm of film was musical enough. Like all his features, *Eroica* is constructed of episodes – two in this case, which were given 'symphonic' titles: *Scherzo alla polacca* and *Ostinato lugubre*.

Part two opens with the arrival of two Polish internees at a prisoner of war camp for officers, 'Oflag'. Munk remarked that, in contrast to the evident suffering in death camps (such as those in *The Last Stage*) the problems in 'Oflag' are psychological and to do with prisoners' solitude. Proportionally there were more 'haunted' ex-prisoners of war at that time than those who had suffered the gross nightmares of Auschwitz.

The story in this part deals with the creation of a hero. Lieutenant Zawistowski (Tadeusz Lomnicki) has escaped from the virtually escape-proof camp. He is a hero, an example to other prisoners who also dream of escape. Two new internees discover that Zawistowski is still in the camp being kept in an attic by two friends, anxious to preserve a heroic legend which provides some hope to their fellow internees. In Munk's words, the internees have built their own "armour", consciously or otherwise. Lieutenant Zak,

a close friend of Zawistowski, has literally built his own wooden shell, the size of a telephone booth, in which he can pursue his private study: "Finally all these armours crack precisely because the condition of a man deprived of liberty is inhuman. It's the impossibility of living within the limits of an abnormal, sham society" says Munk.

And finally Zak's armour does crack; he runs out into the compound knowing that he will be shot by a security guard. From his position in the loft Zawistowski witnesses the death of his friend, and then kills himself. The corpse is smuggled out of the camp in a barrel, with the aid of the German commandant who also decides that it is best to perpetuate the myth.

Both stories are based on authentic case histories. *Eroica* is an ironic, if not sarcastic view of the heroism cult. This 'new way' of focussing on the national experience of war and the Occupation was already becoming routine by 1957/58 and quite apart from its qualities as a movie, Munk's anti-hero had an independent stance.

Many Polish critics noted that the 'second wave' of the Polish School films had as a theme the war and how it affected the behaviour of contemporary characters who bear psychological scars of the war in a way that seriously affects their

Eroica

behaviour; usually the character is 'burned out', incapacitated and unable to act forcefully. This theme is taken up most strongly in Konwicki's *The Last Day of Summer (Ostatni dzien lata,* 1958).

Konwicki's The Last Day of Summer

Born in 1926 in Lithuania, Tadeusz Konwicki is the best regarded novelist among those first published in the early 1950s – ie within the socialist-realist 'system' of the arts. He collaborated on screenplays for films such as *Mother Joan of the Angels* by Kawalerowicz, *Winter Twilight* by Stanislaw Lenartowicz and *A Career* by Jan Koecher. Konwicki successfully made the transition from screen-writer to director. He began with a medium-length feature, *The Last Day of Summer* (1958), which introduced the young and talented Jan Machulski to Poland's cinema screens. His partner on this project was Jan Laskowski and they both co-wrote, co-directed and Laskowski photographed. The music was composed by Adam Pawlikowski ('Andrzej' – Maciek/Cybulski's sidekick in *Ashes and Diamonds),* an eminent music critic as well as an actor and composer.

The story takes place on a deserted strip of beach and has just two characters. It is the final day of a young woman's holidays. While dressing after swimming in the sea, she observes a young man watching her. He follows her along the beach, discreetly but obstinately, and finally makes her laugh. Mad with joy, he leaps into the ocean, forgetting that he cannot swim. She rescues the man, who is some years younger than her. They pass the day together inventing dreams, imagining a house and a town. The woman has withdrawn from life since the war took away the one man she loved. She

does not want to start another, serious affair, but they sleep together on the beach. When she wakes up the young man has gone and she follows his foot imprints leading into the sea.

The Last Day of Summer was a notable début, an intimate and highly personal film about the war's aftermath; it won the Grand Prix at the 1958 Venice Film Festival. Talking to Konrad Eberhardt for the Polish magazine, *Film,* Konwicki reflected on his début, a film made "without official approval": critics and all those in film circles voiced their disdain and disapproval of the man who, almost without experience and for a ridiculous amount of money, made the film. Perhaps he succeeded, he said, because he was "a new man, thus sincere, not conventional, not a cinema habitué". Konwicki's later films are also highly personal and noted for their melancholic nature.

Wojciech Has

Born in 1925, Wojciech Has studied at the Academy of Fine Arts and then at the Cinematographic Institute in Cracow. In 1947 he made a medium-length film, *Harmonia* and then some other shorts including *Cup of the Tatras (Puchat Tatr)* and *Our Group (Nasz Zespol).* His first feature, *The Noose/The Knot (Petla,* 1958), was an immediate success and stirred up a great deal of debate. An adaptation of Marek Hlasko's story, it concerns a day in the life of an alcoholic. Has occupies a place among Poland's leading film directors, but he is considered to be outside the 'school', since he has consistently shown an individual style and approach to his themes. His films all seem to be obsessed with solitude – a fact Has admits to be true, though not as a conscious intention – and he rarely deals with the war in battle terms:

poster for The Noose

"My characters are not weak. They would like to come through but they cannot. You know, it is difficult to live in a positive fashion. If one tries one comes up against not a few obstacles. To live in a regular and legitimate manner, that is a way of solidly rooting oneself, that's what my characters want. I think that the social conditions are OK for a mediocre individual, but for worthier people they are impossible."

Many of Has's characters lack great heroic or positive force. Their passivity has to do with maladjustment to their immediate surroundings. Whether Has's aloofness from the bandwagon of the Polish School movies contributed to the long wait for his first feature is not certain. His attitude to war as drama is revealed in an interview with François Chevassu in *Image et Son* where he says that it is the "ambience of war which alters man . . . each encirclement or man . . . forces him, renders him impotent – and war is the worst of these encirclements".

Marek Hlasko

Has's first feature, *The Noose*, is taken from a story by Marek Hlasko and was made around the time that the author fled to asylum in West Germany. Hlasko was the 'angry' man of letters, a sort of literary equivalent to Cybulski who stars in another transposition of one of his books, *The Eighth Day of the Week* (*Osmy dzien tygodnia*), shot by Aleksander Ford in the same year, 1958. Feliks Falk says of Hlasko: "Hlasko was one of the best Polish writers, especially well-known in the late 1950s . . . he was the first . . . he started to write modern novels based on Hemingway, Faulkner . . . America . . . he was very different . . . everybody talked in Warsaw about him . . . he was the hero of gossips and of many affairs – love affairs, drink affairs – and he was a good writer. But suddenly he was in conflict with the authorities . . . he got a grant for a few months and he went to the West . . . as usually happens, you know, in Poland, he gave a review which made the authorities very angry . . . and then they forbade him to come back to Poland and he stayed all his life in many different countries, mostly in West Germany and then in Israel, then France, then the States . . . and suddenly he died, nobody knows . . . there is a mystery, nobody knows if he committed suicide or he died after taking too many sleeping pills".

Hlasko's first contact with the screen was as a scenarist on a trio of shorts under the title *The End of the Night* (*Koniec nocy*, 1957), about a gang of young delinquents who commit crimes out of boredom. It was a diploma film shot by student directors Julian Dziedzina, Pawel Komorowski and Walentyna Uszycka, and made for about an eighth of the cost of a normal feature; it attracted a big public. The film was faithful to Hlasko's central idea (he was one of six scenarists) although the film was influenced by the work of the Black documentarists.

Described by *Time* magazine in 1958 as a "tall, blond, flop-haired youngster who resembles the late James Dean", Hlasko was likened also to the Beats, to the British 'angry young men' and to a 'Polish Boris Pasternak'. Four of his stories had been filmed. His book *The Eighth Day of the Week* was also given Poland's highest literary award in 1957. At the beginning of 1958 Hlasko was allowed to visit the West. He had a sudden bout of high living (from royalties from Western publishers) and gave free interviews to newspapers such as *L'Express*, to whom he described life under Communism: "The misfortune of a man in a totalitarian country is the feeling, a feeling that never leaves him, of the grotesqueness and ridiculousness of one's own self – the reduction of dreams – the reduction of desires – a moral atrophy – the inability to react to the vileness one sees at every step, every day."

When he asked for an extension to his passport, in order to attend school abroad, his passport was refused. The October 20 1958 issue of *Time* reported his defection to the West, aged 26.

The Eighth Day of the Week

Ford's 1958 film of Hlasko's famous book was co-produced by Ford's unit and Arthur Brauner's CCC Films in West Berlin. It stars the German actress Sonja Ziemann with Zbigniew Cybulski, and deals with two young lovers in rubble-filled Warsaw after the war who cannot find the necessary privacy for their affair.

Agnieszka (Ziemann) cannot bear the thought of making love in Piotr's (Cybulski) bomb-damaged apartment or anywhere cheap such as on a park bench, and certainly not at her own family apartment which houses her vodka-soaked brother (Tadeusz Lomnicki) and her parents. They search Warsaw for a "nice" little room. Government statistics and proud claims about building programmes are set against the dreadful grey reality of Warsaw. Agnieszka is seduced by a journalist who takes her home to his very nice apartment. Full of self-disgust, she tells Piotr she cannot see him again; but after a lecture by her drunken brother she runs after him and there is a happy ending. The title implies that the lovers need an extra day in the week to be able to make it together in the Poland of 1958.

The film had a record run – on the shelf! – of all distributed post-war films. On May 28 1958 *Variety* reported that the film had been banned in Poland after Gomulka had expressed his displeasure that it showed "the weekday in Poland in a bad light". It was also pulled out of the Cannes Film Festival where it was scheduled to represent Film Polski. According to a later *Variety* comment (19 November), "Hlasko has been viciously attacked by the Polish press as a traitor after he left Poland for France . . . Ford . . . still is in Poland but doesn't answer his mail. Poland's Commie chief, Oskar Gomulka (sic) personally nixed showings of the picture."

The film was seen in only a few countries, including the United States. Ignacy Taub, who produced the film, sought political asylum in West Germany which refused to acknowledge the film as a co-production since there were no diplomatic relations between the two countries. Taub made his break for freedom while working in West Berlin, dubbing the film at the CCC Studios. *Variety* further reported the dismissal of the minister of culture who had allowed the film to be made.

Gene Gutowski, later a friend of

Polanski, took up the German language print through his company, Continental Distributing Inc. (US), since no Polish dialogue version was ever allowed out of Poland. It was a shock for old Poles, hoping for a film in their mother tongue, to encounter a very Polish post-war story with a German sound-track and English subtitles.

When finally premièred in Warsaw in 1973 – fifteen years after being made - one French critic described it as Ford's most perfect success. It received many good notices abroad – with the exception of the American *Films in Review:*"This contrived drivel means what? . . . it is a great shame that Aleksander Ford, Poland's best director, should have wasted his talent on this tripe . . ."

Feliks Falk's Idol

Hlasko is the subject of Feliks Falk's new film, *The Idol* (*Idol*, 1984) premièred at the 1985 Gdansk Festival. It opens with a "writer's" death somewhere in Germany; in the film a fellow Pole, also a writer, tries to get into the skin of his hero, in order to find out how he died and what his state of mind was leading up to his death. In its theme *Idol* is almost a remake of *Everything for Sale:* a creator finds that he cannot recreate either the past or the personality of another creator.

Jerzy Kawalerowicz

Jerzy Kawalerowicz is another leading figure of the 'Polish Film School'. Born in Gwordziec in the Ukraine in 1922 and a graduate of the Cracow Film Institute, he spent a period as an assistant director and screen-writer before making his début as a director in 1950 with *Commune/Rural Community (Gromada)* which he co-directed with Kazimierz Sumerski. He then became head of the *Kadr* unit in 1955.

Night Train

Kawalerowicz's *Night Train* (*Pociag*, 1959) is one of the finest achievements of the second wave. Free for once from the ties of literature – an original scenario was written by Kawalerowicz and Jerzy Lutowski – it was a welcome chance to see a first-rate Polish film with contemporary characters.

The film's opening shot is an overhead view of hundreds of people scurrying along a railway platform; on the sound-track we hear the vocals of Wanda Warska in a variation of the Artie Shaw song, *Moon Rays*. The camera moves casually to a number of passengers boarding the train and they form the 'set' of the film in one of the carriages. As the title suggests, the action occurs during a long train journey from afternoon until the following morning, when it arrives at a seaside resort. As with Polanski's *Knife in the Water*, which also takes place in one day

Jerzy Kawalerowicz

without resorting to flashbacks or memories of the war, Kawalerowicz unfolds his story with formal economy.

The plot could be taken from a small newspaper clipping. A 'stranger' (played by Leon Niemczyk, who also plays the cuckolded husband in *Knife)*, a tall, neatly dressed man in dark glasses, pays the conductor to ensure that he can sit alone. He finds one of the two bunks of his compartment already occupied by a young woman, Marthe (Lucyna Winnicka, Kawalerowicz's wife and star of many of his films). She refuses to leave and after a row they agree to accommodate each other. The breaking down of their mutual hostility forms one thread of the film.

Staszek, an impetuous young man, boards the train in pursuit of Marthe who has broken off their relationship. Played by Zbigniew Cybulski, the adolescent behaviour of the man consists of threatening to commit suicide and climbing dangerously to her window while the train is moving. (This sort of bravado was the definitive Cybulski the public had come to expect; with hindsight his near fall from the train as he desperately pleads with Marthe outside her carriage window and his leap onto the moving train at one of the stops en route are chilling presentiments of his death eight years later.)

Passengers comment on a newspaper report about the murder of a woman in the town from which the train departed; suspicions focus on the closed, mysterious 'stranger', Jerzy. Police board the train and go to his compartment – number 16, for their main suspect purchased this ticket at the station. Jerzy declares that he has left his papers "at the hospital" and the police take him in on suspicion. The passengers pass judgment on Jerzy – his dark glasses, his anger over having to share a compartment and other behavioural details establish his guilt.

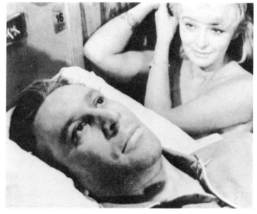

Night Train

Marthe walks to another section of the train and asks the sulking Staszek for a cigarette. Suddenly she sees the man from whom she had purchased her ticket - number 16! He disappears but Marthe convinces the police that the missing man is the killer; Jerzy's bunk was number 15 in the two-seat compartment. The police and most of the passengers hunt for the killer, culminating in a chase across the fields in twilight. Staszek captures the man and protects him from the wrath of the lynch-minded mob; the police take him away.

Following this climax is the final phase of the journey. Marthe and Jerzy reveal themselves. He is a surgeon whose operation the day before failed to save the life of a young girl. Marthe's journey is on an impulse in response to a letter from a boy who "needs" her; she now doubts the sincerity of this letter and whether he will be there at the station to meet her. Like Jerzy she is alone. One suspects that a love-affair will resolve the situation, but when the train arrives Jerzy's wife is waiting for him on the platform. Marthe is the last to descend from the train, in a deserted station.

The action of the film is mainly psychological – fear and suspicion for two-thirds of the story. Kawalerowicz claimed to have higher motives than making a mere crime thriller though he need not apologize: it is the only Polish film to my knowledge which matches the fine American thrillers in the two previous decades. It has often been remarked that the purely psychological 'B-literary' story does not go down well in Poland, but *Night Train* is of course more than a thriller. The reflections on lynch psychology, the easy condemnations on circumstantial evidence and the transformation of ordinary people into mass psychotics all remain firmly in the mind.

Mother Joan of the Angels

Mother Joan of the Angels (Matka Joanna od Aniolow, 1961) was co-scripted for the *Kadr* unit by Kawalerowicz and his literary chief, Tadeusz Konwicki, the Lithuanian-born novelist. The film, like John Whiting's play, *The Devils*, which opened on the London stage in the same year, is based on a real incident at Loudun in 17th century France. There the resemblance ends; Whiting's source is *The Devils of Loudun* by Aldous Huxley. Kawalerowicz reworks an earlier 1942 novel by Jaroslaw Iwaszkiewicz, *Matka Joanna od Aniolow*, which imagines a sequel to the events at Loudun.

The story begins with Father Grandier already burned at the stake for supposedly giving devils to the mother superior and her sister-nuns in the convent. Iwaszkiewicz follows that tragedy with one of another priest who takes demons from the mother superior into his own body by committing a demonic act: the murder of two innocents in an inn adjoining the convent.

The film won the Special Jury prize at Cannes in 1961. Kawalerowicz transposes the setting onto a flat plain in Poland, a stylised art-director landscape. The plastic qualities of the film are remarkable and Kawalerowicz takes every opportunity in the script for formal beauty within a frame or in camera set-ups: for example, the choreographed processions of white-robed nuns leaving the spare Romanesque convent, or the writhing and uttering of obscenities in the courtyard.

Kawalerowicz has said that the film is a protest against the "shackles imposed on Man", whatever his religion, and against dogmatism of all kinds. He approaches the story as an atheist; the nuns' possession is seen as Freudian, a symptom of sexual deprivation. (The one balanced sister, Margaret, visits an adjoining inn, is frequently in contact with more worldly beings and at one stage sleeps with an itinerant nobleman.)

Father Suryn (M Voit), an ascetic young priest, comes to the convent shortly after the death of Father Grandier in an attempt to save the sisters. At his first meeting with Mother Joanna, he is surprised by her calmness and beauty. However, he soon witnesses the signs of the Devil and rejects the traditional methods of exorcists; he prefers isolation and intense prayer with Mother Joan, with whom he inevitably falls in love. Seeking advice he visits a rabbi in the inn who turns out to be a mirror-image of

Mother Joan of the Angels

himself. The rabbi has a worldly solution: only love can cure the sisters. Suryn refuses to accept the physical meaning in this love, except his own sacrifice as an act of spiritual love for Mother Joan's salvation.

Kazimierz Kutz

Kazimierz Kutz was born in 1929 and was an assistant to Wajda on *A Generation* and to Kawalerowicz on *The Shadow*. Although a native of Silesia, Kutz was reluctant at first to make films with a local theme. As part of the 'Polish School' generation, he experienced war as an adolescent which hardly gave him growing-up time. Kutz's early films are very much to do with the national war experience. His first feature, *Cross of War* (*Krzyz Walecznych*, 1959), adapted by Josef Hen from his own stories, comprises three tales linked in time by the end of the war.

Cross of War

The first concerns Francek, a young soldier. Forever ridiculed by his comrades, he proves his valour in battle and is awarded a cross for heroism. Granted leave to see his family, he leaves the camp, now enjoying the envy and admiration of his teasers and proudly bears the cross to show his family. He arrives home only to find scorched earth; there is no-one to whom he can show his decoration.

In the second story a group of sappers return to their barracks in a jeep and meet a stray dog whining for its master; they take it in hand. When they drive past a prisoner-of-war camp, the dog snaps and snarls at the prisoners. The sappers realize that it is a Nazi-hunting dog and decide that as an enemy animal it should be shot. Nobody has the heart to do it and so the men drive the animal away from them with stones. The sad and forlorn dog is left alone just when it was content with its new masters.

A small town preparing to welcome the widow of one of its war heroes is the subject of the third story. The hero's bride has chosen to live in her late husband's home town. Military delegations, children, people with flowers and many pennants await her arrival at the station. Instead of a widow in black, off steps a ravishing twenty-year-old girl who has no intention of opening schools or attending conferences. In fact she has come to look for a boyfriend; the town is scandalised. Eventually the girl disappears from the town which can finally relax.

The Taste of the Black Earth

Kutz's film *The Taste of the Black Earth/Salt of the Black Country* (*Sol ziemi czarnej*, 1969) is an epic period reconstruction of the Second Insurrection (August 1920) against the terror of armed German gangs in the lead up to the plebiscite which was supposed to establish either German or Polish rule of Silesia. Described as a folk ballad, the conservation of folk traditions is also part of the battle for a huge segment of the Polish population who have also waited some 125 years for their land, and who see themselves missing out.

Battles take second place to giving a Silesian colour to the film and in the finale Kutz uses a variation of the symbolic blood on white cloth (used to effect in Maciek's death scene at the end of *Ashes and Diamonds* when his wound bleeds through one of the flapping bedsheets on the line) when his miners in their white shirts flee from a hail of German missiles. Their blood-soaked shirts resemble an assembly of Polish flags in the air.

Part two of Kutz's Silesian trilogy appeared in 1974: *Pearl in the Crown (Perla w Koronie).*

Beads of the Rosary

Kutz eventually returned to Silesia as a source for the third part of the trilogy: the humorous *Beads of the Rosary (Paciorki jednego Rozanca,* 1980). This is an intimate drama about a retired Silesian miner, an old worker hero who presumably won his achievement medals in the same period as Birkut in *Man of Marble.* He refuses to budge from his cottage to be relocated into an anonymous building unit, and to let "them" destroy the home that kept him and his family together.

Roman Polanski

Roman Polanski has never quite 'disappeared' from the Polish film scene. He continued an association with the composer Krzysztof Komeda right up until his first big Western success, *Rosemary's Baby,* shortly before the musician's death in 1969; and for his long-planned *Pirates* he employed Poland's best known cameraman, Witold Sobocinski. After a single Polish feature, *Knife in the Water,* it remains an open question whether Polanski will be coaxed back to shoot something else.

In 1972 the film monthly *Kino* recorded a dialogue between Wajda and Polanski on the subject of expatriate success. Polanski clarified his reluctance to return 'home', saying that he would need a theme that was precisely Polish. In an interview in Paris in 1986 he said: "I truly haven't given it any thought – certainly not lately. I would rather make a film about the war or the end of the war, that period 1944/45 when the German forces were crumbling and the hopes were rising and when finally the war ended and people were returning. I remember that period vividly. I think it's a wonderful canvas for a love-story."

Polanski attended the Lodz Film School then started his career as a bit actor and assistant to Andrzej Munk. He has a part in Morgenstern's *See You Tomorrow,* a 'biography' of the theatre group Bim Bom. He also worked in a puppet theatre:

"The theatre I worked in in Cracow – many years before the time that *See You Tomorrow* was shot – was a theatre run by a couple whose name was Jarema. The man had great ambitions of an artist beyond the form for which the theatre was really created, which was a children's theatre. He was trying to go further and really made shows for adults, but he wasn't very successful in getting these audiences for two reasons; first, that the adults were not so interested in this form of theatre; second, that he was really subsidised to provide for children. But it was a serious puppet theatre like those Czech ones, Trnka, for example, who does the movies... This theatre, called Groteska, combined all forms of puppet theatre, sometimes there were marionette shows, sometimes puppet shows. He had some great artists working for him – painters, graphic artists who later left and went their own ways... you know, the theatre of Kantor was fed by these people later on."

He became second assistant director to Munk on his film *Bad Luck*: "I worked mainly with extras, with crowds and he gave me total freedom. I remember on the first day of shooting there was a scene on the street by one of those gates in the big Warsaw buildings, and I started doing my job, just placing people and directing crowds and I could see immediately that he liked what I did. From then on he left me completely with the crowd and I made it all work in the background. I *directed* them ... I liked that film very much ... This mixture of comedy and drama very often misfires because you don't know which way you should allow yourself to go as a viewer. I think the film is a bit heavy sometimes, that the pace is not rhythmic enough to keep the audience's interest throughout the picture at the same pitch and you lose them from time to time but it's a funny film – I like it." Polanski also played a small part in this film as a tutor.

Two Men and a Wardrobe

Unusually, Polanski was already being discussed as a major new director *before* his first feature. The most famous of his shorts, *Two Men and a Wardrobe* (*Dwaj ludzie z szafa*,1959), is an ambitious student exercise in the Absurd and now somewhat dated for that reason. It shows two men emerging from the sea, carrying a

poster for Knife in the Water

wardrobe through a town, and everywhere meeting with hostility and rejection. A writer accused Polanski of plagiarising his published article. In any case *Two Men* resembles Stefan Themerson's 1937 film, *A Day in the Life of a Citizen* (*Przygoda Czlowieka Poczciwego*), also about two men and a wardrobe, but more a formal experiment in stop-frame and rapid montage:

"I saw it *afterwards* ... I was very much upset about it because I hadn't even known that anything like that was published. I started complaining and telling my friends and started looking for it. The Polish archive man dug it out for me. Indeed it *had* two men carrying a wardrobe in it but it had absolutely nothing to do with it – neither with the article that I was accused of stealing nor my film."

Knife in the Water

Knife in the Water (*Noz w Wodzie*, 1962) was scripted by Jerzy Skolimowski over a few days and then reworked by Polanski into an economic thriller set in the isolated region of the Mazurian lakes. Komeda scored the film which has a middle-aged journalist (Leon Niemczyk – lead in the thriller *Night Train*) and his wife (Jolanta Umecka) on the way to a weekend at the lakes in their small car. They offer a lift to a young blond hitch-hiker (a role Polanski considered playing, but taken by Zygmunt Malanowicz) and take him aboard their yacht for a cruise. A contest of male prowess develops between the two men, leading to a fight and the apparent drowning of the young man. When the journalist swims ashore to seek help, the young man emerges from the water onto the yacht and seduces the wife.

The film made the cover of *Time* on September 30 1963 as the face of new foreign cinema then invading the American art house circuit. *Knife* was a Polish thriller "as sharp as a knife and as smooth as water . . . two lusty men and one busty woman aboard a sailboat".

Knife in the Water

Polanski's need to make movies fits into the pattern of the Hollywood Brats of the 1970s; his involvement has always been a *passion* for film. In a 1960s interview with Boleslaw Sulik he recalled *Snow White and the Seven Dwarfs* as one of his early favourite films; elsewhere he mentions the Errol Flynn pic, *Robin Hood:* Polanski says that he saw these films many times after the war when he was twelve or thirteen. In our interview he talked of what it was like to go to a cinema during the war: "Well, to a regular cinema it was not at all difficult; it was very accessible. These were exclusively German films, but certain cinemas were reserved for the German audiences, only for those Germans stationed in Poland. It was very risky to sneak into *those* cinemas, but for the regular cinema ticket prices were very low. It was unpatriotic to go to the cinema because these were German films and some of them were German propaganda."

The director Feliks Falk recalls Polanski's involvement with the clandestine jazz milieu in Lodz, the subject of Falk's 1981 film, *And There Was Jazz*: "In this group there was, for example, a very famous jazz man, Komeda, composer of the famous tune for *Rosemary's Baby* and for most of Polanski's films. The story also relates to Marek Hlasko. His and Komeda's deaths are somehow connected. Polanski was involved with this jazz group because he was studying in Lodz and some members of this group were also film makers. The group was called 'Melomani'. When Hlasko was in the States he often met Polanski and Komeda. One day they walked in some park and had a few drinks. Hlasko pushed Komeda who collapsed unconscious. After that something happened to his [Komeda's] mind. He was cured for a few months but then he died. And after a few more months Hlasko died . . ."

Stanislaw Wohl continues this story via the memories of a trip to the United States in 1968: "I saw Frykowski who was a friend of Polanski. I went to the Polanskis' house where Frykowski lived and we received the news that Kobiela was dead in a car accident. Frykowski said, 'My God, everyone of our bunch is dead. Cybulski died, Kobiela died, Komeda died, now it's my turn.' Two weeks later he was murdered in Polanski's house. Before this murder he rang me and invited me to come over – the same night. 'You're going back to Poland: Sharon and I would like to say goodbye.' I could not come because I had arranged a meeting with Kaper, Metro Goldwyn Mayer's chief composer. So Frykowski said to take a taxi after my dinner with Kaper. But I spent until 4 am with Kaper and went home. Yes, the same night of the murders . . . One doesn't know how it might have turned out because had I taken a taxi after my dinner with Kaper and gone there with the black driver, six feet six, with a Smith and Wesson gun in his pocket – because they all wear pistols – perhaps it would have all turned out well. On the other hand I could have been murdered with them."

The seeming connection between Polanski's personal tragedies and his films have been commented on in several unauthorised biographies and in the film maker's own entertaining autobiography, *Roman*, published in 1984. His view of other people's versions of his life is plain: "I avoid it. I started reading some of them: it was such crap, I mean complete fantasy. There was no point in reading it. After twenty or thirty pages you realise they were not only inventing my life but even the characters' names and *their* biographies too... They were forced to invent it – people who have never met me because I refused – reinvented my biography... Some pretend to be more scientific and talk about my films but even those... there's no point in reading them, certainly not for me. I think it's revolting."

Polanski returned to Poland in 1981 to direct *Amadeus* on the stage in Warsaw. He revisited the Lodz School and found it "bigger, richer, better provided but the atmosphere is apparently not the same and the results are not very encouraging. That's what I *gathered* from discussions with students and teachers and others... I saw many documentaries, some of them very interesting. It seems that documentary gives more freedom of expression and there are more innovations and new ideas to be found in the documentary or short film than there is in feature production."

Jerzy Skolimowski

Jerzy Skolimowski was born in 1938 and graduated in ethnology, literature and history at Warsaw University in 1959. In 1958 and 1959 he published two volumes of poetry and a play. He was also an all-round athlete, practising in particular football and boxing. Playing in a football team of young writers in 1959 he met Wajda who was then preparing a film on youth called *Innocent Sorcerers* (*Niewinni Czarodzieje*, 1960). Wajda was dissatisfied with the script and asked Skolimowski to rewrite it. The latter did so overnight and became co-scenarist with Jerzy Andrzejewski. He also made his screen début in this film, playing a young boxer.

Skolimowski made three shorts in 1960 and with Wajda's help entered the Lodz Film School in the same year. In 1961 he wrote the first draft of a script for Polanski's *Knife in the Water* - reportedly over three days and nights.

Identification Marks – None (*Rysopis*, 1964), Skolimowski's début feature, was made in a strictly unauthorised way. It comprises several short films made during each year of his studies at Lodz and edited together. Skolimowski plays the main role of Andrzej, a young disaffected university student about to be drafted into national military service. The film follows his last few hours of liberty, encountering old friends and colleagues.

A follow-up to the story was the basis of *Walkover* (*Walkower*, 1965), his second feature. Six years after his military service, Andrzej, still unsettled, makes a living by touring more-or-less suspect boxing events from village to village. It won the Grand Prix at the Arnheim Festival and gained an award at the Montreal Festival. In 1966 *The Barrier* (*Bariera*) was a quasi-third part of the trilogy but this time the character (under another name) was incarnated by Jan Nowicki as a young man travelling across Poland, putting to the test the values of older generations. The film won the Grand Prix at the Bergamo Festival.

Jean-Pierre Léaud stars in his next film, *Le Départ* (1967), a French language Belgian comedy. It is a youth comedy similar in spirit to Richard Lester's *The Knack* and won the Golden Bear award at the Berlin Film Festival and the Critics' International Prize. One of the film's mirror gags is straight out of the Themersons' *A Day in the Life of a Citizen* (1937). In the same year Skolimowski shot the true third part of his 'Andrzej' trilogy – a violent anti-Stalinist film (nine years before *Man of Marble*) called *Hands Up!* (*Rece do Gory*, 1967). The film was banned until it appeared as a surprise special event at the 1981 Cannes Festival.

Skolimowski then began a series of international films beginning with an episode in a three-part feature in Czechoslovakia called *Dialogue 20/40/60* (1968). He went for a relatively big budget in 1969 with *The Adventures of Gerard*, adapted from two Conan Doyle short-stories and starring Eli Wallach and Claudia Cardinale. Set in the Napoleonic era, the film is a satirical comedy on the adventures of a young effeminate officer.

Commercially the film was not a success. He then shot *Deep End* (1970) in twenty-eight days in Munich and London. Starring John Moulder-Brown and Jane Asher, the film was a big critical hit in London and played at several festivals.

King Queen Knave (1972), from a Nabokov story and starring David Niven, Gina Lollobrigida and Moulder-Brown, is Skolimowski's most enjoyable film but was not widely released. In 1978 he gained the Special Jury prize at Cannes for *The Shout* (1977) based on a science fiction idea with potential: a man returns to a sedate English town, having acquired a deadly vocal power from the Australian aborigines. The film is otherwise devoid of much interest – rather an eccentric study of English types at home, at tea or at cricket.

Skolimowski returned to Polish themes in his next two features: the rapidly conceived and executed *Moonlighting* (1982), his response to the imposition of military rule in Poland, starring Jeremy Irons, and *Success is the Best Revenge* with Michael York as an emigré Polish director.

Like Polanski, Skolimowski left Poland some years ago; he now lives in London. He makes his films in various European countries, has written or collaborated on all his scripts, and continues acting in his own films as well as in those of other directors – in Schlöndorff's *Circle of Deceit*, and in *White Nights* as a KGB agent, for instance. In 1986 his new film, *The Lightship*, starring Robert Duvall and Klaus Maria Brandauer, went on international release.

The Barrier

8 : Cybulski : the Polish James Dean

Zbigniew Cybulski and Ewa Krzyzewska in Ashes and Diamonds

"Zbigniew Cybulski may have an unpronounceable name, but women in a couple of dozen countries have developed a sudden passion for linguistics in order to fondle his exotic consonants... " (*Time* profile, 1964).

In 1968 *Kadr*, under Jerzy Kawalerowicz, and *Kamera*, under Jerzy Bossak, could both command impressive lists of directors and films that had passed through their respective units, although only *Kadr* survives to this day. The shake-ups of 1968 led to the death of *Kamera* and the purging of Bossak who oversaw the unit's last film and one of its finest achievements: Wajda's *Everything for Sale* (*Wszystko na Sprzedaz*, 1968).

The 'James Dean of Poland'

"The title was a special one", says Bossak. "It was the end of the unit and 'everything for sale' is typical of a shop which is going to be liquidated, yes?" According to critics of the time the film was another kind of purge: Wajda's sense of guilt. But it is an extraordinary homage to his late friend, the actor Zbigniew Cybulski, the 'James Dean of Poland', affectionately known as 'Zbyszek'.

There is an almost perverse anti-star system in Poland where major actors, who are able to pick and choose their roles, often do brief takes in movies directed by their friends – appearances which have little in common with 'guest' cameos. Zbigniew Zapasiewicz, for instance, shows up in Zanussi's *The Contract* for a couple of seconds as an extra waiting in a telephone queue.

Cybulski, however, is living proof of that special screen property which makes the finest acting craft in the world pale before the magic of 'persona' or charisma that creates box-office heroes. The comparison with James Dean was inevitable; Cybulski as Maciek in *Ashes and Diamonds* represents the same generation, although he was four years older and 'arrived' three years after Dean.

Dean and Cybulski

Both actors were naturals and began as amateurs in student theatre before starting their professional training. Cybulski was taught by the Stanislavsky method at the Theatre School in Cracow where he graduated in 1953. At the same time, Dean studied in New York at the Actors' Studio whose 'Method' was formed from Stanislavsky's precepts. They each had four or five credits before springing their similar and special kind of intensity upon the film-going public.

Dean's 'rebel' without a cause and Cybulski's Maciek each show a hard, cynical surface covering a mass of self-doubt and extreme sensitivity and, in Dean's case, great shame over the weaknesses of his father. Maciek in *Ashes and Diamonds* begins with a definite cause - destruction of the Communist advance in post-war Poland – which is shattered by a sudden love-affair and his contact with the Communist whom he plans to kill.

Whereas two of Dean's films were released posthumously and his sudden fame did not fade with overexposure or physical degeneration, Cybulski declined from a "Hamlet in wind-cheater and glasses" (David Robinson) to a "paunchy, faded matinee idol". But it was not enough to kill the legend. Perhaps it is his face, above all, which best symbolises the face of Poland's perplexed post-war youth. Full of suffering, handsome and hidden behind the black glasses – light green really but they photographed dark – it intimidated a few of his directors, resulting in mediocre performances under lack-lustre direction. Under a firm hand he sparkled, as he did when working with Wajda, although this happened in only four out of the forty or so films he made.

Wajda and Cybulski

Wajda and Cybulski are indelibly associated through one of the most successful films ever made in Poland – *Ashes and Diamonds* – and by their simultaneous rise to the peaks of their respective careers. They were about the same age and both participated as teenagers in the ranks of the Home Army. Their final film together was a segment in *Love at Twenty* (*L'Amour à Vingt Ans*, France, 1961), a compendium of five stories each from an international director, produced by Pierre Roustang. The film's underlying idea was to project a vision of contemporary youth through their eyes and through New Wave directors of varying nationalities – the sort of idea that usually backfires in practice. Instead of looking through the eyes of youth, Wajda looked at youth through the eyes of an older generation – Cybulski.

Love at Twenty

In this episode, written by Jerzy Stawinski, Cybulski portrays 'Zbyszek', a man who has known heroism in a war which has never touched the war-baby generation of twenty-year-olds he encounters. One day in the Warsaw Zoo, a little girl falls into the polar bear pit. The bystanders do nothing, although a young man callously takes pictures. Zbyszek unhesitatingly jumps into the pit and rescues the child. The photographer's fiancée, Basia (Barbara Kwiatkowska-Lass), is fascinated by such heroism and invites Zbyszek back to her home. Their tête-à-tête is spoiled by the arrival of some student friends, and in the ensuing party Zbyszek becomes gauche and absurd. He is shy, cannot dance and can only talk about his war memories; youngsters mock these 'tall' stories and patronise him. He leaves, drunk and embittered. He will return the next morning to his routine job as an electricity-meter inspector.

In an interview with Konrad Eberhardt in the French film journal *Image et Son*, Wajda expressed pleasure in having had this opportunity for a reflective 'pause' in his career and a return to some very personal problems:

"This little film answers the question: if Maciek Chelmicki had not been killed at the end of *Ashes and Diamonds* what would he have become today? No doubt this old combatant in the film *Love at Twenty* who is besieged by old memories and who sees himself surrounded by a new generation for whom his past means nothing. It is a purely Polish drama but one that is comprehensible everywhere..."

Wajda could not pretend to be on the side of the new youth and the film is more like an elegy for his own generation whose youth had been kicked into the attic. The 'old combatants' have slumped into middle age and it seems that they can escape their very dull existence only by recounting old war exploits through a haze of vodka.

Bogumil Kobiela

Cybulski was an experienced, self-taught director. He graduated from the Theatre School in Cracow with his close friend, Bogumil Kobiela. In 1953 they were engaged by the Teatr Wybrzeza in Gdynia. They soon quit to form their own company, Bim Bom, a satirical student theatre in Sopot; a little later they started Teatr Rozmow (theatre of dialogues). As always, Cybulski both directed and appeared in the programmes.

Kobiela co-stars with Cybulski in *Ashes and Diamonds* and co-scripted the autobiographical *See You Tomorrow*, which stars his friend and is about a student theatre in Gdansk. In a tribute to Cybulski, Kobiela recalled:

"He was the main force in the student theatre Bim Bom and was not only full of ideas and invention as an artistic director but what is perhaps surprising – he was a marvellous organiser. The situation of the little theatre was difficult and we had no rich sponsors. Zbyszek worked without rest, doing the decorations, organising the props – we were inspired by his

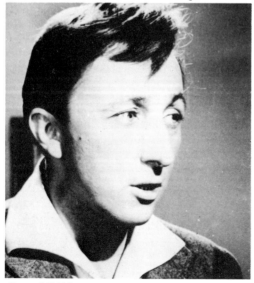

Bogumil Kobiela

enthusiasm. He was a very tough artistic director and electrified everyone with his presence though he was quite helpless in his private life. For a long time he was without a flat; half his life was spent in trains."

Cybulski became a sensation in his first starring role and his sixth appearance on-screen. He was the first Polish superstar in the Western sense, with a marketable image even beyond Poland. The glasses were no affectation; he was short-sighted and rarely took them off, even on film. His fans wanted more though critics became irritated by his 'sameness' and judged him by the standards of the theatre where each role is meant to be unique and unrepeatable. He is a much different character (without glasses) in *The Saragossa Manuscript* (*Rekopis Znaleziony w Saragossie*, 1966), the comedy-horror epic set three centuries ago in a fantasised Spain. Here he displays his known comic talent and was praised for the comical, bemused look he brought to the central role of the count.

The Saragossa Manuscript

Cybulski's death

On January 8 1967 at 4 am, Cybulski ran for his train which was pulling out of Wroclaw station – an express bound for Warsaw where he was to perform at a theatre that evening. He leapt for a foot-hold on one of the doorsteps but slipped and was dragged between the train and the rails. His body was discovered at 6 am and it remains uncertain whether suicide, fatigue or alcohol had been the real cause.

Everything for Sale

An identical scene opens *Everything for Sale*, one of the most remarkable film tributes in the history of the cinema. Whilst the cult status of its subject reached beyond Poland, few of Cybulski's forty-odd films achieved an international release beyond festivals and cinemathèques. The legend arose almost entirely from *Ashes and Diamonds* but this was a subtitled film destined for an art cinema public. It seems that a perhaps unreasonable amount of input is required by the viewer to make the film work - including a knowledge of Polish history (political and cinematic) and something about Wajda himself.

Yet without this background knowledge, the film seemed to work for non-Polish audiences. The US paper *Variety* gave it a lengthy review praising its "timeless probe into the vanities, personalities and vagaries of film creation and its ties with life", and recommended that the film be carefully placed and handled for the effort would be well-rewarded.

Everything for Sale is an exploitation pic with a difference. Hollywood had often raked over its own myths and legends: this kind of exposé was material for films. In an interview with Boleslaw Sulik, Wajda had declared his distaste for films about film making or showbiz: "I don't think it's right that film should feed on itself. I think that it should feed upon reality." Why then this sudden change?

Wajda's picture of the film world is not sympathetic. It is seen as rather trendy and narcissistic and simply a good way to earn money; there is little hint of the ideals which were supposed to have driven the young cineastes of the 1950s. It is also a study of the amorality of art, specifically its ability to feed off itself. Several of Cybulski's friends appear in the film, sometimes as themselves. Bogumil Kobiela expressed his distaste for the project and called the film more a piece of directorial opportunism than a valid tribute. His opposition was expressed both on and off the set – he appears in the film with such views – and it is this blending between fiction and fact that is typical of the film and part of its fascination.

Everything for Sale

The plot is fairly straightforward. The opening scene appears to be a recreation of Cybulski's death. A man runs for a train which is accelerating out of the station; he slips and falls off the platform and is dragged underneath the train. The man resurfaces and asks: "How was that?" He is a film director and has just stood in for his star in a take: we are looking at the making of a movie – also called "Everything for Sale". To everyone's irritation – the director, actors and technicians – the actor has not turned up and reluctantly they begin looking for him, although they are used to his indiscipline and his erratic temperament. We learn that he and his director 'Andrzej' (acted by Andrzej Lapicki) both made their names in a famous film in the 1950s.

The splicing of fiction and reality is further emphasized by several tricks and gags. The actor's estranged wife, 'Ela' (Elzbieta Czyszewska), and his former girlfriend, (Beata Tyszkiewicz), who is now Andrzej's wife (Tyszkiewicz was *Wajda's* wife at the time), go in search of the actor and manage to trace his movements of the previous night. Suddenly, over the radio, they hear the shocking news of his death – a train accident, similar to that staged in Andrzej's film. Andrzej seems more annoyed by the disruption to his project than grief-stricken over the loss of his colleague. He decides to make the star's absence an element in his film, to make a film about an actor, without that actor – which is precisely what Wajda was doing:

"In this film I used all the facts, events and anecdotes that I was aware of or which I witnessed during my many years of friendship with Zbigniew Cybulski. But I could never pretend to make a film of his life or about him in person. *Everything for Sale* will mostly be a film showing the impossibility of defining a man without his presence, a film where the contours and lines of a silhouette even before being established disappear and wear out into nothingness" (Sulik interview).

Daniel Olbrychski

Andrzej then offers the role to a rising

young actor named 'Daniel' (Daniel Olbrychski) who idolises the missing actor and yet seems ambitious to take his place.

Daniel Olbrychski

Daniel begins to adopt the mannerisms, props and clothing of the dead actor but eventually both he and his director realise that Daniel cannot succeed to anything beyond a pale shadow of the original. At the end of the film the director gives up and slumps to the ground, asking his cameraman to take over. Suddenly a pack of wild horses breaks free, and as they gallop around the set Daniel runs off and joins them in a care-free sprint. The cameraman applauds and captures the new Daniel on film. A new star is born, a different kind of idol for a new generation.

Though little is revealed about 'the actor', details of the lives of the actors in the film are parallelled on-screen. Daniel Olbrychski had at that time taken over from Cybulski as the favourite of the young generation. He was chosen over Cybulski for the lead in Wajda's *Ashes* (*Popioly*, 1965), a vast screen adaptation of the book by Stefan Zeromski. Cybulski was embittered by Wajda's rejection and remarked to a friend: "Tell him one day he will need me."

Wajda has been described by a colleague as a vampire who, without a particular point of view, sucks the talents of his collaborators – actors, musicians, scenarists and cameramen – and produces what is sometimes a work of art. Actors would rise to their very best – they loved being vampirised by the director. Certainly the high point of Cybulski's career was achieved in a Wajda film – so too, to date, with Olbrychski.

In *Everything for Sale* the vampirism is there as part of the director's confessions. From the beginning Andrzej the director is making a film about his friend who has failed to turn up on the set; Wajda himself was preparing such a project as a vehicle for Cybulski just prior to his death. Andrzej relentlessly makes use of real facts and rumours about the subject of his movie and casts his real-life wife, Ela, as his co-star in order to play out the 'real-life' strains of their marriage within the action of his film. This is just to achieve some resonance; the pain in the private lives of his actors merely serves as fodder for the director's art.

On January 12 1967 Cybulski was buried in the town of his birth – Katowice in Silesia. For over two hours thousands of people filed past his coffin, draped in white and red, which lay open to the public in the concert hall of the Fitelberg Radio Music House. In attendance were colleagues and personal friends, young admirers and actors and film makers from all parts of the country.

The guard of honour included Jerzy Kawalerowicz who directed him in *Night Train* (*Pociag*, 1959), an excellent psychological thriller which is the closest the Polish cinema has come to the finest American *film noir*. Cybulski (in a support role) is cast to type - the impetuous lover pursuing his girlfriend across the country – and he is to be seen leaping on and off a fast-moving train. One also eerily recalls his first film, *A Generation*, in which his only scene (others were shot but deleted) involves him jumping to and from a moving train.

The funeral procession marched along the streets thronged with mourners. Among the marchers were his wife, son, mother and brother. A funeral oration was delivered by the Deputy Minister of Culture and the Arts who described Cybulski as a man "gifted with a great talent, a colourful and unusual figure, an actor who fascinated the whole of post-war Polish youth".

Kobiela and See You Tomorrow

Bogumil Kobiela died in a car crash, barely two years after his friend's death. Like Cybulski he had a superb comic talent which was only given free rein in Andrzej Munk's *Bad Luck* (*Zezowate Szczescie*, 1960). With Cybulski he co-wrote the scenario of *See You Tomorrow* (*Do Widzenia do Jutra*, 1960), Janusz Morgernstern's feature début. This is a fictionalised account of their Bim Bom theatre in which Cybulski plays Jacek, the director of a students' theatre in Gdansk. He falls for the daughter of a foreign consul but first has to compete with his more cosmopolitan friends, Jurek and Romek (played by Roman Polanski – in between making *Two Men and a Wardrobe* and *Knife in the Water*).

Po Co

The theatre group featured in the story is called Po Co, an actual group which arose under the inspiration of Bim Bom. Po Co was created one winter by students of the plastic arts in a Sopot students' hostel. The special qualities of its work come across in the film. Working to a sound-track of music, sound effects or just silence, the 'performers' were human hands that were highly expressive puppets with the aid of a few props such as a glove, a slipper or a rose. Without dialogue the theatre achieved a special and witty type of animation.

The story-line in *See You Tomorrow* shows Jacek finally winning over the girl when she attends one of his performances. He eventually neglects his work and the group, and spends aimless days with the girl wandering about the city and the beach. The affair is a light one for the girl; Jacek suddenly discovers that she has gone – her father has been posted to another country. Sadder and wiser, Jacek returns to his troupe.

Cybulski in Zbyszek

The cameraman, Jan Laskowski, at the time one of the best in the country, later made *Zbyszek*, a tribute to his friend in a more direct fashion than Wajda's, using some clips from Cybulski's best films. Also involved in *See You Tomorrow* was the jazz musician Krzysztof Komeda who composed the score and whose career later peaked with his score for Polanski's *Rosemary's Baby*. He too died tragically young, in 1969.

Zbigniew Slojewski

Apart from the unstinting hymns of praise to a departed friend, there were people such as the critic, Zbigniew Slojewski, wicked enough to compare the James Dean style of "live fast, die young and have a good-looking corpse" with the physical state of Cybulski before he died:

"Cybulski was sometimes called the Polish James Dean. It was a long time ago. We remember *Ashes and Diamonds*. Cybulski then was more than an actor. He

Ashes and Diamonds

was a myth . . . the essence of manliness, a superman and a superlover. But today we watched him in *To Love*, [the 1964 Swedish film by Jörn Donner, co-starring Harriet Andersson] and he is a completely different actor. James Dean was killed in a car crash and Zbygniew Cybulski had acquired a double chin. It was also the death of a certain creation, a certain acting type that you cannot develop anymore. We cannot imagine an excessively fat James Dean. Dean was a rebellious young man with a fascinating face and sharp gestures; he was passionate, elemental, impatient. Cybulski in *Ashes and Diamonds* represented a similar type of actor but perhaps not so authentic. People close to him said he would improve but meanwhile conditions forced Cybulski to change from this type . . ."

Cybulski's face

Perhaps he succeeded too well too soon. His face had become so imbued with the Occupation complex that you looked at him and knew immediately that he was a man with a wartime past full of exploits and suffering. Everything that happened to the nation, to Poles individually and collectively, was expressed in this face or this "creation" which, Slojewski claimed, was worked out by a team.

The actor's face and its baggage of associations was a common work by Cybulski, his director and screen-writers. It is almost impossible to overcome the association between Cybulski and Maciek Chelmicki, and, whatever he did later on, the complex of those historical, political and individual wartime experiences went with him. Even playing an engineer on his way to Irak he retains an expression reserved for one who stands before a plaque commemorating wartime executions.

Wajda's *Everything for Sale* is the story of a ghost, an identikit picture of a man whose only appearance in the film is as a trail of footstep impressions in the snow. Wajda confided in 1982 that he had lacked the courage to state boldly that the film was about Zbyszek. He regretted the elliptical approach whereby the actor's positive and exuberant qualities are entirely absent in the film.

He had planned a different film but with a live Cybulski: he was in London making plans with playwright David Mercer (another of Cybulski's friends) to create a screenplay around the anecdotes, true or false, which Cybulski used to relate with such gusto. The two men had a great laugh swapping Cybulski stories and agreed to go ahead with the film. But Wajda received a call from Polanski the same evening: Zbyszek had been dead for twenty-four hours.

9 : The Lodz Film School

"When I was sixteen I decided to be a film director . . . a very difficult decision at the time. It was as if, for instance, a young girl went to her mother and said: 'Mama, I want to be a whore.'"

Stanislaw Wohl's decision in 1930 was the natural effect of an enthusiasm for photography, stemming from his parents' presenting him with a camera when he was seven. Less than ten years later, he was seeking a way to enter the cinema. There was a theatre academy in Warsaw for actors and directors, but certainly no school of cinematography nor access to the film world for a technical novice lacking contacts and support from his family. Wohl went to Paris, supposedly to study chemistry, and enrolled immediately in L'Ecole Vaugirard, a school of cinematography and photography. He graduated with his diploma in 1932. Film schools were relatively scarce at that time for in 1930 the cinema was just thirty-five years old – barely older than Andrzej Munk when he made his feature début.

Since it cross-fertilises many other arts – such as painting, theatre and music – the cinema was constantly 'learning', and fixing ground-rules and a minimum of tradition. One country learned from another: for example, in 1905, French technicians went to Rome to upgrade the Italian film industry. Most of them had quit Pathé which soon charged one of its directors with making off with trade secrets and promptly had him arrested. Headhunting was to become the norm for Hollywood in the 1920s when the best European technicians were enticed to the American studios. The Brighton school in England (G A Smith and James Williamson) produced some remarkable films between 1900 and 1902 which inspired a whole chain of directors right through to D W Griffith. In France, the celebrated Film d'Art movement, allied itself to the most eminent men in letters such as Anatole France, and filmed their screenplays. French technicians went to Poland in 1908 and made films on Warsaw life which proved immensely popular and which stimulated national production. The idea of Film d'Art – filming outstanding actors in literary classics – was also taken up in Poland, notably by the Artists' Co-operative (Kooperatywa Artystow), a film studio using actors from the leading Warsaw theatre of the time, the Variety Theatre (Teatr Rozmaitosci). Thus film teaching was more a case of passing on skills via apprenticeship, the hiring of talent from abroad, and simply the influence of watching others' innovations on-screen.

VGIK: the world's first film school

The largest and oldest *institution* for film teaching is the All-Soviet State Institute of Cinematography (Vsesoyuzni Gosudarstvenni Institut Kinematografii, or VGIK) in Moscow. Set up in 1919 with just twenty-five students, it was the first film school in the world. The first chief of the directors' faculty was Sergei Eisenstein who had come to film via the theatre; Pudovkin was one of the school's first graduates. There was (and still is) plenty of scepticism from the professionals with their "it can't be taught in school" claim. This was an irrelevant attitude in 1945 in Poland, with its fistful of surviving film makers determined to get the industry on its feet. Antoni Bohdziewicz and Jerzy Zarzycki among others had run a sort of 'flying university' during the Occupation – clandestine courses for cameramen.

Gomulka's 1968 shake-up

In 1945 a cinema course was set up in

Cracow under the direction of Bohdziewicz, himself a graduate of L'Ecole Vaugirard. Graduates of this short-lived Cinematography Institute in Cracow include Jerzy Kawalerowicz and Wojciech Has. The Institute transferred to Lodz in 1947 and became the National Higher School of Cinematography. Jerzy Toeplitz was its rector, an office he would hold for a record term until 1968 when, in the twelfth year of Gomulka's government, there was a vigorous shake-up in all institutions, particularly those of education and culture, over an ugly underbelly of anti-Zionism and power struggles within the Central Committee. The political infighting filtered through to the arts. In 1968 Jerzy Bossak was Doyen at the Lodz Film School and head of the *Kamera* unit – he was to lose both positions. Toeplitz, too, would resign for it was the key year of student unrest in all of the higher schools and the consequent purges equally affected Lodz. The tensions were noted by Lindsay Anderson, the British director, who was invited by Bossak to Warsaw in 1967 to shoot a small documentary, *The Singing Lesson (Raz, Dwa, Trzy)*, which shows drama students being taught singing presentation by the old vaudeville actor, Ludwik Sempolinski:

"It was a difficult period because it was just coming up to 1968 when there was a sort of anti-semitic putsch and everybody was a bit nervous . . . and although my film was completely unpolitical – if there was any theme in it, it perhaps contrasted the good spirits and innocence of the students with the dourness of the world outside – but when we showed the film at a kolaudacja ('committee of appreciation') they were so aware of the possibilities of trouble with censorship that they were almost unable to look at the film; Bossak turned to whoever was sitting next to him and said: 'in the streets – why is nobody *smiling?*' Then they all started being very

The Singing Lesson

Polish and getting great theories about how this was in fact a film that plainly attacked the system, which was all rubbish – but you had this kind of pre – I mean, auto – censorship . . . in the end a woman from the censorship came down the next day and said 'what a charming little picture.' So it was just a very interesting example of how that climate can affect people."

The Lodz Film School: aims and requirements

In the beginning, the school ran courses in sound, camera and projection, then added those in direction, production, acting and writing. The school opened in Lodz on October 1 1947 at Targowa 61, the site of an old castle. It was a provisional home pending its supposed move to Warsaw a few years later but, like many renowned schools, it is still in its temporary premises. Its curriculum was modelled on VGIK in Moscow and IDHEC, the French cinema school in Paris, and is broadly unchanged to this day.

Its stated aims were: the training of all types of technicians; motion-picture research; the making of educational and popular science films; and popularisation of the cinema medium. It was controlled, via Film Polski, by the Ministry of Culture and had a two-part entrance exam. Firstly, an oral test determining the candidate's knowledge of contemporary Poland; and secondly, a film test of (a) written responses to a questionnaire analysing a projected film, and (b) an oral examination, revealing the artistic sensibility, filmic talent and overall artistic knowledge of the candidate. The candidate had to know at least two of the prescribed books, including: *Ashes and Diamonds* by Jerzy Andrzejewski, *Dead Souls* by Gogol, Dickens's *David Copperfield*, Balzac's *César Birotteau*, *The Doll* by Boleslaw Prus, *Far from Moscow* by Azajew, and Gorki's *The Mother*. Studies lasted four years, the first of which weeded out no-hopers.

To become superhuman

Courses were general, but in the second year studies were partially specialised with more technical subjects for operators and general ones for directors; the-end-of year exams confirmed the specialities for the third and fourth years when directors and operators worked in separate groups. The final examination qualified them to work as assistants, but they were tied for two years to the Film Polski studios, working on films under the school's supervision. Only then was the diploma awarded – a ticket into the profession. Whatever the students' ambitions, they were all to have a thorough grounding in the humanities, politics and ideology. They were to acquire two languages, study all the allied arts, practise composition and drawing and undergo scientific and technical instruction on optics, music, sound, and so on. Directors it seems were to develop an almost superman personality and intellect:

"The director's chief duty is to direct his team efficiently from both the artistic and organizational points of view . . . He co-operates closely with the scenario writer. In agreement with the latter he may alter the scenario or heighten the dramatic interest; knowledge and experience of film drama are therefore essential . . . the director selects the actors, explains and distributes the parts, and outlines the characters of the chief and secondary roles. On the set he directs the action . . . harmonises the photography and the sound recording, and studies the sound effects and the musical score. When shooting is completed he supervises the editing and synchronisation and adds the final touches to the film . . . A film director should be well-versed in political and social questions and have a thorough knowledge of film production, including photographic chemistry, optics, materials, trick shots, sound recording, synchronisation, models, lighting and editing. He should be at the same time artist, technician and leader . . ."

It was obviously no way to 'break' into the movies and it is no small wonder that Polanski is reported to have dazzled American crews with his technical command of the medium. Even falling short in its aims, the school was bound to develop superb craftsmen.

Screen-writing

In 1954 the school produced a crop of graduates who would in future mix their professional careers with spare-time teaching and who would soon fuse with Kawalerowicz and Has in a stream of feature movies during the late 1950s and early 1960s known as the Polish Film School. A graduate in 1954 was Andrzej Wajda. He had served his 'probation' under Aleksander Ford who would guide (and in some respects oppose) his protégé's historic début, *Pokolenie (A Generation)*. In the same year the First International Congress of Film and Television Schools took place in Paris. Delegates included Britain's John Grierson and the Director of Polish Cinematography, Stanislaw Albrecht. The latter, in his address to the Congress, outlined the structure of the school and some of its aims:

"We intend to create a special class for screen-writing and while this may not produce great scenarists or great writing the students will know how to present a subject and transpose literary works into the cinematic language. Equally we hope to create a class for actors but conjointly with the creation of a theatre where they can be regularly engaged as well as making films at the school . . . I should say something more about our professors and stress that we have few technicians and they in any case are fully absorbed by our production. Which is why we invite technicians from abroad. In this domain the Soviet Union has greatly assisted us, sending its best operators for terms of three years . . . we have also had aid from other countries: for several years the well-known Italian director Barbaro was a professor at our schoool . . ."

The difficulties in training scenarists were to be raised repeatedly right up until the present day. At the Fourth International Congress, again in Paris at the time of the 1958 Cannes Festival, rector Jerzy Toeplitz aired the problem. He acknowledged that the weakest part of their programme was the development of screen-writing skills in the majority of student directors who were simply unwilling to film other people's plays. Apart from actual authorship, there was a second level of creativity, vampirising a third party's script – in essence, rewriting before shooting. In either case

some craft or know-how was essential, without obliging a film maker to conceive everything from the ground up or even write the scenario. The discussion touched on the sensitive issue of 'auteurism': who really was the artist in this collaborative art? A French delegate remarked:

"It is impossible to conceive a film maker who is not at the same time his own scenarist . . . in taking an idea from a novel, a play or (another's) scenario he is bound to stamp his own style on the matter in hand. At the point where he imposes his own style he certainly becomes a scenarist himself – without that he is no creator . . ."

Antoni Bohdziewicz, also a delegate, described the tug-of-war between students, anxious to realise their own writing (not always matched by literary or narrative talent), and the professors who preferred to impose adaptations of literary works. Given an existing story, for example, it was easier to measure a student's mastery of the material, his grasp of elements suitable to the film medium and his ability to seek the right means of expression. He stressed that the rigidity of former years had gone, and though the educational aspect of film was observed, it was encouraged only in the broadest sense. There was now a single professor to guide a student's work, and not a commission of many. The conflict of wills – exercises imposed by the professors versus realisation of 'art' by the students – had in Bohdziewicz's view produced a range of subjects far vaster than had previously existed in the profession and moreover it had enriched experiment and research into the film form itself.

The structure of the course

Students actually began filming in their

second year with final prints limited to about 150 metres (5 minutes). This rose to around 900 metres or half an hour screen-time for their diplomas. Toeplitz reported that to date four full-length films had gone on general distribution each comprising three different stories – diploma works by three student groups. In one case the three parts had been written to form a whole. (Jerzy Skolimowski produced a variation by constructing his feature début from exercises completed over the three years). Bohdziewicz outlined the structure of the course:

YEAR ONE –

The student has the right to make a small film from his own idea or from an adaptation of a work chosen by him or by his professor – silent, black-and-white and six to seven minutes long. Furthermore, he adapts and shoots a silent fiction piece based on work prepared by actors in their department.

YEAR TWO –

The student shoots two films, each of around ten minutes, with sound, and in black-and-white; one a documentary, the other on popular science.

YEAR THREE –

The student makes his 'examination film' in either black-and-white or colour, with sound, in two or even three acts.

FINALLY –

The diploma film at around 900 metres or half an hour on-screen.

('He' is a shorthand convenience – there are of course women, though far fewer than men).

The films offered practical work to students from all three faculties: direction, camera and production management. Graduates or final-year students some-times made short films for outside institutions and everyone was expected to work over the holidays with professionals – either on shoots or in laboratories, studios or editing-rooms. In principle there was one consultative professor from 'camera' and one from 'direction' allocated to a student. They oversaw the stages of scenario, shooting script, realisation and editing, and these could only be changed with the agreement of the Doyen; such changes were rare. When a film was finished the consultant professors took 'copy zero', complete with sound, to a kolaudacja or 'committee of appreciation' allied to the Central Office of Cinematography. The film was assessed on its artistic, technical and economic qualities.

In Lodz the colossal personnel compared to the number of students makes it possible for there to be a commitment by working professionals who devote some of their time to teaching – partly for the income as the subsistence wages in the units are rarely enough to live on.

The production course of two years is attended by graduates in economics or law. There are departments for editing, screen-writing and television. The latter (in contrast to the faculty for directors in film and television) is aimed at television professionals to raise their artistic level. Another television school – quite controversial – was started in Katowice in a wing of the university. Jerzy Bossak, a professor at Lodz, is adamant that television sent its people to the film school in preference to Katowice which had in the first place been financed by the television body, Poltel. Poltel is connected only in a commercial sense with the Central Office of Cinematography. It buys in films produced by the units, or makes use of film personnel; it is under a completely different direction. Bossak also says that the Katowice school was transformed into a division of the university with a greater concentration on theory than on the concrete aspects of production.

The structure of the acting department is such that a fully professional theatre is run in Lodz – Studio 83 – and half the productions are diploma plays. The students worked with famous directors such as Adam Hanuszkiewicz or Maciej Prus.

Resources

Politically the school is run by a Senate, elected by the whole school and made up of professors, workers and students. There is a councillor from each department and a headmaster. The head of each institute and the headmaster (at present, Henryk Kluba) are chosen by the Senate, and the headmaster's assistants have also to be approved by that body. The headmaster has to be accepted by the Ministry of Culture and Arts and if the candidate was refused the Senate has to come up with another.

There were (at January 1985) 132 masters and 350 administrative and technical personnel. There is a film archive with 4000 features from all periods and countries, 2000 shorts and 1000 student shorts. There is a library with 50 000 books, a sound studio and editing facilities including ten movieolas (eight for 35mm, two for 16mm), and small departments for costumes and props. There is a lab for stills but not for motion-film, so that professional labs and other institutions (say, for special props, décors or even cameras) are called upon where the needs of diploma scripts go beyond the school's facilities. Graduates making diploma films have the right to be treated as professionals in the sense that they can contract as many professional actors as required – paid for by the school – and, within reason, special props or décor, as well as contracting the musicians of their choice.

The tendency is to use medium-range actors so that the director will not feel intimidated by a star actor who effectively directs the production.

Television

In the year 1983/84 the school spent 100 million zloty (the cost of three normal features) on the whole of film production which included five half-hour works from third-year students and two films of an hour. The latter were fused into a feature called *Fucha (Moonlighting)* which was released nationally. Money from such a film and from outside deals (such as a recent agreement with West Germany's Channel 2) is a bonus and can be used for buying or renewing equipment. The television studio employs a U-matic system and is located at some distance from Targowa 61. The professional equipment for student use includes four new cameras and a mixing-table, a sound-mixer for three tape-recorders and a television studio of normal professional dimensions. The students do exercises here in their first and third years An important television exercise is called the 'Master Shot' which is realised, in one take, from the student's own idea in consultation with the professor. There is also a telecine for 35mm and 16mm transfer to tape.

Entrance examinations

A university degree is not required; high-school graduation is sufficient but Kluba says that some degree of artistic achievement connected with film is essential, but this could be in music, acting, photography, and so on. Age limits are twenty-eight for directors and twenty-five for actors. It is a little more flexible for foreigners but thirty is about the limit. An

Australian student of recent Polish origin, Antoni Borzewski, described in detail his own route to final acceptance as a student for the school:

"As a foreign student the exam takes three days. Before this, however, you have to supply the school with your artwork, whatever that means. I supplied my photography work plus my drawings and two screenplays. The professors have three months to go through it and read everything. Then they let you know whether you are accepted – that is, whether you can come to Lodz for the exams which take three days.

"The first test has two separate aptitude tests: documentary and fiction. They give you a few envelopes and you have to choose two of them. You've got about thirty photographs in an envelope and you spread them all over the floor, choosing eight of them for fiction and five or six for documentary. Then you put them in a sequence as in editing. The second test is that, with either your own or the school's equipment (stills) and the film they supply, you go out for four or five hours and take about ten to fifteen photographs. When printed you can choose up to eight for your story. The subjects are pretty general but it has to make some kind of story. It could be documentary: for instance I went to the cemetery to look for a documentary and I was in luck – there was a funeral going on.

"The second day you have to draw. Out of many pieces of paper you pick one, on which you have a sentence or two as the subject of your theatrical scene – it might say, for instance, 'boy and girl saying goodbye at the station'. You've got twenty minutes or so to think about your own little story on that scene. Then you take actors – students from the film directing course – and explain your intentions to them, in front of the professors. They then perform it on-stage and

you have the right to interrupt and get them to repeat the scene. When it's finished you discuss with the professors what was right or wrong and how you think it could be improved. Then follows a discussion with the candidate, why he would like to study here, what his art interests are and so on. They question you about film, literature, the arts and anything connected with the subject. That's about all."

Costs

For foreign students, the exams are much shorter because of the language barrier; they do not take written tests. But they are just as strictly controlled. Foreigners can be sponsored by the Polish government in accordance with bilateral agreements, for example with France and Italy. Otherwise the student pays for his own education, in 1985 at about US $6000 (600 000 zloties) per annum which still falls short of the costs incurred by the school. For directors of photography the cost is reckoned at 800 000 zloties per year. These figures apply only for the first three years; in the fourth (diploma) year the costs rocket – the half-hour films cost three to four million zloties each.

Henryk Kluba

The present rector, Henryk Kluba, has by no means retired from film making – and has plans for another feature. He is a film maker and actor (appearing in Polanski's *Mammals* and *Two Men and a Wardrobe)* whose career was somewhat checked with the shelving of his feature *The Sun Rises Yet Again (Slonce Wschodzi raz na dzien)*, made in 1967. It deals with the resistance of the inhabitants of a small mountain village to the installation of Communist power. It is still his favourite work and was highly regarded but as mentioned the times were difficult. Kluba affirms his view that art should be taught by outstanding artists:

"We are not trying to reproduce any Hases or Kawalerowiczes or any other artists . . . For each student we try to realise an individual programme that suits his needs and respect his individual ideas and expression even in the first year when in theory the studies are general. Even in the first two years they are making exercises which are individually their own . . . The school tries to prepare the student to be an author, something like a personality, more than just a student. Of course we have to introduce some rules, so this school is organised like a university with separate faculties (ie directors, cameramen, production managers) and they have not changed for the last forty years. But the departments, workshops and 'chairs' – they change from time to time. Right now I am planning to develop an institute which will organise both archive programs and meetings between students and 'masters' who are not institutionally connected with the school – giving them the possibility to work to-gether. It will also produce a quarterly magazine dealing with film history and present day problems . . ."

Apart from Kluba, other personalities who teach at the school include Wojciech Has, Jerzy Kawalerowicz, Janusz Morgen-stern, Andrzej Trzos-Rawiecki, Filip Bajon, Feliks Falk and Janusz Kondratiuk from features, and Jerzy Bossak and Kazimierz Karabasz from documentary.

Andrzej Mellin

Andrzej Mellin, a teacher and docu-mentary film maker attached to the Educational Studio in Lodz, visited the National Film School in Beaconsfield in 1985 for a short stint as a lecturer. He made the following comparison:

"With us the system for the students is harder. They *have* to learn. If they don't understand they must leave the school. Maybe here [in England] there is more 'democracy'– there are excellent conditions for teaching, the equipment is very good – but the students are not *obliged;* it's not serious if they don't work so much . . . As a professor at the school I earn 12000 zloties a month for which I must work directly with the students twelve hours a week. The national average salary is 18000 and the university professors have almost the same as the average. It's very low, unless you've written a book or published some articles. It's completely mad. At my school a woman who works as a cleaner gets more than me."

Mellin remarked that début films were now not so much of a problem for the graduates because the school had just received fifty million zloties to fund students' diploma films under pro-fessional conditions – with the condition that they could be distributed if the standard was high enough. These first features are often done in the *Rondo* unit, headed by Has. Thus diploma films have now become the débuts: "It's not the first film which is tough to make; now it's hard getting the *second* off the ground!" says Mellin.

The school is an integral part of Polish film production and practically the only way into the profession: more than 80% of directors, cameramen and production managers working in films were trained at the school. It is unquestionably a key factor in the regeneration of Polish cinema and it provided the technical base for the flowering of the 'Polish Film School' twelve or so years after the war. There was never a question of teaching that which can't be taught: talent. It was a rational (and very expensive) way of supplying tools for this very complex applied art.

10: *Polish history and literature on film*

The Saragossa Manuscript

In 1794 Boleslaw Worowski, a young Polish officer, incited his people to revolt. Czarina, Catherine II, sent agents to arrest him, but Baron Kemplen (a renowned inventor of robots) hid Worowski in a suit of armour which he described to his inquisitors as a 'mechanical chess player'. Catherine, a chess aficianado, hearing of the wonderful machine, summoned it to Moscow for her personal use. When Worowski, in the armour, failed to execute a cheat move, she ordered the 'robot' to be shot for treason. At the last moment, the Baron substituted for Worowski and died instead. A suspicious Russian officer visited the Baron's laboratory where the dormant robots suddenly sprang to life.

They multiplied rapidly and crushed the breath from the tyrant . . .

Boleslaw Michalek

This curious episode is the basis of a French silent in 1930 – *The Chess Player*. It would be an unlikely venture for a Polish film maker, supported by a tax-paying public perfectly well aware of its history – a fact weighing heavily on any director tackling historical themes. Screen-writer and critic Boleslaw Michalek comments:

"The literature was always obliged to articulate the main national and social issues for a hundred years. This was never the case, say, in France, where literature has always been a game. It is the real tradition of literature in this country, and also to a certain extent the idea of the cinema, which doesn't generally succeed with the purely psychological. It is also quite dangerous, you know, because there is always this continual meditation on serious social issues. It can *paralyse* the film maker because he feels so *responsible*. There is an exaggerated sense of responsiblity; you can't *move,* you get to feel so responsible that every move you make seems to have enormous consequences; it paralyses. You don't feel free to do something frivolous."

It is undisputed that literature played an enormous role in the positive development of Polish cinema, and of what Michalek calls "a certain language, a way of penetrating moral and social issues". Unlike Hollywood, for instance, Poland had only a literature which was dense and difficult for film adaptation – a multi-textured narrative providing not only stories, but also an unusual interpretation of society and human endeavour, with a point of view untypical of feature films:

"Take any film by Wajda, by Kawalerowicz – this is not typical story-telling," says Michalek. "There is always something more – sometimes unsuccessful, sometimes boring, sometimes pretentious, but it always comes out of the literature which in a way was always very pretentious." This perspective of Polish literature which concerns human fate and the problems of society is transferred to the screen treatment; according to Michalek, this is not the case with film making outside Poland, which gives it a certain originality.

Boleslaw Sulik

London-based writer and producer Boleslaw Sulik was the screen-writer for

The Shadow Line (*Smuga Ciena*), a film about the novelist Joseph Conrad and filmed by Wajda in 1976. He describes Polish concern with history as "obsessive". The fact that Poland relinquished its status as a two-nation commonwealth after the Second World War created what Sulik describes as an "upset country", living in its history more than in the present:

"There is a certain sense of neurosis which pervades the country, a neurosis whereby they reject the present political reality . . . they just don't want it, they want something else. No other country in Europe which has suffered a similar fate has the same sense of neurosis that Poland has . . . The lands in the east were lands where Poles were in the minority but lived with other minorities and created a very interesting and quite unique cultural formation. Almost all of the major Polish artists and poets came from that part of Poland. Even now, the most eminent emigré writer, Milosz, calls himself a Lithuanian though he is still a Pole. He comes from Wilno. The demons of the past are still very much alive – in that sense it is an upset country. It's partly what Wajda is about. Half his output if you like is about the absurdity of this compelling power of history . . . the other half, the recent films like *Man of Marble* and *Man of Iron,* is an apology for the same fact."

Wajda

Wajda in some recent interviews expresses his regret that the characters in his early films were ciphers with an existence rendered meaningless in the face of historical forces. In a television interview with Sulik, he said that if *Kanal* were made today he would emphasize the hopes and desires of his characters; their acts would no longer be futile gestures crushed by fate. In spite of the appalling human cost of the Uprising, Wajda had begun to see it historically as a very fruitful experience for the Poles and that it was better for those young people to die suddenly as warriors than slowly in bondage.

"It is impossible to claim that history doesn't matter in Poland, it is imprinted into the citizens' lives", says Sulik. Dates, for example – 1956, to take a recent date – are important in a personal and political sense. 1968, 1863, 1830 – those dates meant, for instance, whether you could get or lose a flat, whether therefore you could marry and have kids, whether you could have any decent friends or be expected to inform on them. Every kind of political change – and one can recall a series of recent dates such as 1949, 1953, 1956, 1968, 1970, 1976, 1980, 1981 – carries a challenge to personal values. "It's an extremely important part of human lives. That's why there is this obsessive preoccupation with public issues in Polish cinema and literature. Yes, there are a lot of films that do not deal with it but the films which are any good tend to be about relations between individuals and the national life rather than about isolated human experiences – which is perhaps a strength rather than a weakness of Polish cinema."

Polanski and Skolimowski

Pinpointing an ambivalence in Poland towards the West and bearing in mind that film 'generations' can occur every five years, Sulik highlighted the generation represented by Polanski and Skolimowski, both of whom had initial access to the West and now work exclusively there:

"That is a generation that was already brought up in Poland, with a sense of deprivation and a sense of jealousy – not too strong a word – in their relations with the West towards whom their feelings are extremely ambivalent. I mean, they are in a sense barbarians; they want it all but at the same time they feel a certain contempt. The Westerners are people who don't know what life is basically about; 'they' have it all and 'we' have little. That's talking in crude terms but there is something in it.

"A prevalent attitude in Poland is that we are wiser and that history is with us because we have been through all that disillusion and all the political suffering, that the West is naive and self-indulgent. But the West is also where all the Polish values come from, at least, Poles like to think so. They reject Russia and they reject the cultural influences of the East. The West offers all the comforts they would like to have – not just materially, but personal freedom. Older artists like Munk and Wajda were much more involved with political themes and values. Skolimowski and Polanski are only at one remove involved with politics."

Henryk Sienkiewicz

The early 1960s saw the first of a series of epic Polish films, labelled "the most spectacular Polish movie of all time": Aleksander Ford's *The Teutonic Knights* (*Krzyzacy*, 1960). It opened a decade and a half of blockbusters in the Polish cinema. The film is taken from the 1900 novel by the Nobel laureate Henryk Sienkiewicz (1846 – 1916). His popular *Trylogia – By Sword and Fire, The Deluge* and *Pan Wolodyjowski*, set in the 17th century – provided material for two other blockbusters directed by Jerzy Hoffman.

Sienkiewicz was born in a rural part of the Russian zone and so was a young man at the time of the 1863 Insurrection and the Czar's ruthless countermeasures. As regards literature the new period brought in the mood of 'positivism', a so-called transfer from the 'heart' (Romanticism, lyricism), as represented by the emotionally charged works of the Paris exiles, to the 'brain'. Prose replaced poetry and the writers responded to a mood that emphasised the practical rebuilding of the nation through *possible* social change, such as the emancipation of women, but above all through a broadly based system of education and the setting up of some enduring institutions as a heritage for the new state to come.

Sienkiewicz expressed his intention, through the novels, to "fortify the hearts of his countrymen, to implant in them the conviction that the Polish nation which in the past had been in tragic situations, could still manage to emerge from these difficulties victoriously." Along with a fellow-patriot, the pianist, Ignacy Paderewski, Sienkiewicz worked constantly in and out of Poland to acquire international support for the self-determination of his country. As a writer his works are comparable to the nationalistic novels of Sir Walter Scott.

Quo Vadis?

Quo Vadis? is Sienkiewicz's best known work, filmed in four versions but never in

The Teutonic Knights

Poland. It is a 'Polish' novel in a very clear sense. Sienkiewicz said that the story – depicting the triumph of Christianity over Rome – was attractive to him as a Pole in its idea of "the victory of spirit over material strength; it fascinated me as an artist by the splendid forms in which the ancient world knows how to garb itself." His heroine, Lygia, was a Samartian, one of the barbarian races in conflict with Rome and from which the Slavs are said to have descended.

The Teutonic Knights

In 1960 Aleksander Ford secured his biggest ever budget to produce a blockbuster, inspired by the most glorious moment in the history of the nation. Ford wanted to produce a monument to participate in the celebrations that year of the Millenium of the Polish State (the Church had its own millenium in 1966).

The film is scripted by Ford and Jerzy Stawinski (author of *Kanal, Eroica* and *Bad Luck)*. At the time when filming commenced in July 1959 through to its première in August 1960, it was a spectacle involving about 1800 people and hailed by Film Polski as "without doubt the most ambitious film spectacle attempted in the history of the Polish cinema"; the claim was probably correct. As several examples show (most notably Sergei Bondarchuk's *War and Peace*, 1967), there is no reason why a Socialist state cannot produce the Most Spectacular and Costly Movie of All Time. *The Teutonic Knights* was to be topped in quick succession by other Polish epics in the following fourteen years.

The action spans the end of the 14th century up to the Battle of Grunwald (Tannenburg) in 1410. The Knights, who described the recent conversion of pagan Lithuania as a sham, attracted Knights from England and France in its just cause against the 'infidel'. Poland/Lithuania represented a considerable military force and an inevitable battle with the Knights took place after years of diplomatic manoeuvres.

Grunwald took place in a day: July 15 1410. Ranged against the Knights and their mercenary crusaders were the numerically superior Polish, Lithuanian and Ruthenian camps together with Czechs and some truly infidel Tartars. The Knights were technically superior and had a psychological edge of 'invincibility'. After a series of reversals the day was won convincingly by the Polish nobility in their finest historical hour. The Grand Master, Ulrich von Jungengen, was dead. It was a blow rather than a decisive defeat for the Knights who continued to trouble the country for the next fifty years, but it broke their ascent.

The plot of the film is as follows. The Knights are in conflict with a Polish magnate, Jurand. Upon his absence they raid his settlement and kill his wife. Jurand swears vengeance and sends his daughter Danusia to stay in safety at the Duke of Mazovia's court where she meets a handsome knight, Zbyszko. They fall in love and he swears he will avenge her mother's death. Zbyszko attacks a diplomat of the Order and King Jagiello is obliged to sentence him to death. Danusia intercedes and the pair are betrothed.

Zbyszko returns to his family home and falls in love with his childhood sweetheart Jagienka, but is faithful to Danusia who is meanwhile abducted by the Knights as bait to lure her father into a trap. King Jagiello dispatches Zbyszko with some envoys to plead for her release. But the new Grand Master, the satanic Ulrich von Jungengen, is looking for a clash with the Poles and the film climaxes with a spectacular battle. In the hands of her captors Danusia has gone mad and dies, leaving Zbyszko free to marry Jagienka.

There were mixed reviews abroad. *Variety* praised "the splendid colour lensing by Mieczyslaw Jahoda, especially in exteriors and battle scenes" but criticised the "propagandistic position " of the script – white Poles and black Germans – and also the fact that "despite some exciting battle and duel sequences . . . the remainder is a generally tedious and talky pastiche".

The Teutonic Knights remains the most successful box-office film in Poland to date. In a poll conducted by the magazine *Ekran*, the public voted Ford as best director and the stars, Mieczyslaw Kalenik (as Zbyszko) and Grazyna Staniszewska, as the performers of 1960 for their work in this film.

The Deluge

The Deluge (Potop, 1974) was directed by Jerzy Hoffman, the ex-documentarist. It was his second 'blockbuster'. The first, *Pan Wolodyjowski,* was, like *The Deluge,* taken from Henryk Sienkiewicz's *Trylogia* and in 1969 was "the most expensive film of all time" – a mantle which passed from one film to another between 1960 and 1974. It may remain with *Potop* for some time, although the film is well down the list of box-office high-earners.

It was probably the nearest you could get to Errol Flynn/Olivia De Havilland in a country with no star system. Unlike a zillion dollar Hollywood flop, a turkey in Poland can hardly ruin its studio (the state, after all). But for that kind of public investment – the build-up as well as the money – it needed all the available hype.

Whilst not the first wide-screen colour production with an army of uniformed extras, it was the first to import American technology, notably Panavision cameras and lenses which performed remarkably well in the temperature extremes. There was much publicity during its three or so years' preparation and some open debate on the ideal star to embody the hero, Kmicic. The part fell to Daniel Olbrychski who had proved his talent in films by Wajda and Zanussi. His co-lead, Malgorzata Braunek, was also a public favourite who had impressed in Wajda's *Hunting Flies* and Zulawski's *Third Part of the Night*.

The final cinema version (as against the splices made into a television serial) lasted five hours and was released inland in two parts but exported in a three-hour version. There were seventy actors in major roles including Tadeusz Lomnicki, the versatile star of *A Generation* who repeated his role of Colonel Wolodyjowski from *Colonel Wolodyjowski*. The UK print achieved mostly luke-warm reviews. The film was nominated for an Oscar.

The Black Madonna

Many national treasures from the time of the invasions were loaned as props to adorn the interiors of assorted gentry homes. These included museum treasures, priceless pictures from churches in Wilno and Grodo, and other antiques from Jasna Góra, the famous monastery of Czestochowa. Here the first real resistance to the Swedish conquerors began and its hero, Father Kordecki, is the subject of another feature. Jasna Góra guards the famous painting *The Black Madonna*, an icon of eastern origin and the target of religious pilgrimages from all over Poland. It is an increasingly potent symbol of the indestructibility of the nation. The defence of that icon by a handful of people against a siege of the massed Swedes inspired revolts in other parts of the country.

The rooms in Wawel Castle in Cracow became film set interiors for the homes of the treacherous Lithuanians, Boguslaw and Janusz Radziwill.

During production of the film, bulletins announced hundreds of thousands of props, including military vehicles, siege guns, cannons, culverins, two thousand complete costumes and "1500 cloaks for Swedish soldiers appearing only in the background". A complete replica of the village Wolmontowicze was built and then burned on location near Minsk. Hoffman co-operated with the Alexander Dovshenko studio in Kiev and borrowed from the Soviet army the regiment of extras who had charged as a cavalry in the Bondarchuk films, *War and Peace* and *Waterloo*.

The Deluge

The background to *The Deluge* concerns a Swedish prince, Sigismund Vasa, who was elected to rule Poland in 1588. For a few years after the death of his father, King John III of Sweden, he became king of both countries and it seemed that a personal union similar to that with Lithuania might emerge. But Sigismund's uncle usurped the Swedish throne in 1600 and a state of war between the Polish and Swedish Vasas culminated in the 'deluge' of 1655/56.

The film's action focuses on Andrzej Kmicic, a colour sergeant sworn to serve the Lithuanian hetman Janusz Radziwill. Realising that his chief is about to betray

Poland to the Swedes, Kmicic tries to warn King Jan Kazimierz (the last of the Vasa kings) who is tricked into believing that Kmicic himself is the traitor. Spurned by his love, Olenka, who similarly believes him a traitor, Kmicic assumes an alias and participates in the defence of Jasna Góra where he blows up a Swedish cannon. He co-operates further in hetman Czarnecki's nationwide campaigns. Pardoned by Jan Kazimierz for his supposed treason, Kmicic commands a Tartar unit. After years of fighting, suffering and beating the Swedes, Kmicic returns to be reconciled with Olenka.

This is a ludicrously slim and unjust outline of a narrative which is crammed with a criss-cross of plots, ever-changing locations and a panorama of politics in 17th century Europe.

Mazepa

More statisfying as drama and set in the reign of the same King Jan Kazimierz are two films based on Juliusz Slowacki's play *Mazepa*.

Slowacki (1809 – 1849) is one of the giant trio of poets (Mickiewicz and Krasinski are the others) who produced their work in Paris between the two famous anti-Russian insurrections of 1830/31 and 1863/64. It is Poland's equivalent of an Elizabethan era which arose from that small island of free Poland in Paris whose emigrés include Fredric Chopin (1810-1848). The poets fused their substantial literary output with political work. Adam Mickiewicz, like the future Pilsudski, set out to establish Polish legions in Constantinople. Slowacki is renowned for his richness of language and the Shakespearian scope of his dramas, of which *Mazepa* is a good example. The author wrote it in Paris in 1839 where it was published the next year but staged posthumously.

The legend of Mazepa has attracted writers such as Byron, Victor Hugo and Voltaire. Brought up on the Eastern borders of Poland, Mazepa was briefly a secretary to Jan Kazimierz. He studied militarism in Holland and commanded the Cossacks in the Ukraine. Several legends have remained – great lover, individualist, invincible swordsman, for example – and the drama takes license with the facts.

In film it inspired the exquisite version by Walerian Borowczyk entitled *Blanche* (France, 1971), a project that he had wanted to realize in Poland.

In 1975 the great Polish actor Gustav Holoubek filmed a relatively straight version of the play, having directed and played in it for television; Borowczyk too is faithful to the main points of Slowacki's narrative.

In Holoubek's version, King Jan Kazimierz (Zbigniew Zapasiewicz) and his page, Mazepa (Jerzy Bonczak), visit the castle of a Voivode (Mieczyslaw Voit), a proud magnate recently wed to the beautiful Amelia, who is at least a generation younger than himself. Zbigniew, the magnate's son by an earlier marriage, desparately loves his step-mother but regards himself as the protector of her virtue. (She is Blanche in Borowczyk's film.) Mazepa has a reputation as a Don Juan and the Voivode continually suspects attentions to his wife. His suspicions are misdirected since it is the King who openly desires the wife and makes plans for her seduction. Unable to sleep that night, the King disguises himself and attempts to sneak into Amelia's room but is beaten off by Zbigniew. Mazepa gallantly deflects the blame from his King and Voivode is convinced that the intruder was Mazepa.

The King dispatches a sealed letter to his army commander. Confronted some distance from the castle by Zbigniew, Mazepa is forced to a duel and wins a bloodless fight. The letter, torn open in the scuffle, reveals the King's plan to abduct Amelia by force and place Mazepa under arrest. The latter hurries back to the fortified castle with the intention of warning Amelia. He steals into her room but before she sees him, her husband storms in accusing her of hiding a lover. Forced to accept her denial over the Bible he nevertheless walls up Mazepa's section as an airtight unit and casts his wife into a dungeon.

Jan Kazimierz, fearing that Amelia has been bricked up, demands that the Voivode tear down the wall. He discovers the unconscious Mazepa who is immediately challenged by the Voivode to a duel. Zbigniew insists in fighting in his father's stead but allows himself to be killed by Mazepa with whom he has established a bond. The dying Zbigniew confesses his love for Amelia. The enraged Voivode refuses to release the king from the castle unless he can retain Mazepa as a hostage. Jan Kazimierz agrees but vows to return in two days.

When Amelia learns of Zbigniew's love she commits suicide and Mazepa blames the Voivode's despotism for the lovers' deaths. Against all honour the Voivode kills Mazepa and ties him onto the back of a Ukrainian horse which he lets loose onto the plains. The Voivode kills himself and the King returns with his men only to see the havoc of his own carelessness.

The story is a meticulous chain-reaction of events precipitated by Jan Kazimierz, with a Hamlet-like series of deaths at the end. Both versions are absorbing films, with good casts and the story slightly less melodramatic in Borowczyk's hands. He casts the superb French comedian Michel Simon as the Voivode, an old man with a fine, smooth-skinned possession in 'Blanche', and there is something repulsive in the husbandly kiss. Her attraction to the handsome young son is

made clear visually whereas in Holoubek's version Mieczyslaw Voit as the Voivode (he plays the priest in Kawalerowicz's *Mother Joan of the Angels*) looks like a man in his prime. Borowczyk changes the setting from 17th century Poland to 13th century France.

Wojciech Has

Has's status in Poland rivals that of the top directors if not quite that of Wajda. He is known for his transpositions of 'impossible' literary works. The critic Krzysztof-Teodor Toeplitz noted in 1964 that Has had never made a war film, which was almost a kind of national service for Polish film makers: "rather as in medieval studios a painter had to produce a Madonna and Child before he could be considered a master".

Has does in fact touch on the war in *Farewells (Pozegania,* 1958) , a film about a couple separated in time by the war which impinges but remains off-screen. It stars Tadeusz Janczar, Maria Wachowiak and a young Gustav Holoubek.

An Uninteresting Story

Holoubek appears in Has's recent *An Uninteresting Story (Nieciekawa Historia,* 1982), an off-putting title which fairly accurately describes spectator reaction, though there are things to admire, such as Holoubek's central performance as the aging doctor dwelling on the hollowness of his life.

The slow, reflective pace of this film leaves one with the impression of reading a quite interesting book that would be good to put aside and return to again and again at leisure, maybe over several weeks and, at the end, appreciating that one has enjoyed a remarkable work, having fully yet gradually absorbed the worlds of its various characters. Perhaps that is why Has is often called a 'literary' director.

Pismak

There is evidently an informed intelligence at work but in the case of the above film and his more recent *Pismak*, shown at the 1985 festival in Gdansk, the whole two hours are difficult to consume in one go.

Both films are claustrophobic works: *Pismak* is set in a jail and many of the exteriors, which occur only in a prisoner's mind, are of moving-train interiors and close two-shots. Added to which – in *An Uninteresting Story* – is the weight of a negative character. Bored or 'victim' characters without any fight or positive force (a good example is *Woyzzek*) are supremely difficult to endure on-screen if they are central to the drama and the only remaining spectator pleasure is an intellectual one: if one is acquainted with the literary source, to examine the director's method of transmitting the work to the screen.

Pismak

The Saragossa Manuscript

In contrast Has's *The Saragossa Manuscript* (*Rekopis Znaleziony w Saragossie*, 1964) is a visual feast and an abundance of action stories, not quite a horror film or committed swashbuckler but with many elements of both. It is certainly an epic, although there are no signs of army-loaned extras. It is the most interesting of the blockbusters and reveals Cybulski as the good light comedian he most probably was. It is one of those rare films where words such as 'hallucinatory' and 'surreal' are entirely apt.

The film concerns the spiritual odyssey of a young captain of the Spanish Walloon guards (Cybulski) whose adventures begin in the arid region of Sierra Morena at the site of a gallows. The film begins with a certain Count Potocki, participating in the siege of Saragossa in Spain, stumbles into a ruined house where he finds an old book and becomes so immersed in its pictures that he is captured by a Spanish soldier. The latter too is enraptured with the book since it is a chronicle about his ancestor, Alphonse von Worden, the captain played by Cybulski.

Taking a short cut to Madrid over the rocky Sierra Morena, von Worden finds himself by the gallows and spends the night in a ruined inn. A beautiful Moorish slave appears and leads him to a chamber where two half-naked princesses declare that he is a descendent of the powerful Mauretenian Gomelez family. He is to be entrusted with important missions provided he succeeds in a series of tests. About to make love to both women, he wakes up near the gallows under the swinging corpses.

Von Worden meets a cabalist and later a mathematician who represent religion and rationalism and each of whom tries to win over the captain's soul. There is much play throughout on this kind of dualism –

spirit and matter, dream and reality.

The film is constructed largely by other people's stories, and by stories by the characters in the stories (Cybulski looks as confused as the audience). It is one of the most cinematic of Polish films and its plastic and visual qualities suggest the touch of an animator such as Borowczyk, rather than a bibliophile. It recalls the more recent work of the American Terry Gilliam, particularly his feature *Brazil*.

Ostensibly a story about von Wordern there are so many interruptions from the people he meets who tell their stories, and from the characters in those stories who tell their stories, that one is unsure sometimes exactly how the events depicted on-screen relate to the 'present'. Again, as with a book, it would be nice to flip back some pages. But the first, if confused viewing is enjoyable for the individual scenes and for Krzysztof Penderecki's rich score, whether a parody of the works of old masters or nerve-tingling electronic effects.

Count Jan Potocki

The chronology of the author, Count Jan Potocki, is also exotic. He travelled widely as a young man, through Italy, Sicily, Malta, Tunis, Constantinople and Egypt, and then through England, Spain and Morocco. He fought in the Polish Army just prior to the Second Partition but avoided involvement in politics. Potocki wrote scientific books on archaeology and ethnology, went on expeditions to the Caucasus and China, and after the failure of the Napoleonic campaigns – Poland's great hope for its re-emergence as a state – he retired to his estate at Podole.

For his private amusement he wrote and staged comedy plays in French. In 1815 he completed his amazing fable, *The Saragossa Manuscript*, said to have begun as an oral narrative to amuse his ailing wife and drawn from his wealth of memories of exotic people and lands. He committed suicide in the following year.

The Saragossa Manuscript

Ashes

Ashes (Popioly) is the Polish *War and Peace*, written by the great Stefan Zeromski (1864-1925), whose books were bestsellers and frequently filmed between the World Wars. *Ashes* spans fifteen years between 1797 and 1812, the year of Napoleon's winter retreat from Moscow. Zeromski describes his own book:

"What is involved here are the deeds of the Polish legionnaires under the skies of Italy and Spain and even beyond the Atlantic ocean. A number of quick scenes show the Polish countryside during the rule of the Austrians with the life of the manors, of the poorer gentry who shut themselves off from everybody else in their estates and of the new magnates who bought their way, with the help of the Austrian government, into the ranks of the aristocracy. Scenes in schools and institutions of higher learning from those times are followed by scenes depicting the debaucheries of the 'golden youth' and the life of the secret Masonic orders. Much space is devoted to love and war. The latter took up many chapters . . . "

Ashes as directed by Wajda in 1965 is a sprawling epic and fully warrants the 140 actors and 1500 extras. It was shot in Poland and Bulgaria; the epic 'storming of Saragossa' was shot in Wroclaw. In fact an abandoned set from *The Saragossa Manuscript* – a large artificial Spanish town – was redecorated for use in *Ashes*. In the spectacular battle scenes two hundred out of the thousand-odd extras were specially trained in the necessary skills and they appear in the foreground of the battles, switching uniforms to fight on each side. An inexperienced young actor, Daniel Olbrychski was chosen to play Rafal Olbromski as one of the 10 000 legionnaires.

Initially Olbromski remains aloof from the Emperor's campaigns but eventually

Ashes

joins an army commanded by Josef Poniatowski. He is wounded and ultimately blinded; these terrible episodes gradually break down any illusion the Poles have that Napoleon will restore their country. In the silence of a wintry landscape strewn with snow-covered corpses, Olbromski hears the wheels of a carriage. Now blind, he is unable to witness a sullen Napoleon escorted by cavaliers en route through Poland after his bitter retreat from Moscow.

The disillusionment with Napoleon is sharply dramatised in the storming of Saragossa in Spain under the Emperor's orders. The Poles are forced to subdue a people who, like themselves, simply cry out for freedom.

Never one to shirk controversy, Wajda's treatment of the widely-read novel excited the hottest and longest debate of any of the blockbusting epics. The black-and-white Franscope epic was written by Aleksander Scibor-Rylski and photographed by Jerzy Lipman.

Boleslaw Prus

Has next adapted *The Doll* (*Lalka*, 1968) from the novel by Boleslaw Prus, a representative of the 'Positivist' epoch in the second half of the 19th century. Prus (real name Aleksander Glowacki, 1846-1912) like Sienkiewicz was a journalist and is regarded as the best Polish writer of realism. He published his quasi-historical *Faraon* in 1897. Concerning a fictional dynasty ruling the Egypt of the Pharaohs, it is less a history than a reflection on the way a country is run, the difficulties of internal reform, the pressures of social groups and the responsible handling, or otherwise, of power.

Kawalerowicz's Pharaoh

The ambitious *Faraon* was taken up by the experienced director Jerzy Kawalerowicz, like Has a fellow graduate of Poland's first film school in Cracow. The film was a fantastic exercise in moving resources and men - "Communism's answer to Cleopatra", as one described it. Film Polski's publicity went further and hailed it as an "anti-Cleopatra epic".

The story deals with the fictional prince, Ramses, heir to the throne of his father, Pharaoh Ramses XII, and commander of the Egyptian army. In part one (it is shown with an interval) the conflict is established between Ramses and a powerful caste of priests. Love interest is provided by a beautiful Jewish slave by whom he has a child and who is a major source of conflict with the priests.

An Assyrian envoy makes a deal with the priests whereby Egypt will relinquish control of Phoenicia. Fearing Assyrian domination the Phoenicians ask Ramses to make war on the Assyrians and try to seduce him into this course by using a priestess with whom Ramses becomes infatuated. While Ramses is busy quelling a rebellion by Libyan mercenaries, his Jewish mistress is murdered through the agency of the priestess.

Ramses succeeds to the throne on his father's death and comes into open conflict with the priests, who as guardians of the gold reserves, refuse to give them to Ramses for his campaigns. The Pharaoh summons his army and plans to charge the priests with high treason. The high priest uses his esoteric knowledge of an imminent eclipse of the sun, appeals to the superstitious masses and claims that the eclipse is a divine sign in support of the caste of priests. During the eclipse Ramses is murdered and the high priest ascends to the throne to carry out the very policies which in Ramses he had opposed.

The exteriors were shot over a five-month period – June to October 1964 – in the Kisil-Kim desert near Bokhara in Uzbekistan. The director was loaned 3000 extras by the Soviet army, and wood was transported 1200 miles from the Siberian forests to build realistic sets, including the Pharaoh's palace and a temple. 10 000 bottles of soft drinks were consumed each day in the 35°C heat.

The catalogue of accessories includes 6000 military costumes, 3000 Egyptian and Libyan head-dresses, 3000 shields, 320 hacked-off rebels' hands (!), 700 bows, 13 000 arrows, and so on. Russia supplied one hundred technicians and builders in addition to the hundred crew and a cast of twenty major actors from Poland. US film stock was imported for the shoot which continued for one month in Egypt for scenes by the Nile. The interiors were completed in Polish studios.

Pharaoh was not a success in the English language market. One cannot deny the obvious intelligence applied to the issues of power and to the ambitions of the protagonists. But somehow, after the first intake of breath looking at all those resources and the scale provided by the desert, sitting out the first half especially is a fatiguing experience: it cries out for the panache of the formula epics. For Polish audiences too, philosophical speculation on power in a culture remote in time and place – however linked by its undercurrent to Polish history – lacks the direct symbolic power of a Grunwald battle or the even more alive issue of *Ashes*, and it certainly has none of the fun of *Saragossa*.

In box-office terms all it could sell was bigger battles, bigger sets, more beautiful women, etcetera. But at the end of it all, those thousands of soldiers and weapons, those months of contact with desert snakes and scorpions, the awesome sands and the heat are all crammed into a few flat tin cans. The most unbelievably spectacular scenes in some of the great Hollywood spectacles were achieved with glass shots and miniatures.

The Story of Sin

Not an epic in production terms *The Story of Sin* (*Dzieje Grzechu*, 1975), Borowczyk's film of Stefan Zeromski's 1906 novel, marked his return to Poland.

Invited by the *Tor* unit to make a film after his recognised success with *Blanche*, Borowczyk already had a reputation as an eroticist if not pornographer. Coupled with his choice of a turn of the century novel which was originally condemned as indecent and included on the Index by the Church, this made his producers nervous. Krzysztof Zanussi, now head of *Tor*, recalls the conferences between Borowczyk and his colleagues in an attempt to thrash out a scenario that had some chance of a green light from the Ministry of Culture. The film was the most explicit to date in Poland, though not explicit enough for Borowczyk's taste.

The plot has Ewa (Grazyna Dlugolecka), the respectable daughter of a landowning family (now settled in Warsaw), falling in love with the married Lukas, who is trying to obtain a divorce. Lukas disappears to Rome where he hopes to facilitate his divorce. Ewa is pregnant

and, unable to care for the child, kills it. She eventually discovers that Lukas has obtained his divorce and married a wealthy young girl.

Sinking into prostitution, she becomes the mistress of a villain named Pochron (Roman Wilhelmi) who plans to burgle the Roman apartment of Lukas, whom Ewa still loves. Ewa prevents Pochron from killing Lukas and in the scuffle she is mortally wounded and dies in the arms of her love.

The Wedding

That other 'Elizabethan', Stanislaw Wyspianski, in addition to being a successful stage designer and painter, was a powerful playwright who wrote *The Wedding* (*Wesele*), a play about a turn of the century wedding between a poet and a peasant girl. The play is spun around the actual wedding of a poet friend, Lucjan Rydel, to a peasant girl from a village near Cracow. The wedding took place on November 20 1900 at Our Lady's Church in Cracow. Wajda's screen treatment in 1972 was written by Andrzej Kijowski, and stars Daniel Olbrychski and Ewa Zietek.

The reception intermixed the intelligentsia (in effect the gentry) with guests from among the peasants – that vast estate of Poland (85% of the population when the Partitions began) who had never been included in the 'democracy' which the nobles had abrogated to themselves. It is the superficial democratic attitude of the intelligentsia that Wyspianski attacks in his play.

Wyspianski integrated his design skills into his writing in the same sense that the plastic skills of Borowczyk as a graphist/animator are evident in his films and screenplays. Wyspianski's design experiments were far ahead of their time and he stands alongside Gordon Craig and Max Reinhardt as a theatrical innovator.

11: *Animation and posters*

Laterna magica, *directed by Miroslaw Kijowicz*

With access to a worldwide heritage – from the first trick films of Emile Cohl in France in 1908 to a spectacular development of the commercial cartoon in America – Polish animators weren't exactly starting from scratch but they were obliged to begin as amateurs and as students of the art. Technically, drawn or 'cel' animation (allowing the tracing of moving parts of characters on celluloid sheets without having to redraw for every frame of the film) reached a peak with Disney's *The Old Mill* in 1937 and with his follow-up feature, *Fantasia*. A frame-to-frame reading of Disney's films was a training tool of the post-war cartoon studios.

Karol Irzykowski

The views of Karol Irzykowski, a critic of the silent film, are respected in Poland today as basic to cinema, despite the technical developments since then. In *The Tenth Muse (Dziesiata Muza*, published in 1924), he wrote that cinema belongs to the "improper arts" (sztuki niewlasciwe), using a "crude reality" under physical and biological processes that have to be respected by an artist. Contrary to the laws of "proper" arts (painting, sculpture and so on) this reality cannot be transformed into a pure art since it speaks from the screen regardless of the artist's intentions ("reality" includes the physique and voice of the actor). The one film form belonging to the "proper" arts is *animation* and Irzykowski even describes it as the film of the future:

"Normal film is just a stopgap for the pictorial film. To deprecate animation because of the development of live-action would be just as absurd as throwing out painting because the photographic mechanism was discovered."

Wladyslaw Starewicz

A truly great pioneering animator who reached his peak in the 1930s, Wladyslaw Starewicz never worked in Poland and strictly belongs to the film histories of France and Russia. He was born in 1882 in Moscow of a Polish family who fled there after the 1863 Uprising. His development as a cineaste was the logical extension of childhood passions: cartooning, modelling, magic lanterns and photography. With a growing reputation as a cartoonist Starewicz approached the Russian producer Khanzhonkov and secured backing for some educational shorts.

Battle of the Stag Beetles

Three out of his first four films concern the study of insects. In *Battle of the Stag Beetles* (*Zukow Rogachi*, 1910) he set up a fight in a Moscow studio. But the beetles, out of their normal habitat, not only would not join battle but expired under the heat of the lamps. Starewicz wired artificial limbs onto one of the creatures and articulated it frame by frame. The effect worked and he recreated a battle with automoton beetles and faked-up backgrounds – one of the first staged documentaries which were so well exploited by later 'documentarists' such as Flaherty.

His next two films are fiction proper: model insects as characters in animated boulevard comedies and human love-triangles. Starewicz continued in Russia, regularly turning out shorts until 1918.

Starewicz's career in France spans an enormous period from 1920 to 1965, when, in addition to trick films, he worked as a feature cameraman and made publicity shorts. His work in the difficult genre of mixed live-action, cartoon drawing and puppet animation remains unsurpassed and he is rivalled only by the great animator-comedian Charley Bowers, a Hollywood contemporary of Buster Keaton.

Starewicz also adapted the Polish classic *Pan Twardowski* in two shorts: *Pan Tvardovsky* (1916) and *Pan Tvardovsky v Rimye* (*Mr Twardowsky in Rome*, 1917), both shot in Russia. But in Poland in the late 1940s there was no one to guide those seriously wanting to take up animation.

Bielsko Biala

The first acknowledged post-war Polish cartoon is the 8mm film, *The Brusky Fox* (*Lis Kitaszek*, 1946), made by Maciej Sienski under Film Polski's Program Department. In 1947 a group of artists formed the Experimental Cartoon Film Studio, a co-operative in Katowice which eventually became the prolific Cartoon Film Studio in Bielsko Biala. The first of its shorts to reach public cinemas was *The Wolf and the Little Bears* (*Wilk i Niedzwiadki*, 1950), typical of the catechism stories predominant in those early years.

In 1952 the group was absorbed by Film Polski and equipped as a professional studio. It sought the co-operation of established artists, including Eryk Lipinski, one of those who developed what is now known as the Polish film poster. For ten years following the war, and particularly after 1948, production was tied to educational entertainment for children where offbeat forms of expression were firmly discouraged. The films turned out were mere illustrations of carefully approved tales or uncomplicated puppetoons favouring clarity over imagination.

The political changes of 1956 brought fresh attitudes to the art of animation. Adult, more imaginative cartoons were released, while the experienced Wladyslaw Nehrbecki made *Cat and Mouse (Myszka i Kotek)*, an international prize-winning short in 1957. Nehrbecki remained a director for children and had extensive credits in *Bolek and Lolek (Przygody Bolka i Lolka)*, the biggest money-spinner of all the cartoon series produced for Polish television. These particularly successful adventures from the 1960s have the typical reduced-animation of television and are evidently aimed at kids, but not for those of all ages. This was not the case with the Bugs Bunnies, Porky Pigs and Daffy Ducks of Hollywood who in their heyday were created for the mirth of their adult makers.

Witold Giersz and the 'Miniatury'

Witold Giersz, one of Bielsko's top animators, moved to Warsaw in 1956 to set up a branch of the Cartoon Film Studio. By 1958 it was a studio in its own right - renamed the Studio Miniatury – and it similarly spawned a unit in Cracow in 1971. (The latter, named the Animated Film Studios, has since become autonomous and produces some of the most interesting 'adult' work around.)

In Warsaw Giersz was joined by graduates of the arts academies and built up a team without preconceptions or any of the set ways that seemed to handicap the Bielsko artists. They began freely mixing techniques: drawn animation, cut-outs, three-dimensional models, collage and so on; Giersz himself took pleasure in

Little Western

diversifying the look of his cartoons, declining to be cramped by a recognizable style. His *Little Western (Maly Western*, 1960) was hailed as the first truly *author's* film of post-war Poland. He animated thousands of celluloids spread with thick paint 'spots' depicting crude characters and backgrounds. In addition to a cowboy and horse, the changing paint textures form part of the animation. His next film, *Red and Black (Czerwone i Czarne*, 1963), was made in the same manner and both films earned Giersz a number of awards.

The identity of Polish cartoons is usually foggy in the mind of many viewers who will often praise as a 'Polish cartoon' a product of Zagreb or Czechoslovakia or Hungary or, occasionally, Poland. By the late 1950s we had begun to notice an alternative form of cartoon peculiar to central Europe. With increasingly inventive means we were treated to witty satires or metaphors attacking those vague areas of war, urban agression or modern man.

A busy commercial side developed in Polish animation, apart from the adult films that win all the prizes abroad. Television consumption is the 'bread and butter' of the industry – mainly series for children – and Jan Lenica points out that only in Eastern Europe are there equivalents of the Hollywood companies equipped to tackle feature-length cartoons in-house:

"To make a long film (in France) you have to put together a studio yourself, to get animators, tracers, painters, background artists and so on. For that reason almost all big animation productions are made in Eastern Europe because there – say at Lodz, Warsaw, Budapest or Prague – you have a Hollywood-style studio with all the stages of production and their specialists. That makes it easier. Elsewhere in Europe the great studios don't exist!"

The Water Babies and Miroslaw Kijowicz

British producers used these facilities in a co-production with Film Polski in 1977 – *The Water Babies*. The Polish element was confined to the lengthy underwater adventures – all in animation – and a leading director from the Miniatury, Miroslaw Kijowicz, took charge of a team at the Warsaw studio. It was not 'full' animation – the short-cuts are evident in the results with their jerky television-look.

It was a bold attempt for Kijowicz who had never attempted anything of the sort. His personal style – well-known in Poland – consists of thickly lined characters against spare backgrounds and look like they could be produced by woodcuts. But he is an original and prominent Polish director in one of the biggest studios and was hired on that basis alone. He said that when the producers in London eventually saw a showreel of his work, (the production was well under way) they were somewhat stunned; Kijowicz was *anything but* a commercial director of fully animated 'cel' cartoons. "Apparently they picked my name out of a computer", he said.

International co-productions are not often 'fraternal' and with *The Water Babies* the opening discussions were ominous. Kijowicz brought to London what he described as lovely background renderings by a Polish artist known nationwide for his fine illustrations of children's books. The contract director (*not* Lionel Jeffries, who eventually directed) grasped the backgrounds – the fruit of many hours' labour – and hurled them across the production office, yelling that they were "shit". The director was soon replaced but a certain cool patronising was bound to be felt on the Polish side. On the other, grumblings were heard about too much arty experiment by the Poles instead of strict adherence to the story-boards.

Unfortunately *The Water Babies* was no more than a commercial job turned in according to contract. As art it fell into that area of animation, with its cute kids and animals, where the only yardstick of comparison is Disney, at a level where art at least meets commerce more than halfway.

The Se-Ma-For Studio

The Se-Ma-For Studio in Lodz began with puppets under the director Zenon Wasilewski, who was the only known film puppeteer before 1951. He completed *The Dragon of Cracow (Za Krola Kraka,* 1947), a project which he had started in 1939 only to see it destroyed in the war. It remains a classic of the Polish cartoon. Wladyslaw Haupe and Gabriela Bielinska began their work here in 1950/51 making puppet films stamped with a funny and rapid style. Their best known short, *The Changing of the Guard (Zmiana Warty,* 1958), features matchboxes in military parades. In ignoring human or animal forms it was a great novelty for its time and won many international awards. Its chief audience

from Szczechura's Mysia Wieza

pleasure lies in the elements used to evoke film life – likewise with the collage cartoons pioneered by Borowczyk and Lenica in the Studio Miniatury.

Technical facilities

Up until 1984 the Se-Ma-For Studio had made 1200 films, 200 of which had won prizes at national and foreign festivals. It has the following technical facilities:
– three camera halls for puppet films (six films can be shot simultaneously)
– six camera stations for cartoon, cut-out and combined-technique films, equipped with CRASS cameras (two of them re-play cameras)
– sound recording and film editing departments.

Working conditions for today's animators

Two of Se-Ma-For's most famous 'sons' are Zbigniew Rybczynski (now settled in the United States) and Daniel Szczechura, who graduated from Warsaw University with a degree in the history of fine arts, and from the director's section at Lodz in

1961. The latter is exceptional for animators, who usually come in as artists or cameramen. Szczechura confined himself to animation and quickly came to attention for his blackly satirical shorts, running free between cut-outs and drawn animation. He outlines the system in Poland:

"We produce in Poland about 120 animation films a year – between four studios. 80% of them are for TV – series films and generally for children. So, the rest are for adults or, as we call them, artistic films. These are necessary for the many festivals and manifestations – for example, the Week of Polish Culture or the Week of Polish Cinema. You've got to show these films even if they have no 'commercial' value. Throughout Europe the cinemas no longer screen a feature, a short and a newsfilm. In Poland, though, we *do* from time to time. Elsewhere as you know there are just the commercials and the feature."

Commercially, the children's films profit from television consumption in Poland and abroad. Artistic films get programmed provided the running time of a feature does not edge it out of the programme. It seems therefore that animation, far from being the film of the future, has become a hybrid. With few exceptions they are free of subtitles and thus have an international currency but within a closed circle of international festivals – Krakow, Oberhausen, Annecy, Zagreb, Ottawa and Cambridge. They have no commercial validity and as one-offs attract relatively few customers abroad. "With us the situation is pretty clear", says Szczechura. "Those with larger ambitions, well, they can make their individual films from time to time and those who want to rake in the cash can make films for children."

Working conditions are very free. It was pointed out that only six or so films have been stopped by the censors in nearly four decades of work – practically nothing compared to the shelved documentaries and features of the past ten years. This is partly because the matters touched on by animation lack the force of a documentary, whose 'real' images are regarded as more dangerous than pictorial art in motion, however sharp its sting. With hardly no dialogue or conventional script, it is difficult too for a censor to 'catch' something censorable.

Projects are submitted as brief ideas either by the author or as a proposal by the studio director. Depending on the studio, the chief of an artistic committee decides on the proposal before clearing a budget. There is a master system whereby a début director is ushered in under the supervision of an established animator. In spite of some complaints about an 'old guard mafia' (keeping young talents at bay), several festival films and those appreciated by the public have, for instance, come from Szczechura's students. He teaches at the Academy of Fine Arts and when he spots good potential he has the possibility of proposing a student's directing début. But he will not push those without basic talent: "In every domain – animation too – you can't drag someone in off the street, hand him a lot of zloties and ask him to make a film. That's an idiotically expensive way of proving he can't do it."

Lenica and Borowczyk

There are many personal styles but a vague first impression when thinking of Polish animation is a mixture of surrealism and very spare graphics, animated in a sort of jerky way with funny rhythms. It is strongly identified with the work of two artists: Jan Lenica and Walerian Borowczyk. Their collages of 1957/58 are

some of the blackest and most bizarre creations ever seen in the cartoon film.

Lenica and Borowczyk use collage and photomontage in a very imaginative way without containing a great deal of actual animation. They were more influenced by movements in contemporary painting and were, as Lenica says, very ignorant of fashions in graphics in the West. In an earlier interview with Marcin Garzicki in *Animafilm*, Lenica describes himself as a barbarian, making use of his new-found tools (stop-frame cameras) regardless of traditional endeavours. Lenica wants the same 'uncontaminated' mind Orson Welles said he liked to possess when embarking on any new film – ie one which strictly avoids watching other people's movies. The graphics came out of surrealism, abstract expressionism and other innovations in painting. Lenica especially depicted archetypal Man as a symbol or metaphor for contemporary dilemmas. Both Lenica and Borowczyk jointly produced the following films:

1957 – *Once Upon A Time (Byt Sobie Raz*, 11 minutes)
– *Rewarded Sentiments (Nagrodzone Uczucia*, 10 minutes)
– *Strip-Tease:* a minute of animation cut into a newsreel
– *Days of Education (Dni Oswiaty):* animated sequence cut into a newsreel
– *Banner of Youth (Szalandar Mlodych,* 2 mins approx.): a publicity film for youngsters, with animation drawn directly onto film.

1958 – *The House (Dom,* 14 minutes): with live-action scenes interpreted by Ligia Branice (Borowczyk's future wife and star of his feature film, *Blanche*).

Borowczyk is one of the few to successfully make the leap from animation to features. A comparable Hollywood figure is Frank Tashlin who continued to use live comedians (Bob Hope, Jerry Lewis and others) in the way he had used drawings in the Warner Brothers cartoons. Though worlds apart in his approach, Borowczyk often treats film actors as 'montage' pieces or marionettes in carefully designed décors. He flattens the personalities of the actors (part of that crude reality which, Irzykowski said, defended live action against art) and he has tried to continue that purest of forms in his features – and back again, as he continues to do animation.

The Miniatury

Other animators from the Miniatury whose work aroused interest were Ryszard Czekala (*Syn*, *Apel*) and K Urbanski (who left in 1971 to start the unit in Cracow). By 1976 the centre was producing sixty films a year and its most honoured shorts to that point were *Red and Black* by Giersz and *The Chair* (*Fotel*, 1964) by Szczechura. The latter (using cut-out technique) has an overhead shot of a committee room. A quorum of the committee prepares to elect a new member and the action shows a kind of chessboard manoeuvering by candidates and supporters, culminating in the triumph of a candidate who tricks his way to the top. The 'dialogue' of grunts and the various patterns of action wittily show the mechanics of power under a 'fly-on-the-wall' gaze.

Jerzy Kucia's Refleksy

From the Cracow unit the best known director is Jerzy Kucia whose *Refleksy* (1979) is certainly an original and carefully animated piece of work. Half of the film has an insect emerging from its egg, like someone squeezing with great difficulty out of a corset. It looks and feels realistic as the insect snaps open sufficient sections of the egg to break free. The setting is somewhere near a puddle of water, by a bus stop. The creature, so recently born, is attacked by a larger predator insect. Wounded and limping it briefly escapes but is overtaken to the fringe of the puddle, and the two forms thrash about in the water, whose thick black and white ripples become slightly psychedelic. The predator kills its victim and in the still water a reflection appears: the head of a man about to board a bus. His foot crushes the predator in the puddle.

Refleksy is the sort of thrilling 'documentary' that Starewicz might have prepared.

Zbigniew Rybczynski

Zbigniew Rybczynski graduated as a cameraman from the Lodz Film School in 1973. He had also worked as an animator at the Miniatury in Warsaw and between 1972 and 1980 made several shorts. One of them, *New Book* (*Nowa Ksiazki*, 1975), divided the screen into nine equal sections, each containing a single take of more than ten minutes – enough footage in all to complete a feature.

Refleksy

New Book

Each of the fixed viewpoints – bedroom, alley, interior of moving bus, interior of bookshop, interior of restaurant, exterior of office building, and other street exteriors – are all contemporaneous: the *external* shot of the bus pulling up with a man entering synchronises with the action *inside* the bus, and so on. Many such incidents link all nine screens so that they are filmed apparently at exactly the same time.

A man goes to an office and finds it closed. He purchases a book, runs into a friend, visits a restaurant, catches a bus and eventually returns to the alley by which he enters his bedroom. End of story. The 'trick' is that each of the screens appear to have continuous motion and you are left wondering whether Rybczynski marshalled nine cameramen with walkie-talkies in nine different locations who could synchronise their shots, or did he edit the apparently single takes in order to cut them together? After all, nine single takes in the perfectly controlled action of the (admittedly banal) story is something you compare with Hitchcock's ten-minute takes in *Rope* or Welles's long opening shot in *A Touch of Evil*.

Tango

At Se-Ma-For Rybczynski produced a 1982 Academy Award-winner in the astonishing *Tango* (1980); it also took first prize at the Annecy Animation Festival the following year. One of the truly outstanding film shorts - animation or otherwise – it is technical brilliance for its own sake and a terrific screen joke, although it is hard to pinpoint precisely what the joke is. It certainly throws light on Irzykowski's enthusiasm for the form. But is *Tango* animation? Or is it live-action

Tango

truly made into a "proper art"? It uses actors but, in its intermittent editing of frames and prolific use of 'masking', the film is definitely a work of animation.

Tango provokes the thought that animation does have a future beyond mere absorption into the frenetic visuals of video promos – in the 1980s the wallpaper of our time. Rybczynski now works with video and produces promos through his company in New York. In an interview with Mark Matousek the director declared "If somebody gave me US $ twenty million to do a feature film or twenty videos, I'd do twenty videos. Film is dying. What's alive is video cassettes." Perhaps Irzykowski was right. Animation – shot on film and transferred to video – is very much part of the 'future'; the new technology has only to solve the problems (compared to film) of poor image resolution and editing inflexibility, then to enlarge a bright, finely-resolved image onto wall-sized screens, at which point heavy film *will* be replaced by the lighter technology . . .

The stunning discipline of *New Book* is taken even further in *Tango* for which there was a reputed twenty-eight run-throughs of the same film in the camera to build up its composition of images. Again there is no story to speak of. The camera retains a fixed view: the interior of a flat or a living-room-cum-bedroom. A ball bounces in through the window, followed by a boy who retrieves it and then climbs back outside. The ball bounces back into the room and again the boy climbs in to retrieve it. Then a burglar enters and steals a parcel from the top of the wardrobe and exits. A man enters with the same package which he puts on top of the wardrobe and exits. Meanwhile the ball and the boy re-enter, followed by the burglar who steals the replaced package from the wardrobe. Several other characters then enter and exit, enter and exit, enter and exit until the room is full of people who, miraculously, never touch one another or disturb each other's consistently repeated actions. Who are these people who don't see or recognize one another – ghosts of previous tenants repeating their most common actions?

Rybczynski himself says *Tango* has no meaning – the actions are carried out to the accompaniment of a slow tango – and the film gives the pleasure of watching the workings of a beautifully built Swiss watch and is also very funny. Intermittent frames have been cut from each of the characters' actions which not only gives an animated feel to the otherwise life-like rhythms but also fits each cycle (between entrance and exit) into a carefully calculated number of frames. *Tango* is trick film of the highest kind and has the advantage of more highly developed opticals than were ever available to Starewicz or Méliès.

☆   ☆   ☆

The Polish film poster

The Polish film poster has a firmer identity in people's minds than Polish cartoons. It began winning attention and prizes from the mid-1950s. There is a tradition of fine

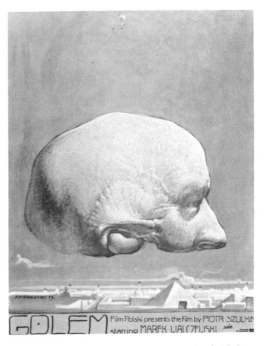

poster for Golem

poster making from the turn of the century, when cultural life was firmly based in Cracow and where, for example, Wyspianski, the playwright and painter, made some very beautiful posters.

Jacek Malczewski

For a more direct link to the dark metaphors we associate with the film poster, there is Jacek Malczewski, a Cracow painter of the late 19th century. His symbolist images, "mythical figures with wings, all mixed up with the nation's history" – are an acknowledged influence on the most surreal and prominent of contemporary designers, Franciszek von biberstein Starowiejski, whose work is uppermost in the mind when discussing Polish posters. (Malczewski, incidentally,

poster for Return Ticket

than, for example, in Great Britain. You could start with graphics, then move into stage design and make friends with the theatre directors, which might then lead you to working in film.

Borowczyk

Borowczyk had a traditional art training and produced several socialist-realist posters, some of them "quite kitschy", according to a colleague. Others were more experimental and innovative – a signpost to his later cartoons with Lenica. Many artists detest the word 'experimental' (Borowczyk and Lenica have both said so in interviews) since the effects they get are exactly those they intend; there are no unexpected flash frames in their films nor do the posters explode. They prefer the word 'original'.

Trepkowski and Tomaszewski

The first generation of designers is represented by Henryk Tomaszewski, Eryk Lipinski, Wojciech Zamecznik, and Tadeusz Trepkowski, about whom Lenica wrote a book in 1956. Trepkowski's trademark is the simple, naturalistic symbol to evoke the *sense* of the subject. The most widely published of his posters is that for Jakubowska's *The Last Stage*, showing a broken carnation against a striped background representing the uniforms worn by Auschwitz deportees. His images would not necessarily appear in the actual film or play. Like Tomaszewski, Trepkowski was prominent in a poster movement that developed in Poland in the late 1930s.

Henryk Tomaszewski is a father-figure to many poster makers. He raised three generations, including that of Lenica who

influenced Wajda in his staging of the film *The Birch Wood (Brzezina)* in 1970.)

The post-war boom of the Polish poster was connected principally with theatre and film. It stemmed from the post-war conditions where the various 'clients' were state institutions and the humiliating (for the artist) client/designer bond was done away with, at least after the Stalinist epoch. Certainly from 1956 artists treated the poster as a medium of self-expression, limited only by their own feelings about the message of the film or event.

Andrzej Klimowski

Andrzej Klimowski, one of the recent generation of poster designers, notes that the movement between graphics and pictorial art is far more fluid in Poland

poster for The Last Stage

in 1952 worked as Tomaszewski's assistant, teaching graphics at the Warsaw Academy of Fine Arts. Tomaszewski divides his time between posters and book illustrations, and is described as a 'literary' designer for the direct association between his poster motifs and the contents of the book or play.

Starowiejski

Apart from Lenica, the second generation includes Waldemar Swierzy, Roman Cieslewicz, Julian Palka, Jan Mlodozeniec, and, of course, Starowiejski. A passionate collector of "clocks, prints, and specimens of calligraphy from the early Baroque era", Starowiejski's work covers a prolific output of posters and stage set designs

plus a couple of film shorts. A *Graphis'* profile on the artist said:

"We should not forget that the film and the theatre are almost the exclusive field of Starowiejski and his colleagues – a domain in which today there is little occasion for plain and honest laughter. These facts constitute a plausible apologia for the shock the observer may experience on his first acquaintance with Starowiejski's posters and drawings – a shock which perhaps appears the more brutal when his work is contrasted with that of a Western artist whose job will normally be to make consumer goods for a pampered public."

Not only were they *not* hired to make consumer goods palatable but their posters were often unnecessary – especially those for the theatre where programmes were often booked out and impossible to get into anyway.

To educate the onlooker

Beyond conveying information, the poster's function is – this is the *artists'* dictum – to educate the onlooker in the street. When paper was relatively plentiful, print runs per poster were from eight to twenty thousand copies and they were distributed to all towns and villages in the country. Lenica says that the street poster is an important tool to mould public taste and educate the onlooker – a sort of primer from which the wider reading and understanding of painting may be learned. He also acknowledges the influence of the British poster movement under James Boswell for the Ealing film studios in the early 1940s – a short-lived movement that was never to threaten the usual mixture of embracing stars, fragments of violent action and hard-sell captions.

The Polish poster certainly ran free for a very long time compared to the short timespans of the Soviet experiments in the 1920s or the heyday of the Ealing group.

Whether it will continue to run and produce generations of extraordinary talents – only time will tell. After the coup d'état in December 1981, many artists either left the country or refused to do bread and butter work for their client, the State, which commissions artwork for events other than films and plays. Also it was part of the economic depression that paper and art materials were scarce and the work simply dried up. As in the film industry, which is saturated with directors and technicians, there are too few jobs for the available talent – nothing unusual in the West, but a new situation in Poland.

poster for Publicity

Publicity/Awans

It is a peculiar state of affairs where, apart from censorship or the rationing of materials, there is little direct pressure or dialogue between artist and client. There is commerce without the commercial art. As regards censorship, several factors come into play, many of them unpredictable. For example, for Janusz Zaorski's film *Publicity (Awans,* 1975), a commission was given to Andrzej Krauze, now in England. The artist submitted a cartoon of a bloated pig swilling Coca-Cola from a trough – an amusing illustration, even socialist-realist with a neat anti-capitalist motif. It was rejected; the bloated body area of the pig allowed plenty of space in which to scrawl, amongst other things, the names of political leaders. For censors it meant the dissemination of ten thousand potential graffiti boards all around the country: so, in addition to turning in a job, the artist must tap-dance over unforeseen readings of his work.

Lenica

Until martial law Lenica continued doing posters for Poland. He now lives in Paris and the speed with which the cinema needs posters restricts him to the theatre, which plans its productions a good year in advance. Sadly his film proposals have been consistently rejected. His current project in France is the exotic Polish story, *Pan Twardowski* - made as a feature in the 1930s and, as mentioned, animated by Starewicz in Russia.

Lenica acknowledges the importance of a satirical magazine, *Szpilki,* which began publication in the 1930s and to which he contributed cartoons long before his poster commissions: "It was anti-Fascist and continued like this after the war with all the best satirical cartoonists. It had a high artistic standard for ten, perhaps fifteen years. After that it became an 'entertainment' magazine without bite."

Similar to the way a film unit vets a script, a syndicate of graphic artists - non-governmental – imposed artistic standards and helped influence the explosion of graphic art in the 1950s. Any artist could attend a film projection arranged for the purpose and then in the following week present a maquette in competition with others. The syndicate, made up of well-known artists such as Lenica and Lipinski, would select one and then arrange for a poster contract with the artist. The design had to be approved at government level and sometimes two ideas would be chosen: one of a high artistic value and the other one more popular.

Technically, they are printed mainly by photo offset method in A1 format (61 x 86cm) and they have to be considered for their effect in the street, not as exhibits in chic exhibitions. The artists all hope that the appearance of a new poster will be an event. It should stand out from the architecture – frequently drab, so it does – and from other posters. Lenica feels that in his most recent walks through Warsaw a certain uniformity had overtaken the designs. His own recognizable style in the earlier years attracted a host of imitators and he was forced more than once to consciously change to another style that would stand out or shout for attention.

Wojciech Zamecznik

In an interview in the magazine *Image et Son*, Wojciech Zamecznik – a first generationer – remarked that none of the great poster makers were "professional":

"To make a good poster you must above all want to do it. An emotional stimulant is necessary. Of course there are professional poster makers in Poland but generally they achieve mediocre results. When you have to turn out as many posters within such and such a time it is impossible to feel sufficient emotion."

Unusually, Zamecznik preferred to work with fragments of photographs, feeling that such fragments of reality, treated and reproduced mechanically, underlined his poster's rapport with film. He often featured the faces of the stars, an exceptional practice in Poland. He stresses that the primary quality of a poster is its perceptibility, that its message should be grasped as much as possible in a single glance.

poster for Family Life

poster for War of the Worlds 2000

poster for The Smaller Sky

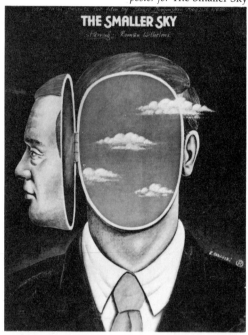

poster for Top Dog

poster for The Conductor

12: Actresses and actors

Leslie Caron

Leslie Caron, born in Boulogne-Billancourt near Paris, made her name in Hollywood. She recently starred in Zanussi's *The Contract*. Now based in Paris, she talks here about the standard of acting in Poland and about Zanussi as a director of actors:

"I thought their actors were remarkable and one good reason is because they practise all day long: they do radio in the morning, dubbing midday, a bit of filming in the afternoon and theatre at night. So they play three or four characters in a day... also they have to go through schooling: you're not an actor unless you've gone to school and you're not an actor in Warsaw unless you're very, very good. The less good actors will be in the provinces... so there is a process of elimination there and if you see theatre in Warsaw you get the very best. No-one improvises himself."

On Zanussi

"Zanussi always asks you to play very slow. He doesn't want fast acting. He doesn't mind if it's slow. He just wants it to be as felt as possible. I don't want to say the word 'profound' because it sounds pretentious but something like that. He doesn't want glib acting so he doesn't ask you to be fast and usually in America they do... they want you to act fast... I'm talking about speech. He doesn't mind if you leave blanks if you take your time, and he's rather interested in what happens when an actor can't remember his lines.

"In *The Unapproachables* [in which Caron plays opposite British actor Danny Webb] Zanussi let the camera roll; we had passed the scene we were supposed to do and he didn't say cut so we kept on acting and we just improvised the moves. Finally we ran out of things to say and the camera was empty anyway – there was no more film, that was it – and then I said to Krzysztof 'Krzysztof, why did you go on?' and he said 'well, it was very interesting'. Several times he's done that to me. In *Contract* he asked me to improvise... a crowd of young people came up and asked for an autograph and I had to glibly talk about travels and so on. I started making up a story and I was running out of things to say and I went on and on and on and he wasn't saying cut and finally I turned to the camera and I said 'that's enough, Krzysztof' and he said 'I was very interested'. Yes, he kept it all and cut it..."

Krystyna Janda

At the time of shooting *Man of Marble*, Krystyna Janda made her simultaneous début in two Warsaw theatres, playing in one Dorian Gray in John Osborne's adaptation, *Portrait of Dorian Gray*. Her rise to fame happened in just one month! Having only seen *Without Anaesthesia*, her next film, you could be forgiven for thinking that she was more a model than an actress – until the final scene in which she pours out her monologue on the gas-heater explosion which has just killed her lover (played by Zapasiewicz).

Without Anaesthesia

"Yes, the story behind this film is very funny because the character I play is the reverse of the character I play in *Man of Marble*. For me it was quite a difficult exercise to play this passive character... it wasn't planned. It happened that one day when I was doing something completely different a taxi came up and took me to the

Krystyna Janda in The Interrogation

studio where they were making *Without Anaesthesia*. It's just that at the last moment Wajda decided I should play that role. But there was no role for me at that time! My character wasn't included in the script. He just decided he would like me to be in his film and play . . . something.

"Agnieszka Holland was asked to write my role into the script and she wrote terribly long and monotonous soliloquies that I was supposed to recite. And when I came they gave me this script – I was dressed up in a historic costume from another film that I was doing – I had a hat and a veil and I didn't even know what it was about. I hated those soliloquies. And I asked him, nearly in tears, 'do I really have to say all this?' Andrzej understood much more than I could grasp. 'Well, can you play it without speaking?' Any other director would say '*of course* you have to say all this'. To dress me for the film he took out a jacket from my present husband

and picked up some other things from the crew and he said 'that's good for your costume'.

"When we finished making the film one night he phoned me and he said 'listen, I've just had a dream that people would think that you were dumb.' And so we shot this last scene after the hero's death and I asked Andrzej 'what am I supposed to say?' 'It doesn't matter what, just say that I've always told you that this boiler was dangerous.' And I was so tense all day I was practising this last sentence that at the end instead of 'boiler' I said 'broiler' to which Wajda said 'don't worry, I'll just run a car noise through that . . .'

"And then the first reviews started coming from Paris and London and they said 'the Angel of Death', 'the Conscience of the Nation' . . . and we were reading all this and I said 'oh God, what am I supposed to say now?' And Wajda said 'well, you see, you do what you feel and they make up the rest' . . .

"The reason I am talking about this is that I think that in this sort of film improvising was a very important factor . . . it is a more general kind of improvising, namely that after shooting that day, you go home, talk about it and a new idea appears of what to do next about that particular scene. And then the next day you go back shooting and the whole idea of that scene changes direction. In my whole life I haven't come across a script that was used in the film in its original form. You can mention some costume films but all the really important films have been made on the spot with terrific effort and mounting emotions . . . something really indefinable.

"Basically I think that my appearance in *Man of Marble* opened a whole new era in film . . . it was a new genre . . . it started this 'cinema of moral anxiety', as this whole movement was later labelled, causing much controversy. Many were against this term but it stuck.

"Wajda was looking for a girl who would interest him, not even an actress, any woman; he was after a strong personality... He learnt about me playing a man in a theatre so he came to a rehearsal and then gave me a test. It occurred to me before to take part in a screen test but everybody thought that I was too ugly to be in the film. So when I came to his test I was furious. I did not have the make-up, I hated everybody straight away. And Wajda, when he saw me, said 'She will play because she can kill'.

"My presence in the film is the outcome of this kind of search. The market is small and if there is somebody interesting, not necessarily in Warsaw or Cracow, and really interesting, they will know. Everything derives from the theatre. Every year a group of young actors graduate from the school, and they are watched by the film directors, because they do their shows. So one can see what new talents appear.

"I appeared on TV, still at school, in *Three Sisters*, and then I was noticed and I got fifteen offers at all the theatres in Warsaw. The truth is that every new director is ambitious and always wants to discover a new face, so they travel across Poland looking for a new talent. The market is not big so it is much easier to be discovered in Poland than anywhere else. Also, in Poland every actor receives training.

"I feel it is very strange how this role, played by me without realising its importance, annoyed everybody so much that it stayed in their memory... And all of a sudden a lot of parts like that were written for women. Maybe that was the time that it was necessary, that women became more active, but it has absolutely nothing to do with Women's Lib, just the opposite... It was a new phenomenon in the Polish

Krystyna Janda

cinema that women started getting more active and significant roles than before. They started writing scripts for women, too... It was never seen before that somebody should be so aggressive on the screen, it was shocking. And now the audience somehow has learned to accept it and nobody is shocked anymore... I mention all this because this period started a new era in Polish cinema."

Maja Komorowska

Trained under Grotowski, Komorowska has become one of Poland's leading actresses and notably appeared in two early Zanussi films, *Quarterly Balance* and *Behind the Wall*.

On Zanussi and his writing

"My first film with him was *Mountain

Twilight, a short film. *Family Life* was my first real fiction film. To have a director who writes scripts specifically for the actors is a real luxury. It doesn't confine him strictly to the text... he doesn't have to justify alterations to anyone...

"Zanussi wrote *Quarterly Balance* and *Behind the Wall* specifically with me in mind – the latter being the first totally improvised script. So in this way I am a creative factor in his films and not recreative. For instance, in his last film [*Year of the Quiet Sun*] Zanussi said himself that Scott [Wilson] and I brought considerable changes to the script as originally written. Zanussi observed us as if life itself was part of the script, like the fact that Scott was speaking English, I was speaking Polish... we didn't know one another and yet every day we tried to communicate by using dictionaries... in this way the film – about the fact that we couldn't communicate and that at the end we managed to – was *true* and this was very interesting... The problem of our communication was written into whatever happened in the script... When Zanussi writes a part for an actor it is very difficult to distinguish between the creativity of the director and that of the actor."

Formation with Grotowski

"It is interesting that a lot of people stress the importance of the period when I worked with Grotowski, for five years. But all in all if I were to state what is the most important thing in my profession it is the crossline between *Family Life* and *Behind the Wall,* because in films like *Family Life* the parts are spontaneous. *Behind the Wall* is a completely different face, a different person. Even physically I would say they were different.

"The most important thing I learned

Maja Komorowska

from Grotowski is a certain way of thinking... not only about the parts but also about work in general... a terrific grounding in work. It's very difficult to specify in a few words but all my roles or parts in the films bear the traces of that 'school'... as in looking for something contradictory in my roles. Usually the characters in films are one-sided whereas things are not straightforward... I am a lecturer now in a drama school in Warsaw and lately I have been trying to pass on to my students the approach that there are many truths... only not all of them are interesting."

The importance of theatre

"I appreciate theatre very much because there it is easy to see if the actor is capable of acting or not... for instance I think that a non-professional can play in a film – himself of course – but he won't play Hamlet because then he has to be professional. Everybody can play one role, themselves, in a film . . . I am very cautious when it comes to scripts . . . I reject a lot of them. I have to know who is the author, who is going to do the make-up, who is going to edit, let alone the director, and the director of photography. And if all those factors come into a whole then it still doesn't mean that the film will work out. You know, because you watch the films. An actor is stretched out over all these elements – like on a cross."

On women directors

"Women's cinema: no, it is no good. Look around: Fellini, Visconti, American cinema – where are the women directors? . . . It is a paradox; I think that women generally become the subject of many films, their life; and there is something that male directors handle in a better way. Film is like a big factory and one has to be terribly strong to pull all that, to pull all the right strings. Yes, there are some female directors – the Hungarian Meszaros – but it is like with surgeons: you have more men. The whole work on a film is like an operation, like surgery in psychological terms – one operates on human psyche.

"From my experience, and based on the world's cinema, it seems that men write better for women. Take Bergman: one may like him or not, but one has to admit that he concentrates mostly on women. I think that a woman can have more to say about a man, but it is no good when she talks about herself – it is usually overdone, there is always too much of something, and I think it is natural. And if you write about cinema, most often men's views on women are extremely interesting. Maybe because women know themselves too well, they cannot write about it. It seems contradictory but only at first glance, if one is deeply involved in something, one cannot assess things properly, one has to distance oneself from the problem to be able to look at things objectively. To stick to this comparison of a surgeon – no surgeon operates on his own family. We could probably analyse the whole problem more profoundly since we know that it exists - the number of outstanding directors proves it. Of course, as I do not want any women to blame me, I have to admit that exceptions are possible here, too - these prove the rule."

An 'unhygienic' profession

"This profession is not very hygienic. I mean that because an actor is concentrated on himself all the time, to stay sane he or she has to be interested in many things apart from his work, and art is a very strange phenomenon – you must not devote yourself to it completely. For me my child has always been most important. It only seems that you have to give everything to art, you have to give and take, this is what I mean by 'not hygienic'. One can only survive by working very hard, otherwise it is like prostitution, it is selling not your body but your soul, which is even worse. This profession can be a devotion but only when one works hard and then it can be wonderful. But if it becomes a profession only, it is not very safe for one's psyche . . . This profession is dangerous because one works under constant pressure, often after perform-ances actors have to relax. A lot of us have broken family life. I think that one has to have constant control over oneself in this profession. A doctor cures and, even if he is bad-tempered, because he is not concentrated on himself only he is in a safer position."

Jerzy Stuhr

It is possible to think of Jerzy Stuhr as a

brilliant new comedy actor simply from his lead performances in *Top Dog, Camera Buff* and *Sex Mission.* He came to films relatively late with the credentials of a classical background in the theatre. His recent feature, *Gaga* (Piotr Szulkin), features Stuhr in one episode only, unlike Szulkin's last film, *Obi Oba,* which stars the comedian. Like other actors Zapasiewicz and Piotr Fronczewski, he seems to be everywhere on-screen: the best actors have round-the-clock work in all media.

Stuhr acts with the Stary Theatre in Cracow, regarded as the finest classical theatre in the country. In January 1985, for example, he opened as the Judge opposite Jerzy Radziwilowicz's Raskolnikow in Dostoyevsky's *Crime and Punishment* under Wajda's direction. Is there a star system in Poland?

"No. There is no such thing. I get invited to many meetings with spectators, mainly student groups, and I go to them. For instance, tonight I have a meeting in a film club in Cracow. This is the only means of contact with the audience. There are no fan clubs and I would never agree to be in something like that. Being popular rather disturbs me. I have no star-like personality."

Science fiction films and comedies

"Well, you know, I had only one experience like that: *Sex Mission,* and I think that is enough. You can do that once. I always wanted to play in a comedy and now I have it behind me. I love contemporary cinema, this whole movement of 'Moral Anxiety'. At the moment it is more difficult with films of this sort but I think it will come back. Falk and I want to make a sequel to *Top Dog* to show what happened to the hero after a lapse of time."

Zbigniew Zapasiewicz

Zbigniew Zapasiewicz, so funny as the face of unrepentant corruption in Zanussi's *Camouflage,* and so moving as the journalist in Wajda's *Without Anaesthesia* (his best central role), is another who shuns cinema's limelight:

"I can see that this conversation is going to be about cinema, but I am not a film actor. During the last thirty years I have made three or four outstanding films, well, maybe five. The rest were for financial reasons or as a favour to my friends. Of course it is nice that these films had some impact on the world, but really and truly I am a theatre actor. The reason why I do not want to talk too much about these differences (between certain directors) is that I am always working for my friends. On the other hand that doesn't mean that I cannot recognize the differences.

Jerzy Stuhr in Camera Buff

Zbigniew Zapasiewicz

"Everyone knows that Zanussi has the ability to create scripts with great precision. His scripts are always very good and he begins work based on a completely finished script usually written together with Edward Zebrowski – in my opinion the most outstanding Polish screen-writer. If Zanussi improvises while making a movie he does it with a pretty clear idea about the whole sequence of events in the film. He always has the whole thing worked out first. His real profession is as a physicist while that of Wajda is a painter: this is the basic difference in their perceptions of the world.

"Wajda improvises to a much greater degree. For instance, while working on *Without Anaesthesia* we didn't know until the very last moment how the film would end. I did not want to talk to my movie wife (during the legal contest for divorce) so the ending was changed, although originally Wajda wanted me and my movie wife (Ewa Dalkowska) reconciled. He was even a bit hurt when I saw it differently . . . I like improvising in a film. With Zanussi you can also improvise and play around with the dialogue since the whole sequence of events is laid out before we begin. In *Behind the Wall* all dialogues were improvised, but I like the scenes to be clearly and carefully arranged and planned."

Jerzy Radziwilowicz

"My situation was particularly difficult because my character already existed in *Man of Marble* , a character we had thought of in different terms because we were unaware of the events which would follow: thus the difficulty for me was in making together two different types of young men. Paradoxically it was easier for me to play the *Man of Marble,* in spite of the gulf between my parents' and my own generations. For the *Man of Iron* I had the feeling of being responsible for each gesture, each word towards those people who had lived in these events so close to all of us. It did not seem possible to me, it would have required some distance and I'm not sure that it would have worked. The story I tell at the beginning of the film on the first hours of the strike, is that of an actual worker – there were four at the beginning – who we followed word for word, gesture after gesture of his actions on the opening day." *[taken from an interview in Cannes, May 1981].*

13: Comedies and commercial films

Weather Forecast

One reason often given for Polish film makers' lack of interest in making comedies is that there is no small talk in Poland when artists get to work. Poles like to laugh, they say, but the best artists do not settle for mere entertainment and besides there is no film tradition for comedies. The type of sharp comedy that the Polish cinema cries out for would of course produce the 'Bugajski' effect: the elimination of all further opportunities for the film maker together with his enforced emigration.

Marek Piwowski's Rejs

Veteran comedy director Stanislaw Bareja comments: "I think that the best comedy of the early 1970s was *Rejs* by Marek Piwowski. But that film aroused such 'disgust' in an artistic supervisor that he refused to supervise it. There was just one copy produced and this copy made its way across Poland, arousing terrific enthusiasm all over the country. After a period of time this film was recognised as one of the best Polish comedies but the director has never made a comedy since."

Rejs (Trip down the River) was Piwowski's first feature, made in 1970 and employing a mixed amateur/professional cast. In form it resembles a Jacques Tati film and the amateurs – among them, for example, a shop girl, a retired worker and a film projectionist – were carefully selected for their acting, dancing and musical abilities.

Two stowaways board the boat at Torun, one dressed as 'Poseidon'. The ship's captain thinks that Poseidon is the organiser of cultural and social activities for the passengers. The character (played by Stanislaw Tym) is a tailor but sets about his new profession with gusto. He appoints a committee to work out a special programme in honour of the captain; rehearsals are arranged and passengers display their talents. During the preparations for the performance, various relationships and romances develop and the climax of the story is a fancy dress ball given by the captain. Everyone is dizzied by the madness of the moment and the ship runs aground; it is eventually hauled back into the water. Later in the night the captain is pulled from his bed and brought up on deck where strange figures emerge from the darkness. A huge choir starts singing - all in honour of the captain whose hair turns grey in full view of the crowd.

Stanislaw Bareja

Bareja himself has persisted with work in the comedy genre, one of the three genres, he says in which it is possible to say something serious – the others being the thriller and melodrama. He began as a comedy and thriller director and continues to work and collaborate in these forms. Bareja's earliest films are *The Husband of His Wife* (*Maz swojej Zony*, 1961), officially considered the first classic Polish crime thriller, and *A Wife for an Australian* (*Zona dla Australijczyka*, 1963), in which a young Pole living in Austrialia returns to his native country to look for a wife.

Even so it has become very difficult to get a comedy script accepted; Bareja worked with Jacek Fedorowicz in co-authoring five or so scripts which were all 'accepted' but of which only two were used. The disappointed Fedorowicz (who then stopped writing film scripts) joined up with Stanislaw Tym who is in great demand in cabarets and theatres. Only two out of their five joint scripts were

Trip down the River

taken up. His recent nine-hour series co-written with two young journalists finally finished up on the shelf: "Of course it is possible to make comedies without touching sensitive areas but in my view that means referring to 19th century subjects, otherwise taking them into acceptable territory tends to make them dull.

"Obviously every allusion to Russia is forbidden. There is a well-known joke. Three people are on a sledge – an Englishman, a Frenchman and a Russian. Wolves are pursuing them and one of them must be sacrificed for the others' survival. Well, the Russian gets up and cries: 'For the Motherland!!' Then he chucks out the Frenchman . . . In my film a group of people want to perform a cabaret which would be acceptable to the authorities, so they change the text of the joke in such a way that the third person on the sledge is from West Germany not Russia. So, when the moment of sacrifice arrives the German shouts: 'For the Motherland' and he shouts it in Russian, then chucks out the Frenchman. So our censor says, 'Why is this German shouting in Russian?' And I say, 'Well, because it's funny. Everyone liked it and you laughed too.' The censor says that no way will the

Stanislaw Bareja

German shout in Russian. So we redo the whole scene and now when it comes to the sacrifice he shouts 'For the Motherland' in German and heaves out the Frenchman but his walonki [Russian boots] come off. So we have another problem. 'Why the walonki?' I reply: 'Well, it's winter.' The film hasn't been released."

Bareja continues: "Let me tell you something that is not so amusing. I had an idea for a film. A man, in order to get a flat, has to present a certificate stating that his father does not own one . . . it is like that here. So he says, 'my father is dead'. 'Well', they say, 'give us his death certificate'. But the man replies, 'my father died in Kolyma, Siberia in 1943'. 'No, it cannot be Kolyma', the censor tells me. So I say, 'Fine, it won't be Kolyma'.

"Bronislaw Pawlik played the role and I was embarrassed to tell him that we would have to make changes in the script. In the end we had to record a new version.

Bronek thus says, 'my father won't come because he died in exile in 1943'. So once again we face a problem with our censor. 'Why *exile?*' they ask. I explain that this term was applicable to all of those removed from the place where they lived to somewhere else; for example, when Germans deported people from Gdynia to Warsaw it was reckoned that those people lived in exile in Warsaw. The censor denies this: the term could only apply to exile in Russia. So we had to change it again. Bronek now said that his father died of 'frosty weather in 1943'. This expression is rather vague and not many people would catch its meaning. Bronek himself was really annoyed, having to come repeatedly just to change a few words – and then for a film which was never released anyway!

"Let's take another film – it was actually released under the title *What will you do when you catch me?* There's a scene including a TV programme in which two groups of surgeons compete with one another to remove an appendix. The losers leave the operating theatre in a fury and declare that everything was pre-planned. *They* had been given a fatso to work on; when they had finally cut through all his fat, the other team had done their operation. One of the latter says, 'Oh, the fat is nothing; what about the inside of his stomach? What do they feed them on in jail?' I had to cut this last sentence out! That's why a lot of people give up making comedies."

Thais

Among commercial 'oddities' are films such as *The She-Wolf (Wilczyca)*, and *Thais (Tais)*, directed by Ryszard Ber. This is a soft-core flick with serious pretensions – a kind of Playboy movie based on Anatole France's novel, *Tais,* about a beautiful courtesan of the same name living in Alexandria in the 4th century AD. An aging Christian (Jerzy Kryszak) vows to convert her to the faith and he begins to succeed. The film stars Piotr Garlicki (the young camp-leader in Zanussi's *Camouflage)* and the attractive Dorota Kwiatowska as Thais.

Seeing some of the 'genre' commercial films such as *Thais,* one is reminded of publishers in wartime France. Since American fiction was banned they set about hiring authors to write 'American thrillers'. Leo Malet, for example, became Frank Harding whose action-sizzlers featured New York cop Johnny Metal. It was a totally unauthentic New York as opposed to Malet's *Nestor Burma* private eye novels set in a Paris you could smell. Some of the Polish 'commercial' films have this same sense of removal: satisfying a sweet tooth with saccharin.

Szyszko's The Millionaire

A pre-martial law example is *The Millionaire (Milioner,* 1978) by Sylwester Szyszko, an engaging drama set in Silesia. It was produced by *Iluzjon,* run by Ewa and Czeslaw Petelski, with whom the director has been associated through most of his professional life: film school graduation in 1956 and then a seventeen-year wait until his first feature, *Dark River (Ciemna rzeka),* in 1973.

The film looks at what happens when a worker/peasant, Mikula, wins first prize in a lottery. His attempts to upgrade his life (better agricultural machinery) - and his gestures of 'reconciliation' with the jealous neighbours (donating a television to the local club) are rather contemptuously regarded as ostentatious. Practically the whole town snubs his wedding and an arson attempt is made on his farm. The townspeople's efforts to drown Mikula's cattle in a lake bring on his mother's heart-

attack. The neighbours change their mind, rescue the cattle and help take Mikula's mother to a hospital.

A Millionaire is a welcome film, full of empathy for a man whose 'crime' is his good luck. It does not attempt a balanced or too-understanding view of mob reaction among 'the salt of the earth' towards one of their own. The film is dosed with humour and the presence of Janusz Gajos who is excellent as the beleagured Mikula.

The Great Shar

A better (post-martial law) example is *The Great Shar (Wielki Szu,* 1982), an encouraging 'commercial' film with a fine script by Jerzy Purzycki (a trainee from the specialist screen-writing course recently developed in Warsaw). It was directed for the *Kadr* unit by veteran Sylwester Checinski and is a contemporary adventure (except for the shot of Edward Gierek speaking on a television – which makes it a 'period' film). Made during martial law, perhaps the sucker-baiting activities of the card sharks in big tourist hotels were things that belonged to the past. More likely the free-spending atmosphere of the film seems more authentic in a mid-70s setting when Poland's economy still boomed.

The film also boasts the talents of Jan Nowicki, one of Poland's best theatre and film actors, as the Big Shar, an engaging newcomer, Andrzej Pieczynski, as 'Little Shar' (noted as one of the extras in Zanussi's *The Contract)* and the fine actress Grazyna Szapolowska (stars in Kieslowski's *No End)* who is wasted as the Big Shar's wife – in an opening scene designed mainly to show us her body.

Big Shar, just out of prison, visits his estranged wife to pick up a grub-stake before shooting off on an odyssey around Poland. In a strange town he is befriended and then plagued by a young taxi-driver

Jan Nowicki

with a certain talent for card playing. There is an interesting ambulatory pace to the film which contains some suspense. It makes one wonder how, say, Clint Eastwood would play Big Shar and George Kennedy the role of 'Mikun', Shar's first big-time sucker, a violent bully of a man but inferior as a card cheat to the great Shar. The role is played by Leon Niemczyk, who bears a passing resemblance to Kennedy. Cheated out of a fortune in zloties, Mikun chases Shar for part of the film. He is pursued too by his annoying disciple, the young taxi-driver, eager to make it into the 'league'. A sinister Charles Manson-like figure also chases the gambler and finally kills him, off-screen, in one of the last scenes. The final scene shows Little Shar, having just squandered a fortune of his brother's dollars in a disastrous game with a big leaguer, spending his remaining change on a pack of cards at a kiosk.

There is also a very interesting 'gambler fever' scene in the film where Shar coolly wins the house, money and Porsche from a young playboy whose own life-style epitomises the tone of corruption and 'looking after number one' that was material for the moral anxiety movies.

There is a case for a diet of caper movies such as *The Great Shar*. It is largely a matter of the script, an area which is admitted to be weak in Poland. The pay is also low and the credit for good story-telling is likely to go to the director anyway. Feliks Falk, who writes scripts for his own films and who won an award at Gdansk in 1985 for his screenplay of *Baryton*, agrees with Michalek: there is no 'B-literature' in Poland, the action paperback kind that provides most of the commercial movies in the West. But could film makers not import American or French books and transpose them into Polish commercial projects? Falk doesn't think so:

"First of all it is very expensive – Bashevis Singer wants to sell two of his novels to Poland and one of the units wanted to do it but his agent wanted US $600 000, so it is very expensive. There should be involved some co-production but of course such novels as Singer's would be easy because it happens in Poland. Now you have only to reconstruct . . . everything is true . . . there were some films based on Western literature but it is very rare . . ."

Some progress is being made with the founding of the new screen-writing course in Warsaw which lasts two years. Scripts are written, better or worse, and there have been some box-office hits, including Checinski's *Wielki Szu*.

Eve Wants to Sleep

The 1958 comedy, *Eve Wants to Sleep* (*Ewa chce spac*), was directed by Tadeusz

Chmielewski who was born in 1927 and who graduated from Lodz in 1953. The film stars Barbara Lass-Kwiatkowska (Polanski's first wife). Before the film she was an actress with practically no experience; afterwards she rose to stardom and became for many a kind of Polish Brigitte Bardot. Chmielewski continued to make genre or 'formula' films as well as the comedies *Where is the General? (Gdzie Jest General?* 1963) and *How I Started the Second World War (Jak rozpetalem druga wojne swiatowa*, 1970), the odyssey of a soldier wandering around the fronts in World War Two. They all fall short of the great high of his début but were great popular successes.

Eve Wants to Sleep was hailed as a "ferocious comedy" partly for the swipes it manages to take at juvenile delinquency and the incompetence of the authorities in handling the youth problem. It combines good light farce with serious reflection. But it had its share of production problems as Bareja comments: "Here the artistic supervisor was Jerzy Zarzycki who himself made films like *The Soldier of the Queen of Madagascar* or *Bachelors Club*. He demanded that the film be stopped because it was disgusting according to him. So, as you see, life is pretty hard on comedy. However, on the other hand, if

one is really patient one will get a film released in the end. Writing a script takes around six months and trying to have it released takes about two years. So you see it yourself."

Antoni Krauze

Krauze was both a painter and actor with the Students' Satirical Theatre and following his graduation from Lodz he became assistant to Zanussi on his feature, *The Structure of Crystals*. Krauze then began making documentaries and found the subject for his first feature in an unpublished manuscript by Tadeusz Zawierucha. It was an autobiographical narrative of the author's early years in a children's home and his forays into amateur theatre and music before settling as a customs officer in Warsaw. The novel, *Selection*, became *Finger of God (Palec Bozy*, 1973): a rare example of a Polish book being catapulted into print because it was being filmed.

Finger of God

The film is a story of a young man trying to break down the barriers which society puts in his way to hinder his ambition – to become an artist. The protagonist, Tadeusz (Marian Opania, the Winkel of *Man of Iron)*, is rejected again and again by the examining board of a theatre school. Trying to satisfy his ambitions he joins a student theatre led by Alfred (played by the director, Janusz Zaorski), a kind of nomadic hippy. Tadeusz becomes close friends with Alfred and his wife. Unfortunately his final plea before the examining board to be taken in as a drama student falls on deaf ears. His authentic desire to be an artist is clear but it is not enough. Tadeusz's mind snaps; his violent tirade against the representatives of the

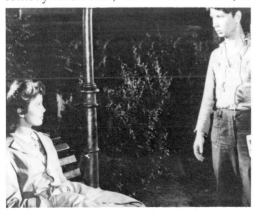

Eve Wants to Sleep

school cause him to be incarcerated in a home for the mentally ill. It is there through a psychodrama played by the inmates - when a man playing Oedipus actually gouges out his own eye – that Tadeusz undergoes a catharsis. That and the death of his close friend Alfred bring him back to a 'normal' starting point in life, from which it is likely that he will pursue some realisable goal.

In an interview with the critic Andrzej Kolodynski Krauze talks of how Tadeusz's fighting spirit becomes "an obsession . . . this in turn drives him to the verge of madness". He also describes his invention of the mental clinic scene (in the book it is an ordinary drama course) as an interesting experience. The scene is played without resorting to the usual clichés associated with such hospitals. Krauze believed that "a convincing and true effect can be achieved when one discards all that which reveals only dull and colourless petty realism".

Weather Forecast

Antoni Krauze's achievement in *Weather Forecast* (*Prognoza Pogody*, 1981) has been obscured by its unavailability. It is a landmark in Polish comedy and, as one of the 'missing ten', has yet to crack even the international festival circuit. A great shame, because it is the richest and funniest comedy to emerge from this country in many years. It lacks the heaviness which bogs down many of the post-1970 movies that tend to counterbalance their entertainment value with an emphasis on background journalistic 'truth', or that simply lack pace. Krauze's film flies free.

Krauze is, however, an ex-documentarist with a realist's eye for detail. In *Weather Forecast*, adapted from Marek Nowakowski's story and with a magical score by Zbigniew Preisner, he

has a vehicle for superb farce, using a cast of septo- and octogenarians, through whose lips the mockery of sacred cows – most of them institutions – lead the film into a limboland of 'limited' distribution – not quite on the shelf but not really off it. A recent request for the film by London's National Film Theatre for a Polish Film Week, for instance, was rebutted by Film Polski.

Weather Forecast

Sadly, therefore, Krauze, a director with a fine comic mind, many never be allowed to develop this too-precious facility in the Polish cinema. *Weather Forecast* is above all a really good laugh in the tradition of the best Ealing comedies of the 1950s.

The setting is an old people's home run by an aging director (Witold Pyrkosz). He and the rest of the staff seem to have no rapport with the inmates, most of whom have vivid and fond memories of life in Poland before World War Two and who have experienced the post-war 'system' through all its phases to today, 1981. The film begins with a close-up of the cook banging a dinner-call cymbal – a pastiche of a J Arthur Rank logo. During the night many of the residents huddle in a living-room penetrated by the October cold. The TV news is on (showing an actual clip from a pre-Solidarity newscast). A woman blandly announces the 'expected' number of old people's deaths from the predicted harshness of the forthcoming winter. The authoritarianism of the institution is established: rigidly appointed meal and sleeping hours along with the 'commandant' character of the director, himself hitting the pensionable age.

In the middle of the night, with all the lights out, a truckload of coffins arrives for storage in an upstairs attic. Discovering the forty-odd coffins, the elders assume that they themselves are marked for liquidation and flee en masse, taking what possessions they can. One or two remain, one even climbing into a coffin to hide.

The next day the director discovers the exodus and is forced to call in the authorities. So begins a round of counter accusations over responsibility for the elders' flight. The coffins are revealed to be an over-production from a coffin factory whose manager made a storage deal with the director. Police and party officials are inevitably involved; helicopters and other resources are commandeered in a panic search since it is feared that the truants will perish in the wilds.

Sleeping for warmth in the back of the lorry, the elders are transported via a motorway to another part of Poland. When the driver (oblivious of his load) parks for a pee, the truants vacate into the woods and stumble across a near-empty but pretentiously elegant restaurant. Treated with disdain by the waiter, they tie him up, lock him and the waitress in a cupboard and abscond with provisions, including plenty of vodka. The restaurant's gypsy band is forced to keep playing when an elder threatens to cut their guitar strings with a kitchen knife.

Making their way over a ricketty narrow bridge, the escapees go deeper into the country. A lone fisherman invites them into his farmhouse in which a group of hippy guests make music on handmade instruments. Enraged by the indecency and drug-taking of the hippies, the elders tie them and their host up with ropes, but then have second thoughts. They untie them all and begin to commune with the hippies, indulging in an assortment of their drugs. One of the old women, dressed in her wedding gown, injects herself with heroin and tries to float Ophelia-like in the river.

The state-wide hunt brings the police to the treacherous single-file bridge and police men fall through the rotting wood planks. The river is dragged and the director looks on, cursing the cussedness of his charges. Eventually the elders are cornered around a night camp-fire and forcibly dragged by medics and the police into a bus to take them 'home'. The director with a change of heart tries in vain to warn his charges to escape. Remaining at the embers of the camp-fire he rekindles the flames and the spirits of the elders (now on their way back) materialise near the fire. The director seems at last to have some sort of communion with his inmates.

Weather Forecast contains a number of barbs and prickles 'for Poles only' – ie it operates on levels best grasped by a home audience, but it does work superbly well on the surface of plot and characterisation

Weather Forecast

– the first rule in demanding two hours of your seated attention. It goes right into a comedy class inhabited by Munk's *Bad Luck* and Chmielewski's *Eve Wants to Sleep*.

Andrzej Kondratiuk

Hailed as a specialist in black humour and the philosophical grotesque, Andrzej Kondratiuk collaborated with the Se-Ma-For Studio in Lodz and made the experimental film, *Obrazki z podrozy*, in 1960. In 1966 he made *Kobiela on the Beach (Kobiela na plazy)*. Kobiela plays a 'medium' in a candid camera film and provokes holiday makers on the beach into some strange conversations.

Promotion/Awans

Made in 1975 and directed by Janusz Zaorski, *Promotion (Awans)* is a comedy satirising the packaging of folk and folksiness for those from the big city. A teacher arrives at a small village – his old home town. He persuades the villagers to cash in on tourism; they accept his ideas and soon the first tourists arrive only to find concrete, glass buildings and garish advertisements. The tourists leave, craving a more 'natural' environment, away from it all. *Promotion* had an interesting poster design by Andrzej Krauze which is discussed on page 108.

Olympics 40

Olympics 40 (Olimpiada 40, 1980), directed by Andrzej Kotkowski, details the extraordinary story of Stalag Freudental XXC – a multi-national camp of mainly Polish, French, British, Norwegian and Belgian POWs. It is 1940. Lieutenant Otto Schultz arrives as the new commandant to boost order and discipline among the prisoners. He encounters Piotr, a Polish officer with whom he was a participant at the 1936 Berlin Games. Piotr refuses to co-operate in a sports plan proposed by Schultz for his charges; instead he organises a clandestine Olympic Games.

A special series of events are organised under the noses of their German captors; medals are struck bearing the emblems of some unusual physical sports. After every event one of the prisoners is delegated to play his mouth organ to the tune of the winner's national anthem. Just when the games seem set to finish – one more event to go - they are discovered! A special guard is placed on the prisoners' quarters. The men devise a brilliant special final event. There is a certain exercise imposed as punishment namely squatting and hopping a set distance in the exercise yard. The competing prisoners break rank in the yard and are 'forced' to do the leg-bending exercise. It is clear, however, that this is the new event. The German officers are non-plussed, but then outraged when the punishment takes on the excitement of a horse race. A Pole wins the event and the 1940 Olympic Games for his country! Piotr, who has been under suspicion, is expelled by Schultz and sent to a concentration camp.

This finale is the film's strong point. While the Stalag was not a death camp, conditions were very low and the invention of yet another code or underground form of existence – here sports – follows the line of flying universities (in the 19th century and after 1976), the underground press, and clandestine courses in theatre and cinema during the Occupation.

Juliusz Machulski

Mention should be made of the 'Holly-Lodz Brat', Juliusz Machulski, an untrained actor and the son of the famous screen star, Jan Machulski – who plays the main role in Kieslowski's *Personnel* (1975) and acts in the features *Indeks* (1977), and in *Constans* and *In Broad Daylight* (both 1980).

Machulski's feature début, *Va Bank*, made in 1980, stars his father as Kwinto, a jazz-playing safe-cracker newly released from prison, seeking revenge against his ex-partner in crime, Kramer, now a successful banker. It is a caper comedy set in the 1930s with an overtly tongue-in-cheek score by Henryk Kuzniak. It is a well-made entertainment and shows a promise that was rapidly fulfilled by Machulski's second feature, *Sexmission* (*Seksmisja*, 1984), an ambitious sci-fi comedy that absorbed most of the Lodz studio facilities for several weeks. The film was an enormous success in Poland and played to generally excellent reviews during its limited London release in 1985.

Jerzy Stuhr and Olgierd Lukaszewicz star respectively as Maks and Albert, two technicians who volunteer for a hibernation experiment – Maks, it seems, to escape from his wife's nagging. The two wake up in *fifty* years' time to find that they are the sole surviving males and objects of curiosity, perhaps experimentation, or even elimination by

poster for Sexmission

an all-female hierarchy which has discovered a way to perpetrate an all-female race. The world has been reduced to the huge interior of a nuclear-free shelter since the outside is said to be still contaminated with radiation. The 'queen' or ruler, however, turns out to be a man in drag who lives in luxury *outside* the shelter; there is no nuclear contamination. Not unlike a Crosby-Hope road movie without the songs, it provides Jerzy Stuhr with his best comedy vehicle and confirms Machulski's talent and zest for screen humour.

Machulski's third film, *Va Bank II*, is a more expensive (seventy million zloties) complement to *Va Bank*, with the same cast of Jan Machulski as safe-cracker Kwinto, Witold Pyrkosz as his friend 'the Dane', and the beefy, Robert Shaw-like presence of Leonard Pietraszak as the murderous banker, Kramer.

The director spent one year in the United States in 1984/85 on a Fulbright study grant. He works with the *Kadr* unit under the leadership of Kawalerowicz.

Va Bank II

14: Censorship

In 1937 a *Motion Picture Herald* report on Poland tabled its main taboos as gangster and mystery films – particularly "those which depict murder, wholesale and retail". In that year a further clause was inserted into the code dealing with state censorship of films: "Producers shall neither produce nor distributors import film subjects including class struggle, riots of a revolutionary tendency, misery as a means of agitation or . . . Russian background."

In 1936 Warner Brothers' *G Men* and MGM's *Public Hero Number One* were banned, although Columbia's *The Whole Town's Talking*, also dealing with gangsters, was allowed in because of its "artistic" merit (entitling the film to a drastic reduction in tax) and its "humorous treatment". The Soviet picture *Love of Maxim*, appearing under the title *The Struggle with the Czar*, made it despite the anti-Soviet current; the change of title was a factor. German productions were generally boycotted – most of the exhibitors and distributors were Jewish – and so UFA bought Filharmonja, one of the largest cinemas in Warsaw, to show German-only films.

Under the Partitions censorship attempted to stamp out the Polish language and culture. The provisions available under the Partitions were retained by the politicians ruling Poland after the Versailles Treaty in 1919 when once again it became a single national state. Newspapers were dependent on government advertising; public policy – in the name of survival of the new fragile state – induced a great deal of editorial censorship.

World War Two

Preceding World War Two censorship became relaxed but newspapers and journals had to be licensed by the heads of the partitioning administrations and whole issues could be confiscated over a small offensive article. There was little room left to the Poles for debate. Nazi occupation brought with it the old Prussian method in a much more brutal form. *No* Polish newspapers were allowed except those issued and controlled by the Germans. Setting up an independent press or mere involvement with one meant death or shipment to the camps.

The Glowny Urzad Kontroli Prasy, Publikacji i Widowisk (GUKPPiW – the Cracow Main Office for Control of Press Publications and Public Performances) was established by the government in 1946, and in the euphoria of September 1956, just before Gomulka's return to power, the Main Office liquidated itself. Journalists, however, formed an ad hoc body to control what was said in the media, in order to curb excessive anti-Soviet statements at a time when dire warnings were being given to Hungary for similar reasons.

Edward Gierek

Censorship soon reasserted itself under Gomulka, but it was under his successor, Edward Gierek, that the most complex and centralised system of censorship was formed. A random series of censor guidelines, transcripts from the *Report on Censored Materials* (the censors' own bi-weekly publication), and other instructional leaflets on the training of censors, were smuggled out of Poland in February 1977 to form the basis of *The Black Book of Polish Censorship*, translated and edited by Jane Leftwich Curry for Random House publishers in the United States.

It was part of the Gierek regime's so-called "propaganda of success" in which the party and its economic and cultural policies had to be given a universally positive image. Leftwich Curry's book quotes from the *Report on Censored Materials* (December 1-15 1974) an excised provocative comment by Stefan Kisielewski in the independent Catholic weekly, *Tygodnik Powszechny*. It contrasts Paul Newman's *The Effect of Gamma Rays on Man-in-the-Moon Marigolds* with an idiotically positive documentary short, calling the latter "bursting with joy, energy and images of prosperity . . . construction, expansion, bright, spacious factory halls, smiling faces, good-looking, nicely dressed girls, colourful streets" and concluding that "after this the American film turned out to be a dreadfully sad experience".

The same writer complains that this consistent window-dressing had only deprived Poland of its own literary and cinematic heritage. Such films *were* being made by directors such as Wiszniewski, Lozinski, Kieslowski and Piwowski, as the release of "ten years of banned documentaries" later showed. As with these films, the systematic control of debate and diversion from the positive government line isolated the leadership not only from criticism but also from any effective reports of economic ills and public unrest on which they could base their decisions – hence the 'shocks' of the price increase riots in 1976 and the August 1980 strikes. Nothing was free from the all-pervasive censorship, including news-paper obituaries – only epitaphs on tombstones seemed to escape the blue pencil.

The Interrogation: the 'Bugajski affair'

More recently, with the advent of martial law, the censor has struck particularly hard on some Polish films. One notorious case is that of Ryszard Bugajski's *The Interrogation (Przesluchanie*, 1981/82).

Bugajski's The Interrogation

Born in 1943, Bugajski studied philosophy at Warsaw University – his old professor, Henryk Jankowski, was a member of the unit's kolaudacja which judged the work on April 23 1982. Graduating from the Lodz Film School in 1973, he translated and staged plays and produced some television plays before co-directing his first feature for the cinema, *A Woman and a Woman (Kobieta i Kobieta)*, with L Dymek in 1979. In 1980 he joined the prestigious film unit *X*, headed by Wajda and including directors Agnieszka Holland, Feliks Falk, and Janusz Zaorski, who managed the group in Wajda's absence.

The Interrogation started shooting in September 1981 – the director's solo début for the cinema and the third of a notable crop looking at the Stalin years (the others are Feliks Falks' *And There Was Jazz* and Wojciech Marczewski's *Shivers*, both of which were also temporarily shelved after the ascent of martial law). Bugajski's film is the account of a young woman who is arrested one night by two security agents and put through the vicious circle of trumped-up charges, tortures to extract confessions, and incarceration for several years until her release and 'rehabilitation' some time after the death of Stalin.

Once completed the film was shown to the committee within the unit, before being presented to the kolaudacja – the advisory body which makes recommendations to the Minister of Arts and Culture or his representative who then decides whether to shelve the film, send it back to the production unit for amendments or give it the green light.

Wajda was in Paris shooting *Danton* at the time of the kolaudacja but had his say in a letter which was read out at the meeting by his deputy, Zaorski. Deputy Minister Stanislaw Stefanski chaired; others present were Bohdan Poreba, chief of *Profil* unit and Chairman of the Grunwald Patriotic Association, an anti-semitic National Front type body; Czeslaw Petelski, head of *Iluzjon*; Ernest Bryll, head of *Silesia* (to be dissolved the following year, along with *X*); Jerzy Hoffman, chief of *Zodiak* and director of *The Deluge*; Jan Rybkowski, director; Maria Turlejska, historian; Jozef Lenart, a 'Party' writer; Marian Kuszewski, deputy to the Deputy Minister, and others including some who, like Andrzej Werner the critic, attended unofficially and were not allowed to speak. (A tape-recording was surreptitiously made of the speeches for and against the film, and later reprinted in full or in fragments in various papers in the West.)

Even those who strictly opposed the present distribution of Bugajski's film praised the skills of its director. It was clear that the comments from the meeting would be no more than advisory, that the final decision would be made higher up, but Stefanski bluntly declared that the film would be shelved for the time being because of its inflammatory quality, that the brutality and tactics of the bullies from the Ministry of the Interior in the film would be read as contemporary, and so applicable to the executives of the current state of martial law.

The writer Kazimierz Kozniewski, a supporter of martial law, praised the film and recognized that it was the first film of its type in post-war Poland. He then attacked the narrowness of the author's point of view, the fact that the persecutors have no background, that they are simply cipher figures performing cruel and unjustifiable acts against an innocent party. Its "one-sidedness" was attacked by others as an intellectual deficiency. Kozniewski criticised it as a distillation of all the nasty stories experienced by the victims of those "painful times".

The Interrogation

This is true, as Bugajski explained. It was not hard to find a wealth of grisly detail – there were people who had been flung in jail after 1948 on unspecific charges and a catalogue of methods employed to make them confess. One can believe that the director 'pulled back' on the torture. There are some repellent enough scenes – Krystyna is forced to drink a concoction of spittle and vodka; she is almost drowned in a small cell which fills with freezing water (really freezing – one of the last scenes filmed just before December 13 1981); she is forced to witness the execution of a political prisoner who is shot in the next room – a phoney execution as it turns out; and she is derobed and given a humiliating medical examination.

Undoubtedly when there is emotional involvement with Krystyna Janda's character, the tortures are tough to take but not as repellant as much of the gore and pain invented for a long list of commercial exploitation pics. Cathartic or inflammable, the same facts were exposed in works that were published shortly before the completion of *The Interrogation*, notably the autobiography of General Kuropieska who was condemned to death in 1952 on false charges of treason and rehabilitated in 1956.

Defending his own position at the kolaudacja, Bugajski knocked back the anti-Socialist charges:

"It's as if you emphasized at the same time that security police practices do constitute an integral part of Socialism. Because if they do not, for God's sake, let's condemn them! . . . I think it is grossly presumptuous to say that I, Ryszard Bugajski, or somebody else may decide, for example, that five million people, or even five thousand people, are in error, and that those five thousand should not be seeing this film. Let's present this film to the public to evaluate it. I would like to propose here a trial run that would help us to decide; let's show this film to people from various walks of life: workers, intelligentsia, clerks, the young and the old. Let's try it! That would be some kind of evaluation I could accept. If these people reject the film, then I would say, indeed, I was mistaken."

Those who decried the film even went so far as to suggest burning the negative – something that happened to several film makers in Czechoslovakia after 1968. Fortunately this was prevented. One print – so they say – rests in the Central Cinematic Administration in Warsaw. However, Bugajski confirmed that there was an underground distribution of the film – presumably in video – *in official circles*.

Completely out of the blue one day, Miss Janda was greeted by a regional Party official, a stranger entirely unconnected with culture or any cultural commission, who blurted out his admiration for her in the film: "You were wonderful. You have such beautiful breasts."

Bugajski, a published writer as well as a cineaste, had simply no outlets for his work in 1985 when he emigrated to Canada.

Script approval

The often absurd system of censorship in Poland is neatly summed up by scriptwriter and director Agnieszka Holland:

"There are two institutions. The first is censorship by the Ministry of Culture for cinema films. Each script has to be seen by a representative of the Ministry of Culture. It is not called censorship, but in fact that is what it is. In order to obtain finance for a production you must have an agreement from the Ministry for the project or for the scenario. Of course many scenarios are censored so they never get off the ground. But during the shooting, until today there was no interference apart from the rare exception. Zulawski, for example, had some problems some years ago with a science fiction film. It was after four months when he had shot about 80% of the script. Then it was stopped; completely absurd because it was so expensive. They destroyed all the sets, all the costumes . . ."

There was always censorship at the script stage but as Michalek pointed out on page 52, the *shooting* was practically unhindered. That has changed, but the script approval is still the biggest hurdle and projects are turned down continuously. Following martial law, the range of taboos expanded considerably. Historical, pre-Soviet conflict with Russia, for example, was an unacceptable background for a movie – not necessarily through any specific pressure from the Soviet Union.

The importance of script approval means that a form of auto-censorship on the film maker's behalf is always present, from choice of subject through to the final cut. Krzysztof Kieslowski, a documentarist, comments on the continuous knock-back of scripts: "It is difficult to understand for somebody who does not know the country, the situation here. It is somewhat different here than in the West and different from other countries in the East. To try . . . it is simply a duty. I am trying all the time, I believe in trying. There is also the matter of pressure. I believe that if I and my colleagues present ten screenplays, they may all be rejected but that the eleventh may not."

Krzysztof Kieslowski

Once completed, however, films may still be shelved. With martial law came the disappearance of several completed films – later nicknamed "the missing ten".

Among them were Bugajski's *The Interrogation* and Piotr Szulkin's second feature, *War of the Worlds 2000 (Wojna Swiatow*, 1981). This was on the shelf but the director fought for its release: "I fought for the liberation of the film for more than one year. Between film makers there are two philosophies: some wait and some fight. I represent the guy who fights for his film. Maybe I wait one year, the others wait two . . . but they are less energetic."

Andrzej Zulawski, a graduate of the Paris IDHEC film school, completed *The Devil (Diabl*, 1972) which was banned. He began shooting *The Silver Globe (Na srebrnym globie*, 1978), but that project was stopped ten days before its completion. He now works in Paris.

Another film, *Robotnicy 80*, was grudgingly released in 1981 and received sporadic distribution in Warsaw. Newspapers were not even allowed to list it. The film is a record of the events in Poland of August 1980 and was made as a result of Lech Walesa's insistence on open negotiations between the government and strike representatives at Gdansk. It tended to play at cinemas which, in the newspaper listings, were "fully booked". Past masters at cracking codes, the punters knew what this meant . . .

Finally, Tomasz Pobog-Malinowski, director of *100 Days (Sto Dni*, 1980), comments on the fact that television, unlike cinema, is free from censorship: "The system is so reliable, staffed by such trusted people, that there is no need for formal censorship. Television is controlled directly by the relevant department of the Central Committee of the Party, and it is the most powerful propaganda tool, albeit incredibly clumsily and primitively run." And in response to the charge that Solidarity went too far the director retorted: "The Communist Party chose to call itself the Polish United Workers' Party – four words and each of them a lie."

15: The Cinema of Moral Anxiety

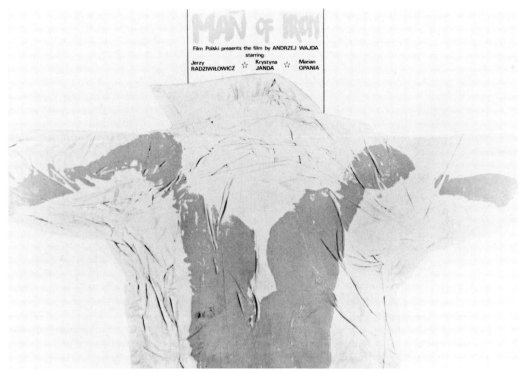

poster for Man of Iron

"As a film historian I know there are always good periods and bad periods and the so-called 'schools' – the trends – they don't last more than four or five years; five maximum. Then a certain fatigue, a certain repetition, then a lapse and we must wait some time until something new appears..." (Jerzy Toeplitz)

'The Cinema of Moral Anxiety' is a phrase attributed to the critic and director, Janusz Kijowski. As a 'school' it ended sharply on December 13 1981, the day of the coup d'état and General Jaruzelski's martial law. It is a generation reflected by the features starting with Wajda's *Man of Marble* and Zanussi's *Camouflage* in 1976 and finishing with Bugajski's *The Interrogation* in 1981 – a film finally in the can just one day before martial law. The films of this period thrust Poland's cinema back into worldwide focus.

The critic Andrzej Werner compared the two "golden periods" of Polish cinema - the Polish Film School, which finished approximately in 1962, and the period from 1976 to 1981. He characterised the Polish Film School as one at war with or estranged from the "social consciousness", that is the traditions or the constant values of the Poles:

"From a very important point of view Wajda of the 1950s was another man. The Polish Film School was against the public position. There was a cultural war between the films of this time and some of the Polish myths. There was maybe not a war but something not constant between Polish culture and the Polish social consciousness. After 1976 all of that changed. Wajda in *Man of Marble* adopted a position of the social consciousness. All of the young directors - for example,

Krauze, Agnieszka Holland, Zaorski and many others – in that period had a kind of war – well, there was a kind of war between a form of official propaganda and the things which are popular in our society. We can say that there was a unification of Polish culture with our social consciousness, and it is that stream which created Solidarity and created a Polish revolution."

Apart from *Man of Marble*, other films which belong to this exciting period are Bugajski's *The Interrogation* and Piwowski's *Foul Play/Excuse me, is this where they beat you up?* The units chiefly responsible were *Tor* (Zanussi, Kieslowski, Zebrowski) and *X* (Wajda, Holland, Falk, Zaorski). Another important unit was the Documentary Film Studio in Chelmska Street, which is equipped for features as well as being the home of the main documentarists.

Political dates

Vital to understanding this movement are several key political dates:

1970: This was the last year of Gomulka's reign. With asinine timing, just before Christmas the authorities put up the cost of staple foods and sparked off workers' riots around the ports of Gdansk and Gydnia. There were a recorded forty-five dead at the hands of the Polish military, but the true figure may never be known. Edward Gierek – party chief of Silesia – became head of state and offered a 'dialogue' with the workers as part of a new deal.

1976: An incredible repetition of the 1970 riots, but this time during the summer and with comparatively little bloodshed. Gierek had withdrawn Gomulka's price hikes of 1970 but re-introduced them in the middle of 1976 without any warning, lowering the workers' low living standards even further. This time the protests and strikes

were in Ursus and Radom, much closer to Warsaw, with widespread support from the intelligentsia. Apart from worker arrests, often on trumped-up charges (a favourite police tactic was to force a poor wretch to smash a store window with a brick), there were widespread dismissals of academics together with several student arrests. It was the first time in which workers and intelligentsia were visibly 'solid' – in contrast to 1968 when workers helped to suppress student demonstrations and in contrast to 1970 when the students in turn ignored the workers' appeals.

The Committee for the Defence of the Workers (KOR) was formed by prominent intellectuals (many of them jailed as students in 1968) and opened the way to a kind of underground state with a flourishing alternative press. Alternative courses, especially in politics and history, took place in 'flying universities' – in private flats at considerable risk to their owners. The state was considered irrelevant to the aspirations of a people who in theory shared its power.

1980: August saw the astonishing appearance of Solidarity, an authentic co-operative trade union, symbolised by the face of an unemployed electrician, Lech Walesa – who inevitably became an actor in the bold film 'happening', *Man of Iron*. Never had the initiative been so publicly taken from the hands of a Socialist state. Starting in the shipyards of Gdansk and Gydnia and rapidly spreading south, these locally-based unions took the general name of Solidarity. It was almost the first stage of an anarchist state – non-military, self-regulating, outside yet part of the political state now governed by an elite which was frightened of the intelligence of its own proletariat. Two governments fell – those of Gierek and Kania – and everyone talked of a Soviet invasion.

Public interest in cinema

The public's interest in cinema revived. From the beginning of the 1970s a group of Lodz graduates revitalised the documentary, a form they considered would ensure the 'reality' of their later features. Among them were Krzysztof Kieslowski, Marcel Lozinski, Marek Piwowski, Antoni Krauze and Wojciech Wiszniewski. They made shorts which, when released up to ten years later, were bigger crowd-pullers than the features. It was a common sight in later years for people to enter the cinema, watch the short and then go home.

Krzysztof Kieslowski

Krzysztof Kieslowski was born in 1941 and graduated from Lodz in 1969. He made his first feature in 1973 with a television film, *The Underground Passage (Przejscie podziemne)*, followed by *The Staff (Personel, 1975)* which took the Grand Prix at Mannheim that year. His first full-length film specifically for the cinema was *The Scar (Blizna)* in 1976. *Camera Buff (Amator)*, made in 1979, brought him world attention after a decade of documentaries and features.

Night Porter's Point of View

Between 1970 and 1978 Kieslowski made a number of documentaries and shorts. These include *Workers (Robotnicy,* 1971, co-directed with Tomasz Zygadlo), *Bricklayer (Murarz,* 1973) and the famous *Night Porter's Point of View (Z punktu widzenia nocnego portiera)* in 1978. This short film is a hilarious interview with an Alf Garnett-like character who loves his work (and uniform) as a factory porter and the control it gives him over others. His

weekend 'relaxation' is to work as a park supervisor, catching and punishing young offenders. The voice on the sound-track is the porter's own. He reels off the ludicrous offences for which he would like to hang, maim or imprison the offenders. Kieslowski screened the film to his subject who was delighted with it. The authorities were not and the film was shelved until 1979 when it was reluctantly 'distributed' at a cinema several kilometres from Warsaw's centre and shown as a support to an obscure oriental feature. Busloads of spectators went to the cinema, watched the support, and then bussed it back home at the intermission.

Krzysztof Kieslowski

'The Cracow Group'

At the Cracow Festival of Short Films in 1971, Kieslowski combined with Tomasz Zygadlo, K Wojciechowski and Grzegorz Krolikiewicz to present a manifesto of documentary film makers. The 'Cracow Group' – as it was subsequently called - declared that the experiences gained from documentaries should be exploited and used in features. This idea is a dominant feature in the 'Cinema of Moral Anxiety'.

Personel

Kieslowski has studied and worked in the theatre and is occasionally asked to direct plays. In *Personel* the action is set in a theatre, but Kieslowski points out that it is not a documentary:

"This is a film I made ten years ago, in 1975. I was an enthusiastic documentarist, which I have ceased to be now. Therefore it was half-documentary, half-feature with no clear dividing line. The point was that theatre is a place in which various fragments of life focus, various elements of reality happen in one place. I called it 'a pill of reality'. That's why I set it in a theatre; it could be made anywhere, in a factory, in an office, it didn't matter. But theatre was more expressive, more clear-cut; it was visually more attractive. It is a place where these conflicts which in reality are so grey and unclear are here very clear. They are obvious, handed on a plate. Furthermore, it was an operatic theatre, which made it *more* expressive."

Juliusz Machulski plays Romek, a young tailor backstage in a theatre and a graduate of a theatre technical school. He is spellbound by the creative process of the theatre but becomes aware of the red tape and backstage politics by which the inspiring part of the theatre exists. He is an observer rather than an actor in the backstage quarrels, but is forced into a corner at the end whereby he must decide whether or not to sign a blank piece of paper denouncing his friend, Sowa.

Kieslowski hired the whole theatre together with the workers who all play themselves in the film. He also inserted his own actors to form the narrative thread.

Camera Buff

Camera Buff (*Amator*, 1979) stars the fine comedy actor Jerzy Stuhr as Filip Mosz, a young married factory worker with a fixed

poster for Camera Buff

FILM POLSKI PRÉSENTE UN FILM DE KRZYSZTOF KIEŚLOWSKI   AMATOR
AVEC JERZY STUHR   LE PROFANE

daily routine in his life. One day he buys a movie camera to film his first child. Filip lives in a small town where his is the only movie camera. As part of the annual celebrations, the factory manager asks Filip to record the event on film; soon he is filming everything that moves, even the manager visiting the toilet. His documentary wins a prize and this opens up a whole new world for him. His life begins to change: his wife leaves him and his relationships with his friends are affected. His new career as a film maker has brought about the changes and he cannot revert to his former life-style. He is faced with several dilemmas: how to adapt to the realisation of being a developing artist; should he begin a new life at the risk of making others unhappy; and whether to exchange a quiet and happy marriage for a career so different and unknown?

With Rosi's *Christ Stopped at Eboli* and Juan Antonio Bardem's *Dias de Enero*, the film shared the Grand Prix at the 1979 Moscow Film Festival. It is a typical Kieslowski film: reality as interpreted from the point of view of the common man, and it is also a personal drama, a small story with a large reflection: worker-manager relations and, by extension, the censorship process in the film industry itself. At this stage a number of Kieslowski's documentaries still lay on the shelf and he had undoubtedly experienced the pressures and 'suggestions' by which film makers can exercise auto-censorship even at the scenario stage. Something of this is present in the story of *Camera Buff*.

Camera Buff

The Scar

Kieslowski's 1976 film, *The Scar*, was the first to touch upon the events in Poland in 1970. It stars Franciszek Pieczka as a man who returns to his old home town in order to build a large chemical works. Wajda acknowledged its influence when he came to shoot *Man of Marble*. As Kieslowski says:

"It was not a similarity of plot. Rather, I touched in a very simple way on the shortcomings or painful areas of reality. I think that Wajda did not know that such a film could be done. He made films about imagined problems. He did not expect that one could show directly – and with claws –

that something is terribly bad here. This film showed him that it could. It was a source of *inspiration*."

Wajda

Wajda was very active in this period – his muscle and personality were as important as his art. He pushed through projects of débutants in his own unit, X, projects which would never have made it under a less independent chief. Ministry men came and went but film makers were there forever and Wajda was a past master at fencing with the functionaries of censorship.

Man of Marble

Man of Marble (Czlowiek z marmuru) was an old project of Wajda's, dating from around 1961. Jerzy Bossak, Wajda's chief at *Kamera* when he first hawked the idea around, had a call from Wajda one evening in 1975 saying that he had been given the go-ahead. Both Wajda and Bossak and the screen-writer, Aleksander Scibor-Rylski, found that plenty of revision was needed on the fifteen-year-old script. Bossak suggested modelling the script on Welles's *Citizen Kane* and thus provided the solution.

Kane's journalist, probing the myth of a great newspaperman through the memories of his associates, was transformed into a student film maker, Agnieszka (Krystyna Janda). Her quest is about a worker-hero of the 1950s, Mateusz Birkut (Jerzy Radziwilowicz). Her commitment to her search becomes an embarrassment to the television head who is responsible for providing the materials for Agnieszka's diploma film. Finally forbidden and taken off the assignment, she continues to search for the missing man since she is too deeply involved to

Man of Marble

give up. It takes her to Gdansk where his son now works in the shipyards. It is implied (and *stated* in the sequel, *Man of Iron*) that Birkut was shot in the food riots of 1970 – one of the many uncounted dead.

The film is a look back at the bad old days of Stalinism, pre-Gomulka. The trouble was that the old days were not so old and the film took on a contemporary relevance. We see, as Agnieszka does, a picture of Birkut put together from old newsreel clips and interviews with his wife and with the director of a documentary, *They Are Building Our Happiness,* which portrays Polish wealth, health and moral goodness as attainable through work, and which features Birkut as the epitome of these values. Birkut is a 'Stakhanovist' or 'shock' worker – ie a showpiece labourer whose fantastic output as a bricklayer makes him a hero, a winner of medals and the subject of propaganda newsreels. In theory these 'superstars' inspired the rest of the working class to achieve similar goals and assist in the great leap forward. Birkut rises to fame as a gullible working-class hero but falls from grace when he defends his best friend from a trumped-up political charge in a show-trial typical of the whole

'Socialist bloc' in the dreadful period of 1948 to 1954.

Held up for distribution for two years, the film was one of the most popular ever screened in the first few weeks of its release. People broke down doors and there were fights to get in, according to Kieslowski. In all, two or three million people saw it and it was the country's largest grossing export film. Eventually it was shown on television for the whole nation.

Man of Iron

The sequel, *Man of Iron (Czlowiek z Zelaza,* 1981), was also written by the late Scibor-Rylski. The film was a speedy response to many crushing pressures, not least of which was time. No-one knew how long Solidarity would last and whether this history-in-the-making could be released without being instantly out-of-date or simply out of joint with the changes taking place every day. Such a film could not afford to be shelved. It *had* to be released immediately with a chance of attracting an audience as a matter of economic responsibility.

A script is woven around the figure of Maciej Tomczyk (son of Mateusz Birkut) who marries the reporter Agnieszka (Janda). Tomczyk (Radziwilowicz) really represents Lech Walesa, who accepted a cameo role in the film. Finished, edited and with government approval just days before the 1981 Cannes Film Festival, the film won the Grand Prix there, giving Wajda the clout he needed for its distribution in Poland and abroad.

Like *Camera Buff,* the beginning of *Man of Iron* leans towards comedy. It opens in a television studio where Winkel, a reporter played by Marian Opania, is briefed on an assignment: to dig up dirt on Tomczyk and to show the workers' unrest as the work of agitators. Winkel is a boozer: he books into a hotel in Gdansk only to find that all drink is prohibited. The one precious bottle he manages to smuggle in smashes on the bathroom floor and he sponges up the liquor into a glass. But, like *Camera Buff,* any comedy disappears in the wake of more serious matters.

The film has an extraordinary mixture of fiction and fabricated document. The real Lech Walesa and the real Anna Walentynowicz (whose sacking ignited the 1980 strikes) attend the wedding of Tomczyk, the quasi-Walesa; the first Secretary of the Pomeranian Communist Party, Tadeusz Fiszbach, plays himself being interviewed on local television; real archive film of military tanks descending on workers in the 1970 riots mixes with newsreel mock-ups such as a group of workers carrying one of their dead on a door hoisted over their shoulders (based on a true anecdote).

There is more exposition and more talk than in *Man of Marble* - an approach which Wajda and Scibor-Rylski believed essential. Once again there are flashbacks – for example, the conflict between Tomczyk and his father during the student demonstrations of 1968.

It is the closest Wajda has come to the documentary approach, a 'common man' perspective on Polish reality. It was not the subject but the *way* in which the stories were filmed that made Wajda very much part of the new generation.

The Interrogation

Ryszard Bugajski's full-frontal attack on the Stalinist era in *The Interrogation* (*Przesluchanie,* 1981/82) was too much for the authorities to stomach. Some of the brutes in those brutalising years were colleagues, many of them now nice old pensioners. The film was shelved and there was even talk of burning the negative. It depicts the arrest, torture and imprisonment of a pretty and very apolitical cabaret singer. The actress, Krystyna Janda, feels that she had her best ever role in this film which is unlikely to be seen for several years. Bugajski – like the documentarist Tomasz Pobog-Malinowski – was left without a future in Poland and as a result emigrated to Canada with his family in 1985. The film is discussed in more detail in chapter 14.

Marcel Lozinski

Another of the documentarists who came to prominence in this period is Marcel Lozinski. As with many documentary shorts, his *Microphone Test (Proba Mikrofonu)* ended up on the shelf and was publicly screened only after the coming of Solidarity. The film is set in a cosmetics factory and is about the presenter of its internal radio system who interviews both workers and management on the way the factory should be run. The clash of opinions and the various social problems which arise show small problems written large. The *signs* of discontent in wall-sized images were all too clear for the authorities to see.

His next film, *Happy End* (1972) co-directed with Pawel Kedzierski is a short without a prepared script which uses a real factory chief, departmental heads and day-to-day workers. Lozinski gave them general situations which might involve them in some sort of moral choice, or lead them to take an action which was natural for them in the given situation. A factory fails to meet its production targets and a special meeting of its internal council turns into a 'trial' of the engineer who is condemned for his attitudes, personal morality and so on. Only at the end does Lozinski pull back and reveal the exercise to be a psychodrama. As a work it stands as a sharp look at the mechanics of a witchhunt.

In a 1974 issue of the short-lived film monthly *Studio*, Lozinski was asked if he treated shorts as a training ground for features: "I'm interested in what you might call documentary creation, that is documentary manipulation of reality. Of course even straightforward recording is really manipulation but I am keen on provoking a deliberate clash among existing elements to elicit certain truths which would be unclear without it. For example, to put your subject in a situation of conflict which forces him to open up, express his feelings and opinions – in short spontaneous reactions."

Marek Piwowski

Dubbed by critics as the 'enfant terrible' of documentarists, Marek Piwowski was a journalist after studying at Warsaw University. His loose-limbed *Trip down the River/The Cruise (Rejs,* 1970) uses a few professional actors to stimulate a cast of 'interesting faces' – working people who make up the passengers. For all its charm and originality, it was taken as proof that the director lacked the know-how to craft a full-length feature.

Foul Play

Piwowski's next feature, *Foul Play/Excuse me, is this where they beat you up? (Przepraszam czy tu bija?* 1976) is a neatly constructed detective story, a true case from the police files of an armed robbery of a Warsaw department store. The main roles are taken by the boxers and Olympic champions, Jan Szczepanski and Jerzy Kulej, as the two detectives. (In fact the film slows down for a set-piece which allows them to indulge in their 'hobby' of

Foul Play

amateur boxing at the station. The sparring match nearly turned into a savage fight off-screen when the staged punches got out-of-hand.)

The film is a story of a young man coerced into undercover work for the police, in return for their dropping charges against him. It deals not just with police morality but also the decisions of the young man who poses as a friend and partner in crime to a criminal. In the final roof-top sequence when both friends flee from the police, the young man, after a moment's hesitation, kicks his partner off the roof into police hands below. Spoiled only by the music – television 'action' music, familiar from countless slick series – it is an interesting version of film noir, shot in colour by Witold Stok, one of Poland's leading young cameramen. What is most striking is the way Piwowski uses the sleazy café/bar underworld in a documentary manner, using non-professional actors.

Lindsay Anderson, the British director who was invited by Jerzy Bossak in 1967 to shoot *The Singing Lesson*, has a particularly high opinion of Piwowski's work. Anderson was curious about the documentaries – which were strictly unavailable – and he insisted upon seeing them; subsequently he met Piwowski. He especially praises the documentary shorts over the later features.

Witold Stok

Witold Stok won first prize at Gdansk in 1976 for his cinematography on *Foul Play*. His own documentary, *Special Train (Pociag Specjalny,* 1978), was awarded at Oberhausen and at the Cracow Festival of Short Films. It uses a subjective camera as a passenger on the final short train ride to the death camp at Treblinka, and is nine minutes long, roughly the time it took for the journey. The only dialogue on the sound-track is that of a child saying "Mama, where are we going?" – an effective reminder that 800 000 people took this trip to be gassed or burned at the camp. Stok's atmospheric *Time Falls* looks at Warsaw's famous Fowazki cemetery, burial ground for the wartime insurgents and many pre-war figures. Fragments of the famous 'September' broadcast by Jozef Malgorzewski over Polish radio during the invasion of the Nazis, and other sounds and voices, such as Jan Kiepura singing *O Marie*, are ghostly echoes hovering above and around the tombstones of the famous.

Still young when he moved to London a matter of days after martial law was imposed, Stok had shot eight features and several documentaries for others. It is the sort of track-record that can only be dreamed of in the West, although the monetary rewards in Poland are comparatively poor at every level of film making.

Zanussi

Born in Warsaw on June 17 1939, Zanussi studied physics at Warsaw University but attended lectures on film at the Institute of Arts in the Polish Academy of Sciences. He made amateur films during his university years (1955-59). Between 1959 and 1962 he studied at the Faculty of Philosophy in the University of Cracow. Graduating from Lodz with the diploma film, *The Death of a Provincial (Smierc Prowincjala,* 1966), which won awards at many festivals including Venice, his first feature was *The Structure of Crystals (Struktura Krysztalu)* in 1969. This film contrasts the lives and philosophies of two physicians, former college chums who meet after many years; the confrontation between two different attitudes to life is a theme Zanussi adopts in his other films.

Behind the Wall (Za Sciana, 1971) is an hour-long film produced for television by the *Tor* unit. Zanussi co-scripted with Edward Zebrowski but changed the script considerably during shooting due to the excellent improvisations of its stars, Maja Komorowska and Zbigniew Zapasiewicz. Two years later he made *Illumination (Iluminacja)* and then went to the United States to try his hand at a formula thriller from James Hadley Chase's novel *I'd Rather Stay Poor – The Catamount Killing* (1974).

The Constant Factor

The Constant Factor (Constans, 1980), like *Illumination,* seems to be about a young man's quest for the purest way to live. This time it is the near impossibility of making straightforward or morally correct choices in a world of corruption, kickbacks and family influence. Like the real-life actor in *Illumination,* the protagonist is a mountaineer, Witold (Tadeusz Bradecki). He dreams of conquering a slope in the Himalayas similar to the one that killed his father. After military service he lands a plum job with a firm organising exhibitions abroad – a job secured through

poster for **The Constant Factor**

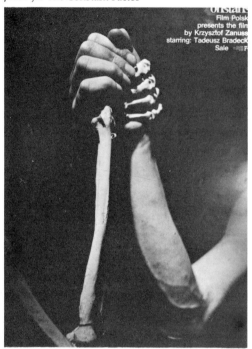

the influence of his father's friends. Witold is shocked to witness the web of perks, black market deals and sheer fraud committed by his boss and colleagues. He finds that his sick mother has been callously left in a hospital corridor because all the beds are occupied. He is offered the blunt hint that a bribe will fix it. Grazyna, a sympathetic nurse, provides the love-interest in an otherwise dry moral exercise.

Kazimierz Kutz

Kutz's main contribution to this period is his third 'Silesian' film, *The Beads of One Rosary (Paciorki jednego Rozanca,* 1980). It is a little like one of the old Frank Capra comedies – an old retired worker sticking with the cottage he loves against the wishes of the mean old commercial developers. The mean old developers here

are representatives of a housing commission who are not cast as villains, but rather as officials with a vast rehousing programme who see the problem in terms of moving a 'mass' of people from their unsanitary, dilapidated homes into cleaner high-rise apartments. The problem is that the old worker-hero, Habryka (Augustyn Halotta) has a confoundedly strong will. His family is at best neutral and one of his sons is openly against his 'foolish' resistance to the move. His wife (Marta Straszna) simply sighs and carries on as a long-suffering helpmate.

The affection between the old couple, the persistent teasing and the squabbling in the kitchen are the funniest moments in the film. The two leads, Halotta and Straszna, are non-professionals and Halotta was actually a retired miner. Straszna's quick waddling and bustling is like something out of a cartoon. She has turned up in other films with a Silesian theme, notably *The Millionaire (Milioner,* 1978) and a recent Kutz war-theme feature made in 1984. This film tells of the plight of the partisans under the Occupation. At one point in the film Straszna strips completely nude and stuns the visiting German commander with her vast body. She saves two partisans hiding in the back room by the ploy.

Feliks Falk's Top Dog

Top Dog (Wodzirej, 1979) was Feliks Falk's third feature and shot him into prominence. It gave Jerzy Stuhr one of his best roles as Danielak, a man on the make in a peculiar line of show business: the dance leader. Eager to be considered as the man to host the forthcoming ball in his home town which will celebrate its 500th anniversary, Danielak, in his thirties, sees himself being permanently stuck on the second rung in his business, particularly as he has been ignored in the shortlist of four candidates for the anniversary. Seeing no other way of making his name or becoming 'top dog', it is crucial for him to land the job. With below-the-belt tactics he gets his name on the list and proceeds to eliminate his rivals by a mixture of blackmail, bribery and the betrayal of his closest friend. One could transpose the story to, say, executive power struggles within a big corporation.

Top Dog

And There Was Jazz

Falks's *And There Was Jazz, (Byl Jazz*, 1981) was photographed by Witold Sobocinski, himself a drummer with a clandestine jazz group in Lodz in the early 1950s. Jazz, like Coca Cola, was taboo, a handy symbol for everything rotten in the decadent enemy states of the Cold War. Times change. It was possible, as late as 1960, for Hollywood to spin a farce around the idea of selling Coke to East Berlin in Billy Wilder's *One, Two, Three* with James Cagney. In the event, jazz was liberated first and Warsaw became an important centre in the jazz festivals of the world.

A group of young musicians in a regular band turn to clandestine jazz for small groups of followers. They want to play bigger houses but even while taking real risks their defiance of official taboos is treated as a game. The times are brought forcibly home; certain supporters and friends are victimised and eventually the boys are discouraged. But when Stalin dies they reunite and achieve their dream of performing in a big concert hall. It is a finale marred by tragedy in an odd pastiche of the end of *Ashes and Diamonds.* The banjo player, Jarpinski, takes a short cut through the railway-yard on his way to the concert. He has a misunderstanding with a gun-toting milicja man and panics, late already for the concert before an expectant crowd of seven hundred. On the run he is senselessly killed by a train. The ending echoes Maciek's death at the end of *Ashes and Diamonds* and Cybulski's own tragedy under a train.

Marczewski's Shivers

Wojciech Marczewski is one of the few film school students to have gone into the profession before completing his studies. Even more oddly, he was enrolled at the young age of eighteen, then quit the film school to enter university which he abandoned to re-enter the film school.

Like *Man of Marble* and *The Interrogation*, Marczewski's *Shivers/The Creeps (Dreszcze*, 1981), made with the *Tor* unit, examines the Stalinist years but from an autobiographical viewpoint. These were childhood years for Marczewski and for many of the new directors in the 1970s. The film is set at the end of that period – over 1955/56, leading up to the workers' riots in Poznan and the eventual accession of Gomulka. But the story takes place before the first Polish 'Spring'.

Tommy (Tomasz Hudziec) is a thirteen-year-old schoolboy whose father is suddenly arrested by the security police. Sensitive and withdrawn, he is picked out of his school class and 'invited' to attend a summer camp with the 'pathfinders' – ideological boy scouts. He becomes the protégé of one girl guide, a sister/mother figure. She eventually wins his soul over to the religion of the new morality where children are encouraged to write essays denouncing their parents and friends. Tommy is gradually built into a Stalinist fanatic and joins the despised bunch of prefects – just at the point where the counter-revolutionary forces take over the government in October 1956. The camp is evacuated and a disturbed, brainwashed Tommy goes out to embrace a new society.

poster for Marczewski's Nightmares

Janusz Zaorski

Janusz Zaorski was born in 1947 and studied in the directing faculty at Lodz (1965-69); he began as an assistant to Janusz Morgenstern on a television series, *The Columbuses*. His début was a half-hour television comedy, *Goodnight (Na Dobranoc, 1970)*, followed two years later by his feature début, *Run Counter Run (Uciec jak najblizej)*. At twenty-five Zaorski was the youngest Polish director to make his début. Zaorski's second film, the comedy, *Promotion* (1975), has already been mentioned.

A Room with a Sea View

Zaorski then made a more serious film, *A Room with a Sea View (Pokoj z widokiem na morze,* 1978). Its drama lies in the conflict between a psychiatrist, Dr Kucharski (Piotr Fronczewski), and Professor Leszczynski (Gustav Holoubek), called in by Kucharski as the best person to talk to a potential suicide. To the psychiatrist's dismay Leszczynski deals with the problem in a thoroughly unprofessional manner and seems to carry on an airy, non-commital chat with the man. What is worse is that he seems to be saying to the man (Marek Bargielowski): "well, if you want to jump, it's entirely your decision of course".

The professor is adamant that force or drugs would be fatal. Meanwhile, appeals from the man's girlfriend and his parents are no use. The young man (only referred to as "D.A.") is finally left alone, at the professor's urging, to make his own decision. He decides not to jump; the professor, exhausted by the struggle, has a heart attack.

A Room with a Sea View is partly a picture of a cross-section of Polish society. The old professor's way wins in the end, talking casually about life, the sea, sport

Janusz Zaorski

and other "silly things". The young, aggressive Kucharski wants more direct methods.

Zaorski had carefully prepared and worked on the physical plan of the film but just under two weeks before shooting was to begin he found that the skyscraper he had chosen was suddenly not available. It was a towering administrative building in the centre of Gdansk, admirably placed with a view of the Baltic Sea and perhaps the only one suitable. It appeared that, unknown to the film maker, certain military or security-related offices were installed in the building. By the time the paperwork returned – with a firm "no" – from the responsible authority, Zaorski had the production all ready to go and his whole set had been blue-pencilled into oblivion. "It was the blackest day of my life", he said, pointing to the building he could never use, during the 1985 Gdansk Festival at which his new film, *Baryton*, won three awards.

Edward Zebrowski

Edward Zebrowski made his début at the age of thirty-seven, though like most Polish directors he was backed by years of experience as a director of shorts and television films and as a screen-writer, particularly for his *Tor* colleague, Krzysztof Zanussi. *Salvation (Ocalenie,* 1972) stars Zbigniew Zapasiewicz as an egotistical research scientist who, after a routine medical check-up, finds that he has a serious illness and ultimately needs a kidney transplant to survive. Committed to hospital, he tries to maintain the pace of his work and remains aloof from the ordinary "boring" people who surround him in the ward. His wife, played by Maja Komorowska, offers to donate one of her own kidneys but the scientist refuses to take mortality at face value.

Transfiguration Hospital

Based on a rare *non*-science fiction story by Stanislaw Lem, *Transfiguration Hospital (Szpital Przemienienia,* 1978) begins in the autumn of 1939 during the first phase of wartime occupation. Stefan, a young doctor, arrives at an asylum for the mentally ill to take up a post. He soon discovers that an amoral scientific and professional code of ethics is practised by some of the staff; different inmates receive cruel forms of punishment either out of vindictiveness or with the argument that the cruelties are radical 'cures'. Electric shock treatment is given to a man with headaches; then the treatment is delayed and the headpains prolonged for the purposes of "study". Not all of the doctors treat patients in this way but a question hovers: will the unformed Stefan be turned into such a professional? Will he lose his ideals or humanity under the persuasive arguments of his mentors?

The Nazis eventually arrive, having decided the fate of the institution: liquidation of all inmates. One doctor declares himself to be a German; a woman doctor, Doctor Nosilewska (Ewa Dalkowska), admits to being Jewish and passively accepts the consequences. Stefan, in the confusion of the desperate scramble to escape by the inmates and staff, manages to flee into the forest, carrying a patient. With the Germans still in pursuit he discovers that the patient is dead. The film ends as the soldiers close in.

Transfiguration Hospital had a browny-orange tint which seems to be a characteristic of several films in the late 1970s. This may have as much to do with the East German Orvo film stock as with

poster for The Hospital of Transfiguration

The Hospital of Transfiguration

any artistic choice. The film is an interesting illustration of Fascism as a creeping disease and of the brainwashing process – something it shares with Marczewski's *Shivers* though it is less exciting and only slightly engages the emotions, another fairly common characteristic of the Cinema of Moral Anxiety.

Leszczynski's Konopielka

As a début feature, the reputation of *The Days of Matthew (Zywot Mateusza*, 1968) is high – somewhere near *Knife in the Water* and *A Generation*. For its director, Witold Leszczynski, it was thirteen years before he produced - for the critics' satisfaction – a film to equal it: *Konopielka*. This rural comedy, shot in black-and-white, is about a young girl teacher arriving in an out-of-

poster for Konopielka

the-way village. She rents a room from a peasant, Kaziuk, the main character of the film, played by the beefy comic actor, Krzysztof Majchrzak. Kaziuk is fascinated and irritated by the girl's behaviour and under her influence he breaks several taboos of his world: he cuts down a sanctified family tree, for example, and engages in illicit sex. Finally, against the will of the entire village he breaks an ancient harvest custom. This incident builds to a dramatic finale.

Aria for an Athlete

Majchrzak also portrays "the strongest man in the world" in Filip Bajon's *Aria for an Athlete (Aria dla atlety*, 1979). This is a film which is unclassifiable in terms of other Polish features. The subject is based on a newspaper interview given by Stanislaw Zbyszko Cyganiewicz (1881-1967), who won the World Championship title in freestyle wrestling, first in Paris in 1906 and then in New York in 1921 and 1922. At the time of the interview (1930) he already looked a very old man.

Aria was Bajon's début but he had made a number of television stories, also about sporting champs. The film is a retrospective on the life of the wrestler – a memoir featuring the man himself (a made-up Majchrzak) and the young hero too. The narrative takes us from the circus to the opera, the two poles of culture to which 'Iron Zbyszko' connected his art of wrestling. His physical strength is treated as just that, a form of art. In a scene towards the end of his career, Zbyszko presents a wrestling show on-stage at an opera house while an operatic song is delivered from the balcony.

Agnieszka Holland

Born in 1948, Agnieszka Holland entered

the Polish film industry as a graduate of the Prague Film School in Famu. Her father, a Home Army veteran, fell out of a window in Warsaw under police interrogation. "They would not have let her into Lodz," said Wohl, "because of her father. Well, no-one knows how he died exactly."

Her first full-length film, *Provincial Actors* (*Aktorzy prowincjonalni*, 1980), was set around the staging of an important Wyspianski play, *Liberation*, in a mediocre provincial theatre. The play was written in 1902, three years before the events depicted in her second feature for the cinema, *The Fever*. An inexperienced director arrives from Warsaw to direct *Liberation* but in a mutilated version. Krzysztof, the leading actor, objects to the cuts which lessen the political import of the play – precisely the reason why they were cut. Krzysztof's adherence to his principles and to the cause of art alienates the company and particularly his wife who leaves him (shades of *Camera Buff*). His missionary zeal in art parallels Leon's zeal in *The Fever* in his disregard for weaker souls.

The Fever

Holland's second feature, *The Fever* (*Goraczka*, 1981), is taken from Andrzej Strug's book, *The Story of a Bomb* and deservedly won top prize at the 1981 Gdansk Festival. With a screenplay by Krzysztof Teodor-Toeplitz, the story takes place in the revolutionary years of 1905 to 1907, the false dawn of the Soviet Revolution. In Poland PPS (Polish Socialist Party) members were inspired to guerilla action against the Czarist administration – forty years after the last Russian recriminations over the 1863 Uprising.

The bomb of the book's title is an intricate construction, lovingly put together by the hands of a chemist in close-up as the credits roll. Soon after he completes the bomb, Czarist agents enter and kill him. A cell of his friends plan to use the bomb to blow up the Czarist governor. Leon (Olgierd Lukaszewicz), son of a rich factory owner (played by Zbigniew Zapasiewicz), is rescued by his friends who ambush a coach taking him to the citadel. He is hidden by the beautiful Kama (Barbara Grabowska) who falls in love with him, but Leon does not return her love. Devoted strictly to his cause – the revolution - he uses Kama's devotion to ensure that she will be so physically close to the governor when she throws the bomb that she is certain to be killed in the explosion. Kama is loved by a rather weak student also involved in the movement and the first part of the film draws a panorama of motives for each individual's involvement in the cause.

The plot to kill the governor is foiled by a farce of fate: he dies of a stroke in his room. The bomb is then stored with Wojtek (Adam Ferency, the leading man in *The Interrogation*) and two years pass. The cause is finished. Leon returns from exile in Cracow and meets Kamil, the student who loved Kama. Kamil harbours a grudge against Leon for causing Kama's insanity and betrays him to the police.

Wojtek, meanwhile, has been waiting for instructions and, impatient, comes back to Warsaw to rally his former comrades, thinking that the underground still functions. Rejected and snubbed, Wojtek is arrested and thrown into the citadel to await execution by orders of the Czarist court. He shares a cell with an anarchist, Gryziak. While Wojtek goes to his death Gryziak is released. He kills the man who betrayed Wojtek to the police and retrieves the bomb. He attempts to blow up an assembly of Czarist police but the bomb, so long in storage, does not function. The police massacre the anarchist and the bomb is eventually ignited peacefully in the depths of the Vistula.

Holland's next feature for the cinema, *The Lonely Woman (Kobieta Samotna i chromy*, 1982), completed just before her exile in Paris, has never been released. She continues to write and make films in Paris.

100 Days and the Monument

In 1980 a monument was built outside the Lenin shipyard in Gdansk to commemorate the victims of 1956 (Poznan), 1970 (Gdansk) and 1976 (Ursus and Radom). It took 106 days to build: three towering steel crosses, each 140' high, welded together at the top, and each supporting a huge ship's anchor which at a certain distance looks like a crucified figure. A ceremony took place in front of the monument, orchestrated by Wajda at the workers' request. It began at 5 pm with the mournful wailing of factory sirens; then followed a spectacle of sound and light, with Penderecki's music and the actor, Daniel Olbrychski, reciting the names of the known dead.

Tomasz Pobog-Malinowski shot an impressive film record of the construction and final welding together of the crosses: *100 Days (Sto Dni*, 1980). The monument remains. Every week schoolchildren leave cloth shoulder badges as a tribute and just as regularly, overnight, the multi-coloured badges are taken away by the henchmen of the authorities. One can always see the remains of the tiny decorations wedged in amongst the sculpted letters of a text honouring the fallen workers. It was the first time in a post-war Communist country that the victims of its ruling forces have been memorised in this way. As yet no monument exists for the millions of victims of Stalinism.

the Monument

Dramatic events

Late in 1981, during a visit to the Polish Cultural Institute in London, a representative from the Polish theatre talked of dwindling theatre audiences. For the first time people were glued to the new programmes on their television sets. The daily headlines were far more dramatic than anything being offered in the theatre. *New Yorker* critic Lawrence Wechsler commented on the fusion of script and documentary in films such as *Man of Marble* and *Camera Buff*: "In Poland today, nothing is more compellingly dramatic than what is actually happening before their eyes. Fiction and documentary are merging in a new epic form." Martial law was declared on December 13 1981.

16: Post-martial law

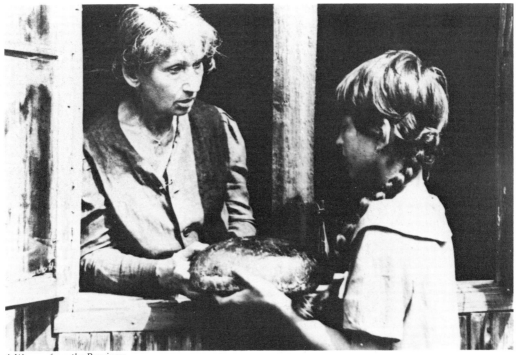

A Woman from the Provinces

The 8th Polish Feature Film Festival, held in 1981, marked a shift of interest from contemporary 'moral anxiety' to the 1950s. Only *Man of Iron* and Zaorski's *Children's Questions* remained as leftovers from a movement that had become repetitious, both for film makers and for the public. This change of direction is highlighted by the writer Krzysztof Jasiewicz and is best illustrated in Filip Bajon's film, *Pendulum* (*Wahadelko,* 1981). In one scene the hero sees the face of Dziadek Mroz (Daddy Frost – a Socialist 're-invention' of Father Christmas) as Uncle Joe Stalin. The hero's childhood is shown as a conditioning in anti-imperialist reflexes during his stay in a sanatorium for pneumonia. His mother, a Party activist, is always too busy to see or to 'love' him. Jasiewicz comments:

"But not everyone had a mother/ activist, not everyone was exposed to such intensive doctrination. Watching Bajon's film we ask: how come not everyone went insane? Marczewski provides an answer in *Dreszcze.* People in love are not normal but their deviation is no mental illness. For Marczewski's hero his first erotic love became an ideological commitment defending itself against doubts . . ."

The effect of "cynical seduction" or the brainwashing applied to our young scouting camp hero in *Dreszcze* remains a question mark at the end of the film. Presumably it did not work. In spite of the boy's joining the camp prefects, and in spite of an ideological outburst to his father, a disappointed love (for the woman who selected him for the summer youth camp) undermines all support for revolutionary commitment. Besides which, the boy is partly Marczewski himself who spent some of his youth in such a camp. Feliks Falk's *And There Was Jazz* (*Byl Jazz,* 1981) describes one form of escape from the mind-conditioning of those years, one of the healthy loopholes by which most people could avoid the post-Stalinist reflexes drawn in Bajon's film.

These, together with *The Interrogation* and Zaorski's *Mother of Kings*, were made by directors who were in primary school in the 1950s. Jasiewicz compares the mentality of these youngish directors with Skolimowski's *Hands Up* (*Rece do Gory*, 1967) which depicts the self-doubts of Skolimowski's own generation in the 1960s. Skolimowski's money-orientated heroes are aware of being disloyal to their ideals: "Skolimowski sees the cause of it in the lies and falsehoods they encountered before reaching maturity . . . they regret not being clean and beautiful like we were in the 50s . . . the system engendered our enthusiasm ... but lost it!"

It seems that these fragments about the 1950s starting around 1981 may well have been the phenomenon of a new Polish cinema. Unlike *Man of Marble* – which went through the era like a steam train – these fragments or little dramas would have been a proper coming to terms and would have provided a deep understanding of the times.

'The missing ten'

The ascent of martial law brought a clampdown by the censors. Very few of the films produced during the life of Solidarity actually made it to the screen before December 13 1981. Ten in particular formed what was famously called 'the missing ten':

Czlowiek z Zelaza (*Man of Iron*)
  director: Andrzej Wajda
Prognoza Pogody (*Weather Forecast*)
  director: Antoni Krauze
Kobieta Samotna (*The Lonely Woman*)
  director: Agnieszka Holland

Przypadek (*The Incident*)
  director: Krzysztof Kieslowski
Matka Krolow (*Mother of Kings*)
  director: Janusz Zaorski
Byl Jazz (*And There Was Jazz*)
  director: Feliks Falk (since released)
Wielki Bieg (*The Long Run*)
  director: Jerzy Domardzki
Przesluchanie (*The Interrogation/The Cross Examination*) director: Ryszard Bugajski
Wojna Swiatow (*War of the Worlds 2000*)
  director: Piotr Szulkin (since released)
Wielka Gra (*Big Game*)
  director: Tadeusz Junak

Rock and roll

In the aftermath of martial law the growth of Polish rock was unprecedented. The things you could not say in the theatre or cinema were said out there at a Poznan pop concert, even on the LPs. Some critics referred to the phenomenon as a "safety valve" for the government which went out of its way to provide equipment, festival space and air-time for this frustrated young generation (ten years younger, say, than a débutant film maker) to release its pent-up anger in the poetry of rock and roll. Another claimed that culture itself was allowed to flourish because the government's hands were full with the political and economic crises; sure enough when stability returned it would then move in to control rock and roll.

One extraordinary documentary, *Koncert*, features the country's top rock and pop groups and shows the incredible explosion of rock poetry. The film parallels the American *Woodstock* and features groups such as ninety-nine-Perfekt, Republika, TSA, Krzak and Easy Rider. The ninety-nine minute film was written and directed by Michal Tarkowski in 1982. Rock lyrics had a freedom that no other branch of the arts possessed. Whether it was a safe area in which kids could let off steam or whether the authorities had other priorities to contend with is hard to say. But it seems that there was less censorship of the arts during martial law than in the period immediately following.

Danton

After the two *Man* films, Wajda pressed on with two projects. *A Love in Germany* (*Un Amour en Allemagne*, 1983) is the second in a three-picture deal with Gaumont in France. The first is *Danton* and the third to be an adaptation of Dostoevsky's *The Possessed*. *Danton* and *A Love in Germany* are intended to be 'Polish'. *Danton* is a Polish product in the same way as Sienkiewicz's *Quo Vadis?* and much of the French critical controversy lost sight of that fact. The way of looking at the terror of the French Revolution came straight from a Polish drama which was written by Stanislawa Przybyszewska, *The Danton Affair*, which premièred in Warsaw in the 1930s.

Danton is a Polish film in French costume. Wajda's script equally weighs the Robespierre and Danton points of view, whereas in the play Robespierre – mouthpiece of Revolution – was clearly the hero. The hedonist, Danton (Gérard Depardieu), has his ruthless past behind him and is clearly more sympathetic than the humourless Robespierre. Danton becomes the victim of an outrageous show-trial, casting its shadow forward to the Stalinist 1950s.

A Love in Germany

Poland was under martial law when Wajda shot *Danton*. He then prepared to make *A Love in Germany*, backed by Gaumont and a Berlin producer. Film Polski refused to participate: although the director was granted a passport his request for Polish technicians and players was rebutted.

The film is scripted by Wajda, Boleslaw Michalek (literary manager of the now-defunct group, *X*) and Agnieszka Holland, a non-person after December 13 1981 as far as the authorities were concerned and probably the root cause of the lack of enthusiasm.

The film looks better on second viewing. Like both *Man of Marble* and *Man of Iron*, it is a story from the past revealed by investigative technique. A man returns to the village where, during the war, his mother was imprisoned in disgrace and her lover, a young Polish prisoner-of-war, was hanged as a result of the affair. (The 'present' part of the narrative is minimal.) It is set in a quiet, colourful provincial village and shot with a French/German/ Polish cast. Despite the presence of soldiers the front seems far away. We catch glimpses of Polish prisoners-of-war as slave labour – one of them a teacher played by Daniel Olbrychski.

Paulina (Hanna Schygulla), whose husband is at the front, carelessly flaunts her love-affair with Stanislaw (Piotr Lysak), a young Polish prisoner under the guardianship of Paulina's two old neighbours. Some in the village know of the affair but shut their eyes or discreetly advise Paulina to avoid him. Her friend, Elsbeth (Elisabeth Trissenaar), whose husband has been killed in action, flies into a rage over Paulina's admission of the affair and her talk of "happiness". A neighbour, Maria (Marie-Christine Barrault), has envious eyes on Paulina's shop. Events lead to the affair being revealed and SS Lieutenant Mayer's (Armin Mueller-Stahl) enforced intervention.

Even the (usually horrible) regulation measurements of Piotr by the adjutant are done reluctantly and incompetently – the scene is farcical rather than an example of dehumanisation. But the commandant's hand is forced – he must condemn Piotr and the tragedy is balanced by farce even in the method of execution.

By 'law' no German was to hang a Pole; it had to be another Pole. The Olbrychski character (Wiktorczyk) is produced – a fellow prisoner-of-war – and Mayer tries to convince him that "for humanity's sake" only a fellow Pole can hang Piotr. Wiktor refuses but Mayer offers him three cigarettes and says that he (Wiktor) is therefore obliged since he has been offered a *regulation* price. Boleslaw Michalek explains:

"This was a certain German spirit of being extremely precise. Just three. Not four, not two . . . three. Even the character of this Gestapo man, giving the cigarettes, he is very human. He said: 'I gave him these cigarettes beforehand, so I trust him! and after a successful hanging I shall give him *another* 3 cigarettes.'"

Wiktor accompanies Piotr to the gallows in a military jeep. When they arrive, any thoughts he entertains of helping a fellow Pole to the gallows vanishes when he sees Polish prisoners gathered to watch the execution. The commandant has no option but to place

the noose himself over the neck of the prisoner. For the first time this relatively decent officer is forced to become a 'killer'. The administrative and moral confusion of the officer (superbly played by Mueller-Stahl) under a welter of absurd regulations in a quiet outpost of the war is a key thread in this interesting film, which is marred only by its flash-forwards: the guilt and close-mouthedness of the characters, forty years on, are of little interest.

Kieslowski and the Tor unit

The present turnover in employees can be gauged by the fact that there are nine major units plus the Irzykowski Studio interested in working with fiction. Each of them takes on around five young people a year which means that about forty young graduates per year enter employment. Kieslowski is sceptical about overcrowding – how many of them really *want* to make movies? The *Tor* unit which he co-manages with Zanussi, far from producing the most films, is nevertheless one of the best, judging from its contribution of films in the boom of 1976-81. It is the smallest unit, making two or three cinema features plus four or five for television each year.

Tor annually publishes a screenplay competition, the prizes for which are permanent posts in the group. The number varies from year to year – three, four or five – but they include the possibility of making a movie. Kieslowski comments: "Now, imagine – that for such a competition – 1983, for instance, we received ten works and the next year, 1984, thirteen works! So *where* are those young people, standing and waiting?!" The competition is strictly for graduates (and they are numerous) from one of the two main film schools in Poland – Lodz or the one in Katowice formed at the outset by Polish television.

Dignity

The characteristics attributed to each film unit have come to be less defined while the division between left and right has become more specific. It is possible to see whether or not a film belongs to one of the 'right' units – Bohdan Poreba's *Profil* or the Petelskis' *Iluzjon* – just by looking at its first few minutes or studying a couple of the credits. Since the middle to late 1970s actors and technicians would go to one or two camps. Actors such as Tadeusz Janczar, for example, would move freely between films with Wajda (*Landscape After Battle*) or Poreba (*Hubal*); now the freelancers will, say, make a film for *Tor* and not move further right than *Kadr* (Kawalerowicz) or *Zodiac* (Jerzy Hoffman), whose chiefs are party members, but try to steer a middle course.

Tor is sometimes regarded as hermetic and very exclusive but Kieslowski is adamant that this is untrue: "No-one tries, to my mind, because no-one wants to. Such a man lies down on the sofa and waits for someone to come and say: 'Hey! I've got fifty millions for you. Would you please get up and make a film?' The school in Lodz has become incredibly artistic and philosophical. But nobody wants to work." He defines it as fear of working rather than laziness: "To analyse screenplays is all very simple but they all fear the moment when they have to get down to work."

The Lodz School

The school simply "went crazy" all of a sudden. Kieslowski blames the isolation of the school from the rest of the film community. In the middle 1970s rector Stanislaw Kuszewski was appointed with a Party task. By the time he was dismissed during the ascent of Solidarity, the students were imbued with the idea that one had to think, to experiment, to analyze: "They suddenly found themselves in a complete void". Kieslowski continues:

"We came to this school, Agnieszka Holland and I, to try and talk to these people: What did they want? What were they up to? What did they do? Since they were on strike all the time they did not study. They were electing a rector and they had no idea whom to elect, but they desperately tried to elect someone. We asked them: 'What do you want, boys?' And they said: 'First we want to learn yoga, we want to get back to the ancient philosophy.' So we said: 'That's fine, but don't you want by any chance to learn to make films?' 'Oh no!' they said, 'by no means! You want to make a vocational school here; that won't do. We will learn yoga!' Such was their state of mind."

Incredibly, students made film exercises because they *had* to do it; they didn't *want* to. The rector fired all of the interesting teachers, so that when the new school in Katowice was established many lecturers went there.

The Katowice School

Katowice was formed as a television school but all of its graduates work in cinematography. The ten competition scripts in 1983 came to *Tor* entirely from graduates of Katowice. In 1984 eight were from Katowice and only three from Lodz. The situation now is not quite as bad as that, says Kieslowski, but this highlights a great lack of ambition among the youth, of the willingness to *fight* for their place in the industry – though he can name now some twenty exceptions who know very much what they want and who work hard for it.

Regarding the new school at Katowice, Stanislaw Wohl said that it was practically finished since no new students had been taken on in the past few years. Ostensibly a school for television technicians, the school was better equipped than Lodz.

However, it also bore the stigma of its founder, Szczepanski, who was an old crony of Gierek's (both were from Silesia) and who rose rapidly to become head of Polish Television in the 1970s. His princely life-style and financial appropriations formed an extensive tip of the corruption iceberg in the latter years of Gierek. Szczepanski was clearly one of the errors that the post-martial law regime committed itself to eradicate.

Kieslowski decided not to make any films during 1985 because he had set himself eleven screenplays to write ("it sounds funny, but it's true"). Amongst the immediate plans of the *Tor* unit was a new film, *Homplet*, by Filip Bajon. It is the story of a family living in Silesia – a big two-part historical film beginning before the First World War and finishing after the Second. Homplet is the family name. Wojciech Marczewski had a contemporary screenplay which Kieslowski hoped would be realized within the year. There would be three débuts with big television feature films.

Piotr Szulkin

Piotr Szulkin (born 1950) is a young director who has created a special kind of film – 'contemporary' films dressed up as the future. The label 'science fiction' irritates Szulkin whose films are set in trash-can futures, with no spectacular new technology – and a lot of what's there breaks down. The environment is often a series of grubby walls or dark corners just like those of today's inner city blocks. He creates an atmosphere such as that in *Soylent Green* which paints a future rife with shoddy technology.

Szulkin graduated from Lodz in 1975 and won the Polish Film Critics Association Award for the best short film in 1977, the animated *Copyright*

(1977). *Golem* (1979, for the *Perspektywa* unit) was his first feature for the cinema. It is also set in a world ravaged by nuclear war. Doctors operate a project called "Mankind Reconstruction" which entails picking up degenerates. The high-ranking cast in this film (Janda, Marian Opania, Wojciech Pszoniak, Andrzej Seweryn) is typical of the confidence displayed by established performers in new directors, at least those with some originality.

His follow-up, *War of the Worlds 2000* (*Wojna Swiatow*, 1982), had more affinity with the Paddy Chayevsky television satire *Network*, than with H G Wells's or Orson Welles's versions of the Martian invasions. It was shelved immediately after the imposition of martial law, along with *The Interrogation* and *And There Was Jazz*. On release in 1984 the film proved to be an amusing but sledgehammer-type satire of television and the manipulation of information.

O-bi O-ba – End of Civilisation (*O-bi, O-ba, Koniec Cywilizacji*, 1984), his next film, screened at the 1985 Gdansk Festival, is set in a vast subterranean bunker – post-nuclear war – in which there is a kind of organised society living for the day when the mysterious 'arc' will be completed to ship them to safety above the flood of

O-bi, O-ba: The End of the Civilization

radioactivity outside. Jerzy Stuhr plays a young scientist whose love-affair with a young prostitute (Krystyna Janda) is shattered by her death fall smack onto a concrete floor under the gaze of a passive crowd. The lassitude of the people is accompanied by the slow beat of bread loaves ejected, with a 'sput' noise, from a long pipe descending like an external colon from the 'kitchen' above.

Szulkin's most recent film, *Ga Ga* (the same meaning in English – going 'ga-ga') was completed in 1985.

Mother of Kings

Janusz Zaorski's *Mother of Kings* (*Matka Krolow*, 1983) was stopped after martial law and remains firmly on the shelf. It is probable that the film is banned because the author of the book on which it is based, Kazimierz Brandys, was already a persona non grata by the end of the 1970s when the only authentic literature went underground. *Matka Krolow* is an epic, spanning 1933 to 1956. Zaorski explains:

"It concerns a very small and poor woman who has four sons in the worst moments of our history: the Second World War and Stalinist times – these take place in the film. She loses these four sons. It is a tragedy, made in black-and-white since it incorporates newsreel from those days. For example, Stalin's death – the minute of silence in Warsaw, the empty streets, where the people and cars stand still, and so on. Also the newsreels from the Second World War and before the war, so that I could put actors into these documentary situations and so on (*laughs*). It's a stupid situation because I'm telling you about a film which I can't show you. Absurd. This woman, Mother King, wrote letters first to the President of Poland before the Second World War because she lived in one room with four sons and wanted to change it for

two rooms or more. Then at the end she was writing to the First Secretary of the Polish Party because she had lost these four sons and the authorities wanted to eject her from this one room. She wanted to stay and wait for her sons."

The above connects to the woman's love-affair with a friend who was a Communist before the war and imprisoned for it. After the war, following his return from the Soviet Union, he is a 'Big Fish' and refuses to recognise or help Mother King even though he is living in the same house! Following the October Spring (1956) the man is sacked from the government and only then – as a nothing – regrets the betrayal of his one-time love.

The film sketches a youth generation of the late 1940s. The four sons have various fates. One, a member of the Communist Party, is murdered in jail through fellow Communists, after a sham trial about his association with the Gestapo. The second son is an alcoholic – drunk every day after the end of the war – and dies. The third ends up in military service and disappears from view. The fourth is a careerist and becomes a Big Fish – but he is also completely demoralised and cynical.

Like many directors who began to interest themselves in recent history, Zaorski's parents, uncles and aunts provided the link and the authentic details. Its germination – from script to screen – did not fall far short of the record for *Man of Marble*. The first script was submitted in 1972, then again in 1977, and was immediately rejected each time. But after August 1980 it was pushed through the *X* unit and made.

The Baritone

The Baritone (*Baryton*, 1985), awarded at the 1985 Gdansk Festival and made for the *Perspektywa* unit under Morgenstern, is a

The Baritone

safer entertainment. Scripted by his friend, the director Feliks Falk, *The Baritone* is a shaggy-dog story that moves with a zing. It has the energy and shape of a good Feydeau farce.

The story takes place on the 29th and 30th of January 1933 – the time Hitler became Germany's Chancellor. The subject, Taviatini (Zbigniew Zapasiewicz) is based on a well-known baritone – a Polish expatriate who sang at La Scala and all over the world. After thirty years he returns to Poland from abroad for his fiftieth birthday and promises a grand concert for the townfolk. Tickets are sold, expectations of the crowd rise... but Taviatini loses his voice. His secretary has an idea: having discovered a private detective in action at the hotel he borrows the latter's amplifier and arranges for Taviatini to mime before the crowds at his window. The crowd love it. There is a minority of Hitler sympathisers and Germans in the entourage who legally bind the artist to themselves. They plan to use him for extensive tours singing only German music. Taviatini conveniently has a number of records already recorded in German for Columbia Records. His managers thus ensure that this world figure will promote the new German

culture. The film boasts a superb comic performance from Piotr Fronczewski, an actor with a cabaret background.

The Irzykowski Studio

At a time when features in Poland cost on average thirty to thirty-three million zloties each – provided they are not encumbered with a lot of studio effects or period costumes – the Irzykowski Studio can make four or five for the same amount.

Until recently the studio – the 'ninth' film unit, formed in 1981 - functioned under the guidance of a five-person artistic council. Since the end of 1984, however, the Ministry of Culture slightly upped their allocation of funds and imposed one director as the single decision-maker over his council advisers – a situation which both the council and the director himself were trying to change, since co-operative direction as well as a lack of funds distinguished it from the eight mainstream units.

The first attempt to build an independent studio working outside the zespoly occured in 1970. Kieslowski, Tomasz Zygadlo and Grzegorz Krolikiewicz, then emergent young directors, hoped to create a studio similar

The Baritone

to the Beli Belas studio in Hungary which had nurtured such talents as Miklos Jansco and Istvan Szabo.

Some mention has already been made (pages 12 and 97-98) of theoretician Karol Irzykowski whose maturity of viewpoint contrasted with the generally unadventurous and imitative commercial cinema of his day. The fact that his set of artistic principles for the cinema ignored the sound era – indeed he considered that technical solutions to the problems of allying sound with image were very far off and that sound was not in any case a positive contribution – makes the modernity of his judgments more surprising.

Irzykowski himself was famous for his criticism but he wrote a major novel in *Paluba*, a Freudian experiment – before Freud was known – in psychoanalytical fiction. The author's analysis of his own characters anticipated the theories adopted by Freud and Adler. The book was also filmed in 1983 as *The Phantom* (*Widziadlo*), with Roman Wilhelmi embodying the central character, Strumienski.

The Irzykowski Studio was formed with Ministry of Culture approval on July 1 1981 and consisted of an artistic council, a literary manager and a production chief. They had total freedom in the selection of scripts, contrary to the Ministry's practice of judging scripts submitted within the regular units. In 1984 their annual grant was thirty-one million zloties – the average cost of a feature – but the studio managed to budget a feature for four to five million. After martial law they continued making films, and in January 1982 they shot a film called *Christmas Eve*, about three women who await the return of their men, not knowing if they have been arrested or interned in a detention camp. Newsreels could scarcely be more contemporary! During the same year actors boycotted

television and theatre and many were keen to work with the studio. Amongst its early films was *Guide* by Tomasz Zygadlo – the story of one of Poland's most famous contemporary cabaret artists, Piotr Skrzynecki, whose cabaret, Piwnica Pod Baranami (Under the Rain's Cellar) in Cracow, had been closed by the authorities.

At formation, the aims of the collective were:

– to prepare film school graduates to work in cinematography and to help them make a good professional début. In 1980 the market for film makers was saturated. From the two schools there were 140 graduates out of work.

– to open the door to everyone, even those from larger film units; to create a place where they could bring unusual ideas. For example: Wajda was refused permission to stage a play by Ernest Bryll (at one time a phenomenally successful commercial playwright and very 'establishment' – he directed the Polish Cultural Institute in London in the 70s). Wajda staged the play in a church and approached the Irzykowski to film it – a typical way in which a project could suddenly develop.

– to organise a "movie enterprise", which means getting their own cinema.

– to publish a regular magazine of 140 pages called *KI*.

One aim the group does share with its namesake is to act as a watchdog – to monitor good film making in Poland, and to care for the artistic and professional qualities of films, especially in guiding début works, sometimes resulting in up to eight or nine changes in the film.

The studio is regarded by some as a safety valve for film makers while the restrictions are so heavy elsewhere. But the achievements and aims of the group are recognised by established cineastes and critics such as Toeplitz. Many of their shorts and features have achieved awards – most recently, *Custody* (*Nadzor*, 1985) by Wieslaw Saniewski at the 1985 Gdansk Film Festival.

An earlier Gdansk festival featured Waldemar Dziki's film, *Postcard from a Journey* (*Kartka z podrozy*, 1983), a psychological study of a middle-aged Jew living in the Warsaw Ghetto. The postcard of the title was a standard order from the German command to report and prepare for deportation. The film is a strange study of fatalism and of one man's obsessive "preparedness for his voyage". It won the 1983 Andrzej Munk Award for a début work. The second national film festival after Gdansk is held every summer in Lagow. In 1983 it awarded a prize to Irzykowski Studio for its work as a whole, and to Wit Dabal for his cinematography on *Postcard from a Journey*.

Postcard from a Journey

Until the end of 1984 the studio's output was forty films – mostly shorts and documentaries but including nine features – all of which had been produced for the sum of one hundred million zloties. The studio can top up its yearly allocation with profits on the sale of its films to the cinema.

Women directors

As elsewhere in world cinema, Poland's film industry is largely male-dominated. The 'Moral Anxiety' films, however, have shown a certain trend in dealing with feminine subjects and two female directors of note emerged: Agnieszka Holland and Barbara Sass-Zdort.

Agnieszka Holland

Holland began as an assistant to Zanussi on *Illumination* in 1973 and eventually moved to Wajda's X unit where she made a remarkable début in *Provincial Actors*. She was one of those to whom Wajda admitted he owed his graduation into a more 'reality-based' form of film making. Up until *Land of Promise* (*Ziema obiecana*, 1975) he had rarely moved away from a kind of grandiose fatalism – the 'sweeping historical forces' represented in the subjects he adapted and the violent way in which he filmed them. In Holland's script for *Without Anaesthesia/Rough Treatment* (*Bez Znieczulenia*, 1978) he seemed at last to have time to look – in minute detail – at the life of a contemporary man.

Without Anaesthesia

The film is semi-autobiographical (for Holland). We are introduced to the protagonist, a rather smug, very successful international news reporter, telling anecdotes on a television show, which is partly a celebration of the guest journalist's career. At this moment – the peak of his career – his young wife (Ewa Dalkowska) chooses to leave home, taking with her their only child. The abrupt shock (Zapasiewicz in his richest screen role to that date) has a numbing effect on him. He scarcely notices the small details surrounding his life which suggest that he is being subtly down-graded and relegated into a non-person.

The journalist figure is based to a small degree on Ryszard Kapuscinski (*The Emperor*) who is far from being a non-person. The process of destroying a man's career and then the man (who dies a banal death when a gas-heater explodes) presumably matched that which led up to the death of Holland's own father – who 'fell' out of a window under police interrogation in 1960. The film was a welcome departure for Wajda who was too experienced to fall into the trap of shooting "talking heads" – exemplified in the brilliantly effective divorce scene where the shots focus on Zapasiewicz and Dalkowska as the contestants. How much of this is due to the actors and how much to the director is hard to say. Zapasiewicz has said that he argued his case to say absolutely nothing in the scene. It is obvious that he loves his wife and she him, while around them the lawyers talk, the judge calls witnesses, the witnesses talk and the wife's counsel (a gleefully 'bent' personality embodied by Jerzy Stuhr) destroys the couple's marriage.

Holland's début was a television feature, *An Evening with Abdon* (*Wieczor u Abdona*, 1974) following her graduation from the Famu Film School in Prague in 1971. Her last, unreleased feature, *The Lonely Woman*, deals with a professional scientist in her thirties for whom work is everything. Proud of her position she conducts herself without any consciousness of her own womanhood. Her sense of priorities are up-ended by an encounter with a young woman who tries to commit suicide because she cannot have children.

There were elements of this film in her fine television piece, *Sunday's Children* (*Niedzielne dzieci*, 1976), which opens with the wedding of an average-looking young couple. When it transpires that, after many attempts, the wife cannot have a child, they visit the state-registered adoption agency but find that they will have to wait a long time – 'red tape' time – for their suitability to be assessed. On another visit to the agency the husband hears a distraught young girl seeking advice on an unwanted baby. He offers to buy the baby from her when it is born. Two stories occur, side by side – a slightly farcical few months in the life of a wife who increases her 'pregnancy' for the benefit of friends and parents. There is a scene in which one of the friends wants to feel the distended tummy and the baby 'kicking'. The wife wants to stop the charade. Strangely, the wife *does* become pregnant and the couple instantly forget the deal made with the young woman who is finally reconciled to her own need for the child and the possible rupture between herself and her parents.

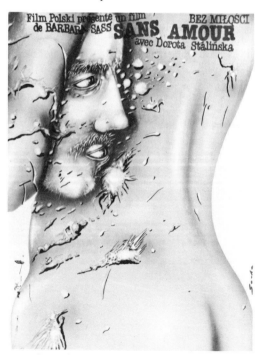

poster for Without Love

Barbara Sass

Barbara Sass began her working career directing television films for Wajda's X unit but later switched to Kawalerowicz's *Kadr* for whom she has made the features, *Without Love* (*Bez Milosci*, 1980), *The Outsider* (*Debiutantka*, 1982) and *The Scream* (*Krzyk*, 1982). All star Dorota Stalinska, an interesting screen actress judging by her work in *The Outsider* in which she plays an idealistic young architect who hero-worships a genius architect (Andrzej Lapicki). He is washed up creatively but still directs a team of young architects like an Old Master.

The Scream

The Scream tells of the release and 'rehabilitation' of a demi-monde girl, Marianne. She is given a job in a luxury old people's home where she is constantly humiliated and verbally lashed by her charge, the old man, Nestor. Marianne lives in a sordid house in Praga and her only hope is an affair with a young male nurse who has the prospect of obtaining a co-operative house. Two trade union officials come and inspect the old people's home suspecting that some of the inmates have no right to be there and that Nestor is a corrupt ex-Party official who escaped into the home to avoid imminent corruption charges. There follows a soap opera sequence of events in which Marianne splits with her boyfriend, her hopes for a new apartment are dashed, and she kills Nestor in a fit of rage. To make matters worse, Nestor was not the villain everyone took him for. This realisation, on top of her other torments draws forth the scream of the title at the end of the film.

What is odd about the film is that it raises the 'period' film to new heights of absurdity. The setting is "last year" – 1981

Dorota Stalinska

– when the country is "tension-ridden". The mind boggles at the thought of scripting a film, which would normally take a couple of years to reach the screens, with the setting "one year ago" – one year *after* the script is written . . .

Story of a Crime

Andrzej Trzos-Rawiecki's *Story of a Crime* (*Zapis Zbrodni*, 1974) is taken from a true police case in Poland in 1973. Two young ruffians hijack a taxi for a trip north to the Baltic but they kill the taxi-driver in the attempt. En route north in the Fiat they murder a carpenter for his money and some provisions. The latter crime is reconstructed first in flashback from prison – after the two have been caught. The film had a very restricted release in Poland. Contemporary crime movies are a rarity in any case but the documentary flavour imparted by Trzos-Rawiecki, including the (by then) fairly clichéd use of a handheld camera, gives the film the impression that the disease of senseless violence was as much part of the fabric of Socialist life as anywhere else in the world. Its treatment was fairly compared to *In Cold Blood*, Richard Brooks's film from Truman Capote's novel.

The director made an equally interesting feature screened at the 1985 Gdansk Festival: *Objection* (*Jestem Przeciw*). This is a harrowing documentary-style story of a juvenile heroin addict. Much stronger stuff than *Story of a Crime*, though I was told that 'drug films' were old hat. One press critic even muttered that it was "fashionable" and implied a certain opportunism in the director. It is hard to accept that; it is not the director's first film about drugs.

The setting is a voluntary drug rehabilitation centre run with an iron hand by Grzegorz (Daniel Olbrychski), a cruel-in-order-to-be-kind type. Addicts commit themselves once only. If they leave the rules say that they cannot be readmitted. Unable to stand the rigorous disciplines – physical work, no drugs, the harshness of obligatory group psychotherapy – a young Jacek (superbly played by Rafal

The Year of the Quiet Sun

Wieczynski) escapes with his girlfriend, Jola. She dies in hospital and Jacek tries to be readmitted to the institution. He is rejected by fellow addicts in a harrowing group session in which his pathetic excuses provide a framework of flashbacks for much of the film's narrative. The lost cause of Jacek, the stupid death of Jola, and Jacek's horrible withdrawals under the helpless gaze of his father make this a passionate warning against the escalating effects of narcotics.

The Year of the Quiet Sun

Zanussi's *The Year of the Quiet Sun* (*Rok Spokojnego Slonca*, 1984) was nominated for the best foreign film in the Academy Awards and provides Maja Komorowska with one of her finest screen roles – in her first feature film since martial law. The film is about the fate of a small family – mother and daughter (Komorowska) settling in a village in the Western territories – ex-German soil now part of Poland in the country's 'shift' (involving four to five million people) to the west following the Yalta Agreement. Komorowska plays a middle-aged widow imbued with a feeling of having no right to personal happiness, until she meets an American officer temporarily stationed in the village. He is involved in some gruesome excavation work – uncovering mass graves of murdered prisoners-of-war, mostly allied pilots (such as the group from the true story on which the novel *The Great Escape* was based) who were machine-gunned by their captors in these wartime German lands.

A co-production between Poland, USA and Germany, the film was almost disowned by Film Polski. It is one of the director's best – definitely his warmest – due to the superlative performances of Komorowska and the American Scott Wilson.

Ewa Dalkowska

in Soviet camps – were murdered by their captors and buried in mass graves in 1940. Or 1941, claim the Soviets, implicating the Nazis – since it was never admitted for inclusion in the catalogue of Stalin's crimes after the dictator's death. Zanussi himself has scorned the idea of any Katyn association.

The 1985 Gdansk Feature Festival

Much gloom surrounded the 1984 event. There was plainly no point in tendering scripts that touched on contemporary reality, even in a disguised or compromised way. Scenarios with 'popular appeal' stood the only real chance of approval: musicals, shockers, nudie-pics or even film noirs – preferably set in the Gierek years or better still in the 1930s. However, an experienced director survives on a contract salary: he rarely directs because he needs the work and is never obliged to shoot someone else's ideas. The assumption has generally been that he is an artist or author who films because he *must*, and whose film is his dialogue with the contemporary public. That assumption is mostly correct and if the only option is to escape into some genre movie then many directors simply will not function – a sad waste of talent and highly expensive training.

The film concerns Norman (Wilson), a lonely displaced soldier (Zanussi compared him with a Vietnam veteran), and his painfully developing love-affair with Emilia (Komorowska). Their very moving communication is achieved through gestures and monosyllables (sometimes of one another's language). Norman promises to take Emilia and her mother to America, represented in the womens' minds by Monument Valley which they saw in an old John Ford movie. Norman arranges to meet them in Berlin but Emilia's mother dies and she sacrifices her own happiness to help a prostitute neighbour (Ewa Dalkowska) get out of the country with the aid of greedy black market intermediaries. A likely contributor to the film's 'offence' are the excavation images which for all their historical accuracy, make one think of 'Katyn', where the cream of Poland's pre-war leadership – all prisoners-of-war interned

No End

At the 1985 Festival it was the new Kieslowski film, *No End*, which excited the hottest discussion. According to the director it had been seen by an audience of 150 000 and would later go on wider release.

No End (*Bez Konca*) contains two stories. A radical lawyer (Antoni) is defending a

No End

worker accused under martial law of leading a strike. The defence plans to admit the charge and plead the defendant's right to have acted according to his conscience. Antoni suddenly dies and his colleague takes an opposite view. State evidence is weak; if the accused would only co-operate he could be acquitted by ordinary process. The accused eventually agrees not to stand on the issue of human rights and is quickly acquitted. However, he alienates his wife and friends who had hoped for a public martyr. When the film begins Antoni is already dead. As played by Jerzy Radziwilowicz he is a ghost, and the second story concerns his pretty widow, Urszula (Grazyna Szapolowska). Surprised by the depth of her love for Antoni, she fails to fight off the impulse to rejoin the spirit of her husband and the film ends with her suicide (kitchen gas) on a strangely upbeat note.

Va Bank II

Va Bank II (*Kadr* unit) is written and directed by Juliusz Machulski and it won the special audience vote as best film. Machulski is a sort of Wonderboy – the

nearest thing in Poland to a Hollywood Brat. His three features, *Va Bank*, *Seksmisja* and *Va Bank II* are excellent action-comedies. He stands alone in his authentic relish for the entertainment movie.

Both *Va Bank* films star his father, Jan Machulski, who was a leading man in the 1950s. He plays Kwinto, a jazz-loving ex-con who matches wits with Kramer, a murderous banker who was once Kwinto's partner in crime. Both films have revenge stories at their core and are set in the 1930s. According to Machulski, *Va Bank II* cost seventy milllion zloties compared to a present average of thirty five million; an irritating jazzy score reminds us of the bootleg 30s. His films are exactly the sort of commercialism that the State-producers want. With a few more directors like Machulski and without their country's history they would have a point. Certainly his scriptwriting skills and his grasp of pace should not be lost on his colleagues. Many, more serious efforts cry out for producer control for other than political reasons.

Yesterday

Yesterday (*Rondo* unit), directed by Radoslaw Piwowarski, was a sure audience

Va Bank II

Yesterday

hit and about the best Beatles film I have seen. A man in his thirties is waiting in a corridor; he daydreams back two decades to his youth – 1964, the time of Beatlemania. Four high-school lads in a provincial town ape the music and appearances of the Beatles, and even take on their names. Their ambition is to play as a band at the high-school concert. The story focusses on 'Ringo', whose bigoted aunt keeps trying to sheer off his mop. The boys manufacture their own instruments and at one clandestine rehearsal 'John' is electrocuted by his guitar. The parents and school authorities force the boys to separate and to have their hair cut short.

The narrative takes us through the rivalry of 'John' and 'Ringo' over their love for Ania (Anna Kazmierczak), Ringo's suicide bid and his subsequent incarceration, and his reconciliation with Ania in a 'happy end'. The story flashes forward to the corridor, 1985; Ringo and Ania are called into court to argue their case for divorce. This is hard-edged nostalgia and very entertaining.

Custody

Piwowarski shared the 'début' jury award with Wieslaw Saniewski whose *Nadzor* (*Custody*) was made for the Irzykowski Studio. This is an excellent prison story which never lapses into documentary or becomes a mere study of the inmates. Klara (Best Actress award: Ewa Blaszczyk) is a young bride, arrested at her wedding on charges of embezzlement. The year is 1967. Klara is found guilty and packed off to a women's prison where most of the action takes place.

The *Nadzor* budget was sixteen million zloties and the film looks as good as a thirty-five million zlotie movie. It was needlessly shelved after an initial release owing to protests from the courts and part of the legal community. In fact it is an engrossing narrative on the fate of Klara and the wardens and prisoners are less

Custody

sadistic than might be expected from a similar Hollywood product. Saniewski made use of actual prisoners and his set was made up of two real-life prisons.

Woman Wearing a Hat

The Grand Prix film, *Woman Wearing a Hat* (*Kobieta w Kapeluszu*) was a safe choice. It came loaded with a Silver Medal awarded at the Moscow Film Festival but it is an unexciting, if intelligent, study of a fairly dull actress and her desire to play a 'real' role. Stanislaw Rozewicz directs. The Special Jury Award went to *Woman from the Provinces* (*Kobieta z Prowincji*), directed by Andrzej Baranski, with a wonderful performance by Ewa Dalkowska. This is a funny film: a series of memoirs covering fifty or so years in a woman's life. The events are ordinary in themselves but they serve as a panorama of recent Polish history as seen by those in the countryside.

Gdansk is a national festival which is made accessible to English-speaking visitors and the reception people (many of them from Gdansk) are pleasant and helpful. Sadly, in 1985, it proved impossible to buy a map of Gdansk in Gdansk.

Woman Wearing a Hat

Stanislaw Wohl

Sadly Stanislaw Wohl died a few months after our interview. His most emotive reflection concerned the poor technical state of the industry – specifically run-down equipment and particularly in cinemas beyond Warsaw, but also in the professional studios. More serious was the loss of specialist talent, the artists responsible for the plastic qualities of film – make-up, woodworkers, tailors, painters:

"We had *marvellous* specialists. There was a school in Warsaw for them but it was liquidated. It's all gone, and one cannot build it up again. It takes years. The Czech cinema has preserved all this. Not in our country – sad. They, the grips and others, won't work because they don't make any money... our equipment is broken already and old... The terrible thing in our cinematography is that we have very few cinemas and of those few cinemas only ten per cent are perhaps really cinemas. You can't imagine what a typical cinema in Poland is like – in Warsaw you can't see it – but in a smaller town you have terrible cinemas – cold, very uncomfortable, bad projection, incomprehensible sound and so on. So now the cinema is the worst in Europe, the last place... worse than Albania. It's terrible because the possibilities for Polish cinema are very big. We have really talented people and the management of all this is terrible. It's a miracle that films are still produced, a miracle."

Interview with Andrzej Wajda

Interpreter and translator:
Maria Zurawska-Denus

Q:
I am interested in one of your current projects, based on *The Emperor* by Ryszard Kapuscinski. Is that imminent?

Wajda:
I've been interested in making a movie of the book ever since it was published, but it has been very difficult to have it made in Poland; not so much for censorship reasons – the book wasn't well received . . . The difficulty in making a movie from the book lies in the number of characters involved . . . also there is nothing in it of any interest to us [Poland] so I've been trying to interest someone like the Gaumont Corporation and I'm thinking about collaboration with an English company.

Q:
But you have a project in France at the moment . . .

Wajda:
Yes – *The Possessed* by Dostoyevsky. It will be done in the fall this year; it's to be shot in Finland; the actors will probably be either French/English or French/German . . . I asked David Bowie; it's a fantastic role, the most enigmatic person, Stavrogin. He's a man of the future and David Bowie has that expression and mystery about him. He has not given me an answer yet; the question is whether he is familiar with the novel.

Q:
Was Kapuscinski himself the actual model for Zapasiewicz's role in *Without Anaesthesia?*

Wajda:
Yes, the first part of the film set in a TV studio . . . the interview comes directly from Kapuscinski . . .

Q:
Leaping back to a different period I'm curious to know something about Cybulski and his theatre company Bim Bom. When were you first associated with Cybulski?

Wajda:
I got to know Cybulski when he graduated or was about to graduate from the Actors' Studio. He played in my first film *A Generation.* The censor would not allow two of his scenes so I had to delete them . . . very important scenes. He had an important role in the movie but after the two scenes had been cut there remained practically nothing. I don't have these scenes anymore which is a great pity. Since then I had always wanted to use him. He was initially to have starred in *Kanal,* my second movie . . . however he starred in the next, *Ashes and Diamonds.*

Then I worked with him in the theatre. We did two plays together. The first was *A Hatful of Rain* which played at Gdansk.

Then at the Ateneum (Warsaw) we did *Two for the Seesaw*. So I started *my* theatre career at the same time as Cybulski. Later there was a rumour that I wouldn't work with him but this wasn't true. Since I offered him such an outstanding role in *Ashes and Diamonds* it was very difficult, later, to find something appropriate to match the image. You think that people will live forever and not that one day they will die *(laughs)*. I thought that we had a lot of time left.

Q:
Did you have contact with his theatre group Bim Bom?

Wajda:
No. I saw this theatre but never co-operated with it; it played a very important role. A lot of its actors played and still play an important role on the Polish scene. For instance, Cybulski and Kobiela, the actors, the playwright, Mrozek, then Czeslaw Niemen, the rock musician... many interesting people. Also, a very important factor at this time – the era of Stalinism – was that everything was restricted or limited. *They* introduced a childlike style, naïvety . . . the very term 'Bim Bom' . . . in those days in the theatre everything was bombastic, very serious, politically defined. This theatre was striving for privacy; some private aspect of people's lives had at last entered the theatre.

Q:
In a television interview you said that official criticism of your first film, *Pokolenie,* was like a "cold shower", and that after the sudden shock of those attacks you were ready for it in the future. Do you look forward to contrary opinion of your work?

Wajda:
Yes, very much so. I believe that a film is made for a public and 'what kind of public?' I ask myself; the kind of public that I am myself as a human being; that does not mean a one limited by a certain education or by the fact that I am a film director. If my films are not accepted by everybody that's because they are limited by my own psyche and if the films do not appeal to anybody it is not the audience's fault, it's mine. Further, I look for themes for different subjects in all possible directions. Sometimes I happen to make a political film, sometimes they are entirely different like *The Maids of Wilko* or *The Birchwood* – that is, I want to be a film director such that if some expect me to make a political film I don't have to do it.

Q:
In the French/Polish co-production *Danton* you had the actors from the Robespierre camp speak in Polish and those with Danton, French. Why was this?

Wajda:
It was a necessity out of which I tried to make a virtue or extract some meaning. I knew that I would never find an actor better suited to the role than [Wojciech] Pszoniak who played the role in Warsaw [i.e. Robespierre] on stage so I made it a point. Through him I wanted to show other actors how much I was on the lookout for hysteria. Because Pszoniak spoke only Polish the pace of his role was set by the Polish text he had learned. The dialogues were taken from a play; and for him to embody that role he could only do so in Polish. I decided to surround him with Polish actors. Actors speaking in two different languages tend to speak slowly; there's a moment of hesitation when they respond. There's a whole group of people who speak with him but Robespierre only meets Danton once and he speaks very little. Otherwise he talks a lot in meetings

with his own circle of friends which is why I decided to make that group speak Polish; of course, I understood that there should be French actors gathering round Danton, speaking in French. These kind of decisions are fundamentally the director's.

I started from the Polish group that I found easy to direct in Polish and shot their scenes first. I showed the results, the Polish scenes, to the French actors to illustrate what I was seeking . . . and, later on, I didn't have to explain in words what I was driving at. It's always very difficult when it comes to making movies in a foreign language, even if you know the language very well . . . you have to seek solutions. There was the question of dubbing voices into French and there is always a loss there . . . inevitable. There's as much truth in one's voice as in the picture in a scene. Any dubbing in any language is a violation.

The problem comes up again in *The Possessed*. I would be very happy to make *The Possessed* with English actors. The problem here is not only that actors speak a different language . . . they also *act* differently. There are things that appeal to English actors, different things to German actors and completely different again to the French. To unify all this the director has no time – he has to make a movie and cannot have classes for the actors; that's why they always look artificial. They appear false.

In *Danton* the situation was fortunate – the French picked up the Polish way of acting and everyone thought that that was a result of us making a film about a revolution . . . and this is true. *We* know what such leaders look like here – taking Solidarity as an example. Leaders are always . . . hysterical, always panic stricken and not having enough sleep . . . so *Danton* is not just about a revolution as the title would suggest, but something else, the *psychology*. Revolutions last only a short time . . . that's what every revolutionary is afraid of because time is always running out before they can introduce more changes.

Q:
You said some time ago that trying to make a film in America was like working in another world. Is this a possibility open to you?

Wajda:
I would love to make a film in America. It is a wonderful country to work in. I've worked twice in American theatre – once with the Yale Repertory Theatre at Yale University. I was the first director who ever had Meryl Streep as an actress on stage (*laughs*) at the time she was attending the Actors' Studio.

Robert Brustein was the director of this theatre and had seen *The Possessed* in London when I was there with my company from the Stary Theatre in Cracow. He invited me to Yale to restage it. And Meryl Streep was a student but it was plain to see – you could really sense that she was going to be a film star. Everyone seems to have the impression or image of a woman who wants to be a movie star in America as aggressive and with a will of her own. Streep had none of it. All she had was her talent and her own natural beauty . . . and it was my feeling, well she's going to make it, she's going to be a star, and three years later she made it! – first in *The Deer Hunter* with Robert de Niro and then *Manhattan*. I saw these films in America. I love the way they work there.

Polanski was right in saying to me one day years ago . . . I asked him why he was going to make films in America (not Europe) and he answered: I'm making films in Hollywood because when I hold out my hand they give me a hammer – how the hell do they know I want a hammer? They read your mind and this is really incredible . . .

The one we were working at was a student theatre – they were so efficient! I came to Newhaven from Warsaw – I'd never worked before in America, I didn't know what to expect – it was on a Sunday and I suddenly see the poster – yes, the poster – saying *The Possessed* directed by Andrzej Wajda with the hour and date of the opening night. I thought, well what if we don't make it, if we run out of time? And they looked at me as if I was crazy and said "Why shouldn't you make it on time?" *(laughs)* Fantastic . . . Oh well, I don't know if I will be able to work in America . . . but now that *Danton* as well as *A Love in Germany* have been accepted in America I could maybe find a producer . . .

Q:
Presumably you would like to work with your Polish crew?

Wajda:
No, I would prefer to work with Americans. It all comes down to the subject, the theme. I would like to find a Polish theme – there are five million Poles living in America, probably six by now; you have Chicago, the second biggest Polish city in the world. Well, we've never made any Polish films describing Poles in America. On the other hand there are plenty of 'Polak' jokes and you have the Pole in *A Streetcar Named Desire* with Marlon Brando: *this* is the image Americans have about us, and I'd like to reverse it. I'd like to make a movie about Brzezinski, about someone who made it in America . . .

All the Poles that emigrated to America did so in search of food – bread – or for financial reasons. That was the first Polish emigration. The ideological one happened in the 1940s after or during the war. Prior to that it was all for money . . . But we never created a lobby like the Germans or

Jews. What the Poles like in America is that there is no sense of snobbery, because they were always too low to know the social standards.

Q:
Did you hear many Polish jokes in America?

Wajda:
Those kind of jokes come to us – we hear them here as coming from Russia *(laughs)* like a detour. The New York Jewish humour I feel to be truly Polish. The most gifted 'Polish' humorist is Woody Allen – his is the kind of humour that appeals to us most; it's the pre-war humour of Polish cabarets . . . for example, that of Tuwim or Slonimski [cabaret poets] and when you read Woody Allen jokes it's very much like reading Tuwim's or Slonimski's work *(laughs)*.

Q:
Do you envisage making such a 'Polish comedy' film in the States?

Wajda:
I have always wanted to but it is always difficult to find good scripts for comedy – it has to be funny when you read it. In Poland humour has died. We, as a people or a society, have a great sense of humour but we don't seem able to translate this into movies. Apart from Mrozek, there is no other playwright around able to accommodate it.

Q:
Can you see a situation in which you would again use Polanski as an actor?

Wajda
In fact I talked with him about it – I wanted him to star in *The Possessed*. The problem was that he started shooting his project *Pirates* and was extremely busy with that. He wanted to play in one of my movies and was very definite about it. He is a

fantastic actor. He has this extraordinary ability to imitate; he knows how to imitate anything. In his biography there is one anecdote missing that I will describe to you.

At the time he was playing in *A Generation* we were shooting some scenes in Wroclaw and there was another crew working there. And in the studio there was a great comedian, sitting there for hours. His name was Adolf Dymsza; he starred in many pre-war comedies – many roles. He was telling jokes and we listened to them and never said anything. But Polanski couldn't resist the temptation. He was a small boy and short. He stopped him – Dymsza – and *he* told a joke. A great silence descended . . . there was this little bugger stopping the maestro - interrupting him. Dymsza was playing with a coin and he did a trick where finally the coin ended up in the sweet. He had all these manual tricks. He gave the coin to Polanski and said "When you learn how to do that come and show me." And he was sure that he'd finally put Polanski down – Polanski went out. Twenty minutes passed – less than that – Polanski came back and said: "Maestro, I've learned it!" This is Polanski – he's able to learn just anything.

Q:
I know that there are always battles with censors as to what you can put in the scripts. Were there any peculiar instances whereby you 'got away' with something and hadn't expected to?

Wajda:
Now I will have to be more general. First of all I must say – because ideology comes in words – censors control words more than actions – that's the first point. You may have different scenes and say more *through* them and it's very difficult to censor them. But words come first with censors so they are most particular about

dialogues. Furthermore the only way to fight the censors is to make something which is *generally* not censorable. If I were going to make some scenes that were political per se, people would cut them out and there would be nothing left (within the film). So what you have to do is try to make every scene so fit with the ideology of the film that there is very little (individually) for the censor to cut.

I will give you an example: *Ashes and Diamonds*. There were different things they wanted to cut out – for example, the final scene in the garbage dump. Luckily enough they didn't succeed. The film was basically not censored because of the role that Cybulski was playing – and in the circumstances of those days, when the film was being made the character that Cybulski played was negative. Because he is the one who is aiming to shoot the Communist. But the moment he plays it –

the way he does – he's such a nice guy . . . this is totally uncensored; you cannot censor it. After that all the rest follows. I mean what in particular are you going to cut out – the scene where he laughs? There is nothing to cut out. And that's the real problem in making a movie and fighting the censor.

It was the same situation with *Man of Marble*. The general treatment of the subject was not to be censored because this is the country of workers. Why should workers be prosecuted? If he is an honest man he cannot be prosecuted. So everything put together cannot be censored. Whether they cut out some scene at the beginning or some dialogue in the middle or some at the end does not matter. The whole film stands for itself. The whole movie is a challenge.

Q:
You were technically in the Home Army during the war. There were several witchhunts against the Armia Krajowa members during the 1950s. Did you suffer from any of this? How big or wide was the witchhunt net?

Wajda:
In the 50s only those suffered (among film makers) who had some links with the past. For instance, a real victim was Jerzy Zarzycki who made a movie called *The Warsaw Robinson Crusoe*. This was a very interesting film. You can see this movie in its original version – they have two different versions. When they started to make the movie it was called *The Warsaw Robinson;* when they finished it was called *Warsaw, Siege City.*

This is an extemely interesting story. They wanted to make a film about a single man living among the ruins of Warsaw – there is an ocean of ruins and there is someone living in them. It's a psychological movie – how to live, being alone on a desert island, in this case with Warsaw as the desert island. Instead of that they turned it into a movie about the Russian army entering and rescuing Warsaw. That's really a thing from the 50s – it was a remaking of the film right from the very beginning.

In the second version – the 'official' one starring the Russian troops - everything begins from a commentary which abuses the underground army. Well, Jerzy Zarzycki was an officer of that national army. During the Warsaw Uprising he made some movie footage about the rising and these pictures were buried in some cellar and he sought help from his colleagues, Aleksander Ford and Jerzy Bossak, who were very important in those days, and they all waited for the house to come down and recover the pictures but they were never allowed to dig them out – his is a real drama but not one that happened to me. I was then beginning my career at a very fortunate moment. It was already 'October' and Gomulka was coming to power. I started to make *Kanal* and the good days started. I was fortunate . . .

Here we get another incident in a small place in the mountains called Wisla. There was a conference of Polish film directors somewhere in maybe 1952, maybe 1954 – well in the early 50s . . . and this conference set the political orientation of Polish movies; and in Wisla at that time the accepted version of *The Warsaw Robinson* was shown. That year they dealt with all directors who held a different point of view. It must have been in 1954 because I wasn't yet a film director; I was too young, in fact just about to start. It was a terrible moment. By sheer luck this didn't last long because in 1955 and 1956 all this collapsed. But that was a terrifying moment. *Kanal* was then possible. It was made in 1956, shown at Cannes in 1957 and sold later.

Q:
I saw the film recently and was quite struck by its beauty – in spite of its setting: amongst shit in the sewers. Could you tell us something about the setting?

Wajda:
All those canals were built in front of the studio (at Lodz) on location. There were some holes drilled on the wall to enable us to put in lamps. The canals were filled with water. It was all very well fabricated by the same designers who worked on *Ashes and Diamonds*. Since the film was being made in Lodz, some thread was wrapped around some carbon tubes which were then cut into pieces; then the carbon becomes very like fluff, like cotton and when you put these into the water they don't sink but float on top and there you have your image of sewage. *(laughs)* A *special* invention. We always come up with them.

Q:
What happened to the Korczak project?

Wajda:
That's a very long story so I'll try to make it short. When I was director of a film unit prior to the 13th of December 1981 I asked her to write me a script on Korczak and I wanted to make a movie out of it. It all started two or three years before – to be exact 1978 – somebody came to me, an American producer whose name was Larry Bachmann – the producer of *Whose Life is it Anyway?* based on the stage-play. He then asked me to make a movie about Korczak. He suggested as scriptwriter John Briley who later did *Gandhi* which won an Oscar. Now a famous scriptwriter but he wasn't then. He started work on the script and actually finished it.

The script was all very detailed in its description of Korczak's life. It made me laugh because it was not Doctor Korczak,

more Doctor Zhivago. It was a very well written script but not for a film by me. It could well have been made by a different director. And you would have to cast two or three different actors to cover the span of time.

Then I suggested to Larry that Agnieszka Holland write the script. At that moment she went to Paris and then in Paris, during martial law, she wrote the script. I brought it here and it was only a couple of weeks ago that it was accepted. So then I was supposed to go to Paris, talk to Larry again who was to decide about meshing the two scripts. In the meantime Agnieszka's script reached Hollywood and it was sent to Richard Dreyfuss. He read both scripts and he preferred Agnieszka Holland's because it's more dramatic. It starts in 1939 and ends in Korczak's death. Therefore he is always the same age and there is no need for more actors. He is an old man at the most dramatic period of his life. They didn't want to make that kind of movie, fearing that it would become another *Holocaust.* I am of the opinion that it is an entirely different subject . . . about how the world changed the man . . . should we teach children to steal in order to survive because that is the way the world has turned out; while he teaches them to respect others, that they should not steal, they should not kill and so on, by so doing he condemns them to death. And that's the real subject of the movie and Agnieszka Holland's script basically sees his life this way.

There is in any case nothing I can do with this project without Larry's decision as the producer. I knew that it was possible for me to make the subject more dramatic in my style, but I couldn't do the other version, something that I do not believe in, that I couldn't believe in. And another thing is that I would like to make it in Poland; it was only very recently that it was accepted . . .

Interview with Krzysztof Zanussi

After an initial discussion on co-productions, notably his own **The Year of the Quiet Sun** *(Poland/USA/West Germany) and Wajda's* **A Love in Germany** *(West Germany/France)*

Zanussi:
I've made quite a few films in Germany. Wajda's was an old project which he wanted to make with Brauner, the German producer of Polish origin, and he was backed by Gaumont. I'm usually backed by one of the television channels such as ZDF. I'm now starting a new film with French/German co-production.

Q:
Can you say something about that?

Zanussi:
This project has a funny title: 'Paradigm'. But nobody understands this, at least most

people, so I'll have to add a subtitle, something a bit funnier because it is almost a comedy. I *hope* it will be a very heart-breaking melodrama, with comic overtones, about a young theologian advocating that evil doesn't exist as such; which is my personal polemic on a certain state of mind whereby I reproach this kind of light-hearted approach to life, and absence of recognition of evil as a dynamic power, and human beings as able to choose evil consciously.

Sometimes I am exposed to the evil which is far more visible here – that's why I made the film. It's set in the 1920s and has Vittorio Gassman and Marie-Christine Barrault as the leading actors, so you may imagine how excited I am. It will be shot in French and redubbed in German.

Q:
It has nothing to do with your Gombrowicz project?

Zanussi:
Oh no – you're very well informed. The Gombrowicz project is hanging in the air because the rights are in the hands of [he names a French producer] who is rather reluctant to make any moves; she's one of the most difficult people I've met. She commissioned the script which we wrote. So the script is there plus a lot of interest from various television heads. I bring these people to her; they're always getting very discouraged, saying, 'well, we can't deal with this lady', and she's unwilling to give away the rights, so I'm lost. In terms of mood it's not very far from 'Paradigm' . . . I seldom touch other people's writing, but once I do I think I learn something.

Q:
Because you've done most of your own screenplays without going to literary sources.

Zanussi:
Yes, some 80% if we generalise.

Q:
This subject of evil has come up many times in your interviews. In a *Newsweek* article you claimed that a moral sense could almost be fabricated by chemical means. Is that true?

Zanussi:
Well, I don't believe that it has been proved – not to my knowledge – but I consider this as a major menace for – how can I say it? – our consciousness, our way of thinking. We're challenged now by the discoveries of science which provides quite a new knowledge about the material structure of our existence which is in eternal conflict with our own understanding of our life and our own subjective consciousness. So the eternal problem of philosophy – is it a dualist world or a monist world: is it all material or is spirit something that really physically exists in a way; is this existence orthologically well grounded? – is such that it revives now under the new pressures of science and that's what I find very interesting. Also, on a practical level, I have to think about it, knowing that the kind of violence – the tools that science provides to any tyrant who wants to possess my thinking or at least to block my activity – is there and is enormous.

There was one semi-documentary – I don't think it was one of my best but it was quite a relevant, important subject – I made it in Germany about seven years ago and it was called *The Lesson of Anatomy*; it was a study where I tried to revive the 'language' I had developed in *Illumination*. I don't know if it worked that well but the premise lay in the story of a Chilean exile, a student of medicine, and intercutting his fictitious story with documentary pieces on the knowledge that science provides about all kinds of violence that have been

recently developed – which was to *me* very illuminating.

I now know quite well what is imagined, what can and cannot be done, and how much can be done. We were working on the basis of Amnesty International research so we had quite a specific knowledge of what is done where and we see quite clearly that there are some schools and tendencies and some groups of countries who use certain kinds of violence; and some other countries are inclined to use different kinds – different drugs, different treatments . . .

Q:
Are you talking about prisoners?

Zanussi:
Oh yes, prisoners and people who are detained for political purposes and are either treated to extract their confessions or treated in order to block their faculties – which are two different goals.

Q:
Can I digress and refer you back to an old interview with Boleslaw Michalek in which you mentioned an incident that you filmed in your third year at Lodz, which caused you to repeat that year. It was to do with an actor who did something totally unexpected, something you filmed and incorporated into your project.

Zanussi:
I did that from the beginning of my career and have repeated it several times since. I think I may now look more distantly at this interest. Theoretically speaking I do believe that in cinema, by contrast with the theatre, what is unique and specific is a record which is in a way unrepeatable. It happens only once and will never occur again; we're extremely excited by it – you can look at any shot of a dog or a baby on screen . . . we feel some sort of special excitement that this happened, that it was

filmed; and when you see anything in the background you feel that it happened only once, one coincidence which was caught by the camera, one mood which will never be reproduced.

I think it is particularly exciting, so it is something which by connection is the very substance of film making: that's why I was interested in things that were slightly improvised or films in which something unexpected would happen - even now when I am dealing with professional actors I try very often to provoke something which happens only in front of the camera, which has not been rehearsed. Sometimes I think it is refreshing, something far more convincing and far more private, far more credible than whatever is fabricated by the actor's craft.

Q:
Will you go back to using non-professional actors?

Zanussi:
No, I can't do that anymore now, working most of the time abroad, because my control and command of another language is not good enough – also my project control is smaller. I am far more master of my own work here where I am producer in a way plus the director and writer and have a big credit. So I can do more in terms of credibility – people give me the chance to make the film and they won't enter into details as to how I do it – so there's a chance to reshoot and restructure something if it doesn't work.

In the West it is a miracle if I can continue doing films which I have wanted to do all my life. As I said, we like to complain; it is one of the Polish charms – we like to talk of things that are not going well just to contrast with the Americans who like to say everything's fine. We think in a way it is a charming and very conservative approach to say everything's fine – I think it's far more creative to say

everything's awful and impossible and unacceptable.

Anyway, comparing these two attitudes, and subscribing to one – I am always complaining – I happened to be talking this way to Antonioni just after Venice this year – I know him quite well – and I saw how angry he became, telling me what do I expect!! If such a master as Antonioni is fighting six or seven years on a single project and can't manage to make it, while I make one film a year - and they are films I really wanted to do from the very beginning; I didn't really compromise; I made two or three less important films in the West but none of which I would like to disinherit or regret; I did mostly films I've written, mostly those I wanted to do – so how dare I complain?! I couldn't *expect* more than that.

Q:
How did *The Catamount Killing* come about?

Zanussi:
Well, this is on the edge of being regretful but even in this film, which I made ten years ago as a first approach to the United States and the American market, (it placated my desire to make an American film that most young film makers share because they know that America is the country that is able to impose its film making into a product all over the world, so the temptation was enormous) even in this film I have at least twenty minutes which I would sign with satisfaction saying that this is precisely my film making . . . another twenty is maybe something that even today I would do the same way. Perhaps there is something in the basic structure which I wouldn't do again just knowing that this kind of compromise will never pay off and won't work. The film is halfway . . .

Q:
What was the problem? Was it working with a foreign crew and producer?

Zanussi:
No, no, it was just a problem of the subject matter. I was coming as a foreigner to America to tell the story which was conceived – well, the story was imposed on me, it was not my story – and in this story, which was written by James Hadley Chase and which made it even more difficult because it wasn't true to life as I had expected, there were many elements which I basically felt alien to me. But I tried to add something and the second half of the film is rewritten and added by me and that's what makes the film very disturbing and uncommercial – unsuccessful – but that was what I was proud of.

The film is about a crime – the nub of the film is an invitation to crime, something which tries to convince the audience that the crime would be a natural and absolutely justifiable solution to the problem of the leading characters and the *second* half of the film is a reproach to the public of "look what you wanted – how shameful that you wanted this ugly girl to be killed – look what it means". It has a cosmic dimension to kill a person and it's not just a piece of action; so the final message was very Dostoyevskian, let's say done in a very poor way, but it still has this intention.

Somebody says at the end that remorse is so heavy that punishment would bring freedom . . . I thought that this was the message which they *wanted* to bring to an American audience, not sufficiently aware that this was a wrong cannon to shoot that ball, that it was another kind of film. And it was not the kind of writing which could convince people, at least bring them to think about *my* thought. Nevertheless it is not enough to dismiss this film. It is one of the films least loved by me. If I have to throw the cans from my boat, probably this would be one of the first that I could get rid of . . .

Q:
Do you have a desire to make an efficient thriller or a Western or a film of any specific genre?

Zanussi:
Well, no – a genre film: if the genre structure may serve to say something I'd like to say, of course I would use it without hesitation. I haven't had the occasion yet and I wouldn't like to be trapped by 'genre' or kept within its limits; this doesn't interest me even when these genres are esteemed and respected highly; it is not my glass of Chianti and I am old enough to say I know what I like or dislike, where I'm good and where not.

So genre – especially the thriller as an experience of fear and of actual crime and tension – is something which I know probably far more about than most of the directors who talk about it on the screen. Just living here I'm far more familiar with tensions and pressures and extremely refined plots designed in order to trap an individual – I know a lot about it – so there *is* a lot of experience. And I think that this is something that Polanski brought from another period but from the same experience, and he's very good at telling people now what he knows metaphorically. I know the flexibility of Roman to go that far away using different stories and telling his own contents. There is no doubt – in *Chinatown* I recognized every bit of it as something we have lived through – never having been exposed to American corruption but knowing our own corruption . . .

So, I wouldn't be tempted to make a film which is only designed as a 'genre' film, but I would love to make a big film and probably a period picture is closest to something that I'm *likely* to do in future.

Q:
Will you go back to contemporary films and contemporary problems?

Zanussi:
Well, I *try* – I'm working quite a lot and have quite a few projects, in fact one of them in England which is very likely to be done this year. It is a contemporary project; you can imagine how hard it is for a foreigner to write a story which takes place in England – and I did I think receive from the Film Finance Corporation some development funds so it looks rather positive – with Channel 4. *'Paradigm'* was set in the 20s just because it was more suitable.

I have quite a few other projects, including stories about Eastern Europe, at least you call it 'Eastern'. You know we hate to be called Eastern bloc. We have to swallow some things which are the sad consequence of others' treaties. One never said 'Eastern Europe' before the war, it would have been quite inexplicable – so, I have another story about Polish women, adventurous women in their conquest of the West which is a contemporary story and is connected with many of my own observations of the abnormal muscle that people get when they leave the system in this country and go to fight against a society which is far less protected against such kinds of people. Probably the first generation of the steel barons and all these people who built American industry – they knew how to protect themselves. But not the grandsons who are innocent which these ladies are not. That is a very interesting clash. I have observed it you know in quite a few spectacular careers.

Q:
Where is that going to be set?

Zanussi:
In America – I hope so. This is one of the stories I have in mind.

Q:
When you made your films in the 1970s, they were seen by London critics as reflecting problems within Polish society at that point. Was that part of your conscious intention then and do you still see it as an exciting reason to make a film or as a rich source of stories? I am talking about contemporary problems which are tied to the moral choices people are forced to make. What about drug problems in Poland, for example?

Zanussi:
This is a symptom. There may be many reasons for widespread drinking and so on but my interest lies more on the other side. I am interested in, let's say, the existential perspective of our life. 'Morals' are a perspective which tests our freedom because the choice is the moment when our freedom is executed. We can't be free if we make no choices, no conscious choices or dramatic choices . . . so I am interested in choices – in moments where people may go left or right. These moments create drama in general and I hope that whatever describes my own society, if it is universal enough then it applies to another society where you will find the same choices everywhere even if they will act in a different way. The basis is the same. That is my goal. I am very angry when people watch my films abroad in order to learn something of Poland. Well – they like to interpret it this way; I prefer that they talk of these films to learn something about themselves. It is far more relevant. Our interest in exotic countries is always limited while our interest in ourselves is unlimited.

No, I'm not my own critic so I have to comply with all critics whatever they write because I depend on them enormously. I cannot afford to ignore them because in the kind of film making I attempt, critics are of crucial importance. Vincent

Canby in New York was able to delay my American career for ten years just because he gave me three negative reviews – at least one of them based on total ignorance from his side. It was in *Illumination* – he expressed some sort of divergence, believing that I must be ignorant myself in talking about science. *I* am a physicist and I must rebuff this accusation. I don't think that he is very up-to-date on what happens in science – but it was enough. One bad review and the film never opened, because of one man, who is a dictator – against his will I don't doubt but it is a social fact. It is the same in theatre.

Q:
Well, they are exceptionally powerful in America.

Zanussi:
Right. In London you have at least five critics who are not necessarily of the same opinion and that's very encouraging. Otherwise it's a big problem.

Q:
What about more direct responses? You sometimes promote your own films. What kind of response do you get?

Zanussi:
I am very cautious in talking about it, because I know that the promotion of films is a separate profession, a separate quality of an artist who may be great as the artist but not such a good promoter or the reverse. An artist promoting his work – a film director or a film actor – makes some kind of show and entertains the public . . . You may if you are good enough achieve a positive reaction with the audience for whatever product you bring just by the strength of the blackmail that you create, appearing for the screening before and after. I've seen it working quite often with other people. So I am fighting for my own warm reception but whenever I get it I

always suspect that maybe it is my good 'performance' and not necessarily my good film. Very seldom I participate in discussions incognito and that's the most interesting because then I see a more objective reaction from the public without any manipulation . . . it is highly interesting: if I make films it's because I am seeking contact, communication with other people.

Q:
Have you had any peculiar reactions? For example, have you taken your films to factories?

Zanussi:
Oh yes, quite a few . . . also quite a few in other countries. I was trying very hard to continue these meetings – in Poland I was really travelling around with all of my films and as part of the aspect I mentioned, I still believe that it is extremely interesting and necessary to be with your films and see these reactions. I was travelling from military concerns to milicja concerns to seminars for priests; I showed one of my films in a prison many years ago for juvenile delinquents. How extreme can you get? It was almost everything . . . in ministries and factories of course.

Q:
What was the delinquents' response to your films?

Zanussi:
Ah, they did not respond to the film at all. They did respond to my presence enormously; they realised that I had the kind of life they would like to have and they were only interested in knowing: what is the price? How do you get it? Especially since I was trying to tell them that this *was* conceivable; it was not given, I am not the son of a great producer, it is open for almost everybody and so on.

Q:
Did they get your message?

Zanussi:
I think so, yes. They were interested. There were a hundred questions . . . how to do it?

Q:
You mentioned some years back that you had an ambivalent attitude towards actors and actresses. You said something to the effect that these perfomers are essentially prostitutes and therefore you sometimes felt yourself to be a whoremonger.

Zanussi:
(*Laughs*) 'Prostitute' is a very impolite way to say it. Yes . . . it is an ugly metaphor but it is absolutely apt . . . I agree with it. Of course art is a sort of vivisection if you hate it enough or it is a sort of strip-tease done in public, something which is exhibition-istic and will remain like that. And I have inhibitions and am very embarrassed in doing it but I have a very deep need to do it, I want to justify it . . . I know that people are making just 'genre' films and entertaining the audience. They remain well protected by the group-genre . . . they're not artists, they're craftsmen. An artist is someone who tells something about himself.

Q:
What do you suppose actors do then? Do you respect their craft?

Zanussi:
In a way I learned to respect it because I met so many good, outstanding actors. I've worked with them and now I am meeting more and more, in foreign countries – incredible actors . . . It is a growing fascination. It is true that as a person brought up in a university and having a different life-style I don't feel very much need for actors who have a

natural tendency to abuse their craft in life. The craft is to imitate feelings and to create, to manipulate the public. I feel very often that they do it in life as well.

Q:
In personal relations?

Zanussi:
Oh yes, and that is very embarrassing to me. But still, I am fascinated . . .

Q:
Did you like working with Leslie Caron?

Zanussi:
Oh yes. I've worked quite a few times with her. I worked with Robert Powell – one of the most beautiful experiences of a director's relationship with an actor.

Q:
Going back to that Michalek interview we didn't quite get to the point. You mentioned that in your third year you filmed something that was rejected . . . that it was the reason you had to repeat a year at Lodz Film School.

Zanussi:
I had a very bad start in film making, on many levels. Later on when I made my first full feature, *The Structure of Crystals*, the film was totally dismissed by my production unit and – out of friendship – they considered putting this film on the shelf. They thought it would be better for me not to show it at all. It was a very, very delicate decision: the first feature which later on – for me – was quite successful. It still plays . . . which is rather unusual for a film that is fifteen years old. Then it was something new and fresh – the film was very 'undramatic' with an amateur actor in the lead part.

I remember the final suggestion of my colleagues which in a way was right. They said, make it as short as you can. I just cut it down to the shortest standard for a full-length feature which is one hour and seventeen minutes, something like that. It was exactly cut down with almost half of the film thrown away as useless. But then it worked quite well as quite a good film. Still it was on the edge of moral bankruptcy because I felt that I had done something so embarrassing, that I'd started off on the wrong foot right from the beginning. It was a very crucial moment.

Q:
Can we talk about film economy? Leslie Caron said that when you both met at a screening of Robert Altman's *The Wedding* you expressed horror at the wastage involved. You later said that both yourself and Wajda made a decision to be very efficient as far as shooting ratios, economics and keeping under budget were concerned. I saw *Potop* here some years ago and had the opposite impression. It seemed, well, you could use the army, you could use just about any kind of resource that would prove too expensive in the West.

Zanussi:
Yes, but with *Potop* it was not critical because there was a tremendous profit, even being so expensive a film, so it was alright. To make a big commercial film you're entitled to take some risk. My idea with Wajda was to westernise our production because we felt that as long as we made art films that were totally subsidised by the state we should feel like clients of the state – we should feel totally dependent on someone who's giving us this money. We could be spiritually independent yet economically we know that our whole existence depends upon the state, that is the Ministry. That was the moment when we said, no, if our films are relevant we must find sufficient support from the audience and on the other hand we don't

wish to be debtors of the state so we will try to make our films well, very inexpensively, to be sure that we are totally on top – on the red side. We are saying: we have a right to take loans from the state because we bring this money back.

I was very worried about it, especially with regard to our colleagues who are protégés of the state or the regime. They have been spending a tremendous amount of money and making heavy, propagandistic films that no-one wants to see later. So it was not so much against those people who made *Potop* but people whose films were never seen. They use big budgets and are heavily supported. They get all the green light from the government and then make lousy, heavy films that nobody watches. We wanted to say that that has nothing to do with us; we are not in the same position.

Q:
So it was a conscious choice for efficiency?

Zanussi:
Yes, just to be efficient. It is not that we believe cinema has to be commercial and we haven't gained financially from this. We regarded it as showing that our cinema is healthy, that the public wants us to make our films; this was particularly important. Also to change a certain mood because some of our older colleagues have the approach that many opera directors have; this slightly academic approach: I am a great academician, I am somebody, I am a national treasure so I have to be subsidised, that is the nature of my existence . . . which allowed them to make films slowly, heavily. Even if they were not good they were always defending themselves saying, we have the right to do this.

Q:
Is a low shooting ratio very general?

Zanussi:
A low shooting ratio is very important because it concerns something that is most painful, our raw material: the negative which we're short of. So we must make films on Eastman Kodak. You know, some countries like Romania – I've just come back from there – they're shooting in black-and-white. They cannot afford colour. They were doing films in colour but not anymore and they have quite a big output – about thirty films a year.

Q:
Amazing, because in the UK it's un-economic to shoot in black-and-white just now.

Zanussi:
When I made *The Imperative* – it's mostly in black-and-white – I had a very bad time because it was a free artistic decision; it was so hard to find a lab. Still, the low shooting ratio is just part of our misery. We're willing to make all our films in colour, at least almost all of them, at a very low shooting ratio. In a film with Leslie Caron it was 'one shot'. If there was something wrong with the shot I had to depend on some reverse angles to cover. It was a completely different technique of shooting. One has to be very aware. Also, in this film I was hurried enormously, having a very clumsy production house. We were not allowed to reshoot. With all my other problems I had to make it in, I think, seven shooting days which is quite low.

Q:
How long did *The Year of the Quiet Sun* take to make?

Zanussi:
We were not that rushed so we shot it within two months. I think we had thirty-six or seven shooting days which was quite generous. I didn't need any more

and could have done it faster but there was no particular need to rush.

Q:
When it was screened at the London Film Festival a questioner referred to a scene where the mass grave of airforce pilots was dug up. To him it alluded to 'Katyn'. Was it in fact to do with the pilots from the story of *The Great Escape*?

Zanussi:
Yes. *The Great Escape* was the biggest story of this sort. There were several others which were smaller affairs. The graves of the pilots in *The Great Escape* were not found. A couple of them were found but they were all shot individually and buried in different places.

Q:
In the movie version of *The Great Escape* the pilots were all machine-gunned together.

Zanussi:
Right. But there were others who were shot together. So all this is on the edge of being something specific and not specific. This happened in the last stage of the war; but most suggestions were taken from *The Great Escape*. And then the rest from the graves that were found in the late 50s, not that it matters – there were some other graves that were as big but they were mixed with allied and Russian soldiers shot together. There were several mys-teries that the Germans were trying to cover up in the Western part . . . the part that was German before the war.

Q:
What about the film *Golem* made by your unit? Is that new?

Zanussi:
Golem is relatively young or new; it was shot five or six years ago and Piotr Szulkin, the director, is very active with a very

good film now – *two* films shot recently. In fact I recommend that you see Kieslowski's new film *Without End*. It may be really difficult but perhaps he can pull a string for you. That is really an outstanding film. It was produced in my unit and I am very proud of it. It took us months to liberate it – a story set at the time of martial law. It is about the trial of a worker who is accused of inciting strikes against Jaruzelski and he very openly says this is right, this is what he was trying to do. There are several lawyers who have different techniques on how to get him out of jail and obviously every technique is backed by a different philosophy, different values, what is good and bad and what is not. You have in the film a very small English episode – the same actor I brought over from Britain for *The Year of the Quiet Sun*: Danny Webb. He appears in this film in a role which is a typical part for a foreigner – somebody staying at the Victoria Hotel.

Q:
You have done some theatre work, haven't you? Do you interchange much between the two disciplines?

Zanussi:
I've only done one play in Poland which was *One Flew Over the Cuckoo's Nest*. Then I produced *Slaughterhouse* by Mrozek the Polish writer, in Milan, then I did two English plays in German: *Night and Day* by Tom Stoppard and *Duet for One* by Tom Kempinski at the State Theatre in Bonn. I wanted to do the latter with Leslie Caron in Paris but I was unavailable and somebody else took the option using another actress.

Q:
You made a film with the Pope as the subject. It stars Sam Neill but I was under the impression that the film was made as a documentary.

Zanussi:
You know, in some languages the word 'documentary' describes exactly what I have done . . . that is a fiction about a real subject, which is partly nonsense. It has some documentary sequences in it, like forty minutes, and the rest is obviously fiction. You don't expect the pictures to be the real thing. Still they watch it and say, oh it's a documentary. There is a script of the film published in English.

Q:
It was all filmed in Poland?

Zanussi:
Yes. And some at the Vatican, but very little. In the region of Cracow there was a funny scene where an American satellite detected that there were Soviet tanks, in the Old Town. And they thought maybe now there was an invasion. One sequence I repeated in *The Year of the Quiet Sun*. I actually took a negative from the Pope film – the producer gave it to me, so two shots were saved. There was more film on Poland and about times in the Stalinist period . . .

Q:
I wonder finally if you could tell me something about the actor who played Franciszek in *Illumination*?

Zanussi:
Oh yes, Stanislaw Latallo. It was very tragic because he died just a year after the film was completed and his own life-story is so close to that in the film in a way. He was my student.

Q:
Training to be a director?

Zanussi:
Yes. He first trained as a cameraman, then he was trained as a director. In fact he made two films on which I served as

advisor. I wanted him on my crew; he was meant to be a camera assistant and ended up being the actor.

Q:
He had quite a remarkable screen face.

Zanussi:
Yes. His voice was not very good, not trained, but he had a very good presence. He had a very strong personality and the biggest trial in the film was *his* trial, which was quite moving. After a very big row his wife abandoned him. He had a hard time – all this is real life – and she went to join her parents who were Jewish emigrants in Germany. With a group of people who were friends we had to give some sort of guarantee to the government that he would come back. They granted him a passport to leave Poland, which is usually very difficult to obtain . . . Nevertheless he didn't manage to convince his wife to come back and he lost his son, which was very dramatic. The German court gave the child to the mother. And being depressed by this turn of events he joined a Himalaya expedition.

I called a friend of mine who was the boss of this expedition to warn him that Latallo was not an experienced climber. And besides it is very dangerous to take somebody in that state of mind. Nevertheless, he proved that he was competent and he was to be the cameraman on this expedition . . . the circumstances under which he was found, frozen to death, indicate that it happened because he cared for somebody else who was thought to be lost and who in fact survived. It is very moving and full of pathos, the end of his life. There was a long investigation to establish the causes and there was somebody accused of making an error in not telling him that he was refused permission to come . . .

Q:
Perhaps I could press you finally for some off-the-cuff anecdotes.

Zanussi:
Hmmm. You know *Sun* was the first big international co-production being done in Poland after the martial law. It was made with Americans and created a special kind of excitement around it. We obtained for the production a walkie-talkie which is considered, like a Xerox machine, equal to a machine gun – the most dangerous devices you can use. So we had two policemen in charge of this and all the time they had it in their own hands and were supervising and watching for private conversations. I asked my collaborators, hundreds of times, to behave and talk strictly in a decent manner. But we often had to talk to the American actor and sometimes to Danny Webb on the walkie-talkie.

Eventually, after all these precautions about foreign NATO members present in military uniforms on Polish territory, we discovered that we were on the same frequency as the Soviets who were just storing some rockets in the forest close to the film's location. So there were some conversations in English and some in Russian on the same frequency. It was probably highly secret. Then somebody reacted and the walkie-talkie was sequestered. We were not allowed to use it anymore without explanation – until somebody discovered that the 'interference' was in fact a Russian voice.

Wajda can tell you some stories about his fights with the censors which are endless.

Do you know the story of my *Camouflage*? This was not a political film but created a political reaction. You know even the military government banned it at the beginning. For a year it was on the newly-banned list of films, which makes

poster for Camouflage

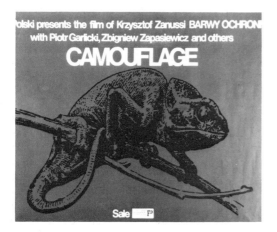

me very proud. They banned *Man of Marble, Man of Iron, Camouflage* and two or three others as deeply subversive . . . There is always a question that all Western journalists ask: how is it possible that the government allows things which are considered anti-governmental? It is the sort of certification that the government has provided. Somebody who has signed the film, who has signed the script and given it the OK will be motivated to fight for the reputation of the film saying, the film *is* OK because I signed it and I'm not a fool; I haven't been fooled by the director! So they always declare for your side even though they hate you.

In the case of this film one of the very high-ranking government officials called on me and asked me to make some cuts because one of the ladies in the film, an actress, was a founder of the movement for the defence of the workers, so her appearance was considered something particularly painful. Well, I said, I am going to compromise. (I am a realist and I know that the other side must have some victories) so I said, alright, though I think it's unfair. I will cut some but not all of it.

Then we started the negotiation: he said, well, you can't have her portraits. I said, all right, the close-ups will go but I will leave the medium-shots. He said, all right but – ah – could you tell me, what's a medium-shot? I made a drawing on his desk and he said, oh that's a portrait! In Rembrandt you have portraits down to your belt. And I said, no, in film *this* is a portrait and he said, oh, you never make portraits like that; *this* is a portrait and you're trying to deceive me. I said no. He said, oh no, it won't do; the medium-shots are absolutely unacceptable. So I said, all that is left are American shots. He said, American? . . . alright, leave in the medium . . . So these are the arguments in each film. Somebody is always cutting something . . .

In *The Contract* the trouble is I cut away a small bit with Joanna Pacula, the later star of *Gorki Park*. We had a lovely small scene but because it was wrong for the film I cut it. She was a nurse in the hospital where the man works and there is a very strong hint that she is his lover – a pretty, young, aggressive nurse. Unfortunately I cut her away. Now she's more famous than any other actress here . . .

(*On a door-handle in the flat which Zanussi shares with his mother hangs a clean, white truncheon – objet d'art of the milicja. He swung it back and forth like a pendulum and grinned: "a sign of the times".*)

Postscript

At a conference of the Film Makers' Association during the 1985 feature film festival in Gdansk, Janusz Zaorski surprised his colleagues by proposing an additional (ninth) major film making group. He contended that, whilst the Irzykowski Studio (initially a co-operative, now directed by an appointee of the Ministry of Culture) was a valuable stepping stone or 'experimental' outlet for directors, the industry needed such a group on a higher professional plane. He proposed *Dom* (house), with himself at its head, as a new unit to fill that gap.

Dom was officially approved and formed at the end of April 1986, comprising Zaorski as chief, plus seven young directors: Wieslaw Saniewski, Radoslaw Piwowarski, Krzysztof Magowski, Maciej Wojtyszko, Jan Kidawa-Blonski, Robert Glinski and Piotr Lazarakiwicz. It was allocated a budget for two theatrical features in 1986. From 1987 it is to be funded on a par with the eight other members of the Zespoly Filmowe. *Dom* immediately hired three eminent literary researchers to assess the right projects – Edward Zebrowski, Filip Bajon and Maciej Wojtyszko – and set about scouting Poland for a small town "somewhere in the south" as a suitable location for its feature début, *I Love Movies* (*Kocham Kino*), scheduled to commence shooting in September 1986.

Whereas most film groups have offices in Pulawska Street, adjacent to the Filmoteka archives, *Dom* occupies space alongside the Irzykowski Studio whose work it will complement in the production of features, half-hour shorts, videos ('experimental' or for clients) and so on.

Zaorski's own *Boden Lake* (*Jeziora Bodenskiego*), which he directed as a member of *Perspektywa*, played at the summer festival in Lagow and then at the festivals of Locano (Italy) and Gdansk in 1986. Andrzej Wajda's *A History of Romance*, from a Tadeusz Konwicki story, is the director's first all-Polish production for some years. Set in Wilno in Konwicki's native Lithuania during August 1939, the film comprises a cast of unknowns, "fresh new faces right out of acting school". Konwicki himself speaks the narration. It also played at Gdansk in September 1986.

The continuing crisis in the economy is reflected by a downturn in feature films, from forty in 1985 to thirty in 1986, ignoring those made for television.

Chronology of Polish cinema

1892-94: Nearly a century since the Third Partition (1795) wiped Poland off the map. Polish Socialist Party (PPS) formed in 1892, led by Limanowski. Jozef Pilsudski, PPS member, writes and prints *Robotnik* (*The Worker*), a clandestine periodical. Poles invent 'living photography': Piotr Lebiedzinski, Jan and Jozef Poplawski and Kazimierz Proszynski all build ingenious devices. Proszynski, with his 'pleograph', shoots several fiction and documentary shorts. The country is partitioned between Austria (Cracow), Russia (Warsaw, Lodz) and Germany (Gdansk, Poznan, etc.).

1895: Birth of cinematography with the Lumières.

1896: First public screenings in Poland of the 'Cinématographe Lumière' in Cracow (November 14), Warsaw and Lodz.

1897: Boleslaw Matuszewski, Polish cameraman, pioneers medical cinematography and shoots newsreels for the Lumières throughout Europe.

1898: Matuszewski publishes *Une Nouvelle Source de l'Histoire; La Photographie Animée* in Paris – the first ever theoretical summary of film. He actively promotes film archives.

1899: First permanent cinema, in Lodz.

1902: First active film studio – Towarzystow Udzialowe 'Pleograf' – which shoots and distributes short films starring Warsaw actors.

1905: Nobel prize for literature awarded to Henryk Sienkiewicz.

1905-07: Revolutionary activity in Poland.

1908: First Polish feature: *Anthony in the Capital* by Pathé cameraman Jozef Meyer, starring popular comic, Antoni Fertner.

1909: Aleksander Hertz, Polish film mogul, founds Sfinks studio which will produce many features up to 1939.

1911: First literature adaptation: *The Story of Sin* from Stefan Zeromski, by Antoni Bednarczyk. Several companies in business. Influence of the French Film D'Art movement – using outstanding actors in classic literary works. Film studio Kooperatywa Artystow uses leading actors from Teatr Rosmaitosci in Warsaw.

1913-14: First film periodicals: *Scena i Ekran* (Lwow) and *Kinoteatr i Sport* (Warsaw).

1914-18: First World War. Sfinks the only company in operation. Hertz establishes a group of stars: Pola Negri, Mia Mara, Kazimierza Junosza-Stepowski, Jozef Wegrzyn. Negri's screen début in *Slave of Passion*.

Pilsudski forms the Polish Legions (1914). The Germans occupy Warsaw in the summer of 1915. The country is split into two occupied zones. Writer Sienkiewicz and pianist/composer Ignacy Paderewski organise committee for Polish war victims and push Poland's cause for independence. *The Warsaw Secret Police, The Czar's Favourite* and *The Czarina*, all by Aleksander Hertz. First film cartoon appears in 1916.

November 11 1918: Poland becomes a state, after 124 years of oblivion, with Pilsudski as head.

1919: Number of cinemas approximately 400. Formation of the Film Industry Alliance which produces 21 features and 61 shorts. Ignacy Paderewski becomes Prime Minister in January; resigns December.

1920: First films on the theme of

independence. The Polish-Russian war, ending in the Treaty of Riga (1921).

1922: American films begin to dominate the market. *The Shot,* directed by Hertz, launches Jadwiga Smosarska: the first major star in the new state. Actor/director Wiktor Bieganski breaks with the predominant theatricality in his more cinematic *Abyss of Repentance* and *Jealousy.* Adaptation of Wl. Reymont's *The Peasants* by Eugeniusz Modzelewski. Pilsudski abdicates; government instability.

1924: Literary critic Karol Irzykowski publishes *The Tenth Muse,* one of the first major books on the aesthetics of film. His ideas apply well beyond the silent cinema. Nobel prize for literature to Wladyslaw Reymont.

1925: Production chiefly of farces, melodramas and sensational movies, notably Bieganski's *The Vampires of Warsaw* and Henryk Szaro's *One of the 36.* 426 cinemas. 9 Polish features produced.

1926: Smosarska makes an impact in *Leprosy* by Edward Puchalski. Henryk Szaro's *The Red Clown.* May 12: 300 deaths in a coup d'état – Pilsudski dictates behind a puppet head of state.

1927: Former critic Leon Trystan becomes director. Notable débuts: *The Revolt of Blood and Iron* and *Szamota's Mistress.* Newsreel production coalesces into the official body PAT. Ryszard Ordynski directs *Tomb of an Unknown Soldier.*

1928: Top inter-war director Jozef Lejtes makes *Hurricane* on the 1863 Warsaw Uprising. *The Dot on the I's* (Juliusz Gardan), *Early Spring* (Szaro) and Ordynski's adaptation of the Mickiewicz poem, *Pan Tadeusz* – typical of a larger group of poor screen transpositions of 'high literature'.

1929-30: 827 cinemas. Around 17 features per year. 1929 noted for sensational and erotic films. Avant-garde group of theorists and film makers formed, registered later as START – founded by Eugeniusz Cekalski, Stanislaw Wohl, Wanda Jakubowska, Tadeusz Kowalski and Jerzy Zarzycki; later joined by Jerzy Toeplitz, Jerzy Bossak and Aleksander Ford. It fights for the "socially useful" film typified by the shorts made by Ford, Cekalski and Zarzycki. Michal Waszynski makes *Cult of the Flesh* in Vienna, hyped as the first Polish sound film projected with a phonograph record.

1930: Impact of Constructivism and the avant-garde: Stefan and Franciszka Themerson produce *The Chemist.* Numerous literary adaptations, including Gabriela Zapolska's *The Morality of Mrs Dulska,* characterised by contemporary social critique: the first talkie wholly produced in the country. Establishment of the Main Office for . Propaganda and Educational Films, concurrent with many film makers' efforts along these lines. Appearance of the first popular film weekly, *Kino,* and of the more serious periodical, *Film News.*

1931: Decline in production to 10 features per annum. First export success: Jan Nowina-Przybylski's *Roughneck,* sold to 13 countries. Polish census: 32 million inhabitants, including 10 million "minorities" (Ukrainians, Bielorussians, Germans, Jews etc.).

1932: Critical and public success of Ford's second feature, *Legion of the Streets,* said to be a forerunner of 'neorealism'. The Themersons produce *Europa.* Lejtes's *Wild Fields.* First sound cartoon by Jan Jarosz. Non-aggression pact with the USSR.

1933: Ford's *Sabra*, shot in Palestine – disappoints at the box-office. Adam Krzeptowski's *White Track*, the first Polish entrant in the Venice International Film Festival. Successful Polish/Czech co-production, *Twelve Chairs* by Waszynski and Fric, starring the popular comic, Adolf Dymsza. Formation of the Association of Short Film Producers. Hitler elected Chancellor of the Third Reich (January).

1934: Non-aggression pact between Poland and Germany (January). Formation of the Main Council of the Polish Film Industry to govern all matters on Polish film activity, home or abroad. First dubbing of foreign movies into Polish. *How About Young Lucyna* by Gardan, typical comedy product with leading popular stars such as Smosarska and Eugeniusz Bodo. *The Young Forest* from Lejtes. Ford's *Awakening*.

1935: Pilsudski dies (May 12). The military asserts control ("Government of the Colonels"). First international festival awards: in Moscow for Lejtes's *The Young Forest* and at Venice for his *Day of the Great Adventure*. START disbands.

1936: Lejtes's ambitious adaptation of Zeromski's *Roza*. Ford's ciné reportage, *The Road of Youth*, about a sanatorium for children. Venice festival award for Cekalski and Wohl's *Three Etudes*. Formation of the Association of Film Artists and Technicians.

1937: Record level of production (27 features, 102 shorts). 769 cinemas. 429 foreign movies are shown. Ford and Zarzycki direct *People of the Vistula*. Jules Gardan's *Halka*, from Moniuszko's opera. Lejtes's *The Young Ladies of Nowolipki*. Creation of the Co-operative of Film Authors (Spoldzielni Autorow Filmowych – SAF). Polish-American Joseph Green stimulates a dynamic Yiddish film industry. Michal Waszynski's *The Dybbuk*.

1938: First and only film realised by SAF: *Fears* by Cekalski and Karol Szolowski. Liquidation of Polish Communists by the political police in Moscow.

1939: Wanda Jakubowska's *On the Banks of the Niemen*. Leonard Buczkowski's *White Negro*. Other features interrupted by war.

1939-45: Germany invades Poland (September 1 1939). The Soviets invade the Eastern territories (September 17). Total occupation and partition of Poland.

American documentarist Herbert Kline (in Poland at the time of invasion) shoots and smuggles out film for *Lights Out Over Europe*, shown worldwide in 1940. Auschwitz created as a concentration camp (1940) in tandem with Jewish city ghettos. Bohdziewicz and Zarzycki establish 'flying courses' on film making and camera work. Cekalski goes to Great Britain, then in 1943 to New York, where he makes several shorts for the Polish Information Film Centre. The Polish Army Film Command established in the USSR (1943) under the helm of Ford, along with Bossak, Wohl, A and Wl. Forbert and Ludwik Perski. Katyn (1943): mass graves of 4-5000 Polish officers found by the Germans in retreat out of Russia.

Warsaw Ghetto Uprising (April 19-May 6 1943). Bossak and Ford film *Majdanek*. With the support of the Red Army, new Polish government (the Polish Committee for National Liberation) established at Lublin (July 21 1944), then in Warsaw. Warsaw Uprising (August 1-October 2 1944): 90% of the city destroyed. Hopes of Home Army to assert political control dashed. Warsaw liberated January 1945. Legal government, which fled to Paris, then London, powerless to combat Soviet-backed 'provisional government'. Power struggles and near civil war continue through to 1947.

Practically all cinemas, all technical houses and facilities destroyed or put out of action. Decimation of Poland's film personnel. Only a few dozen of all the artists and technicians survive the war.

Film course established in Cracow by Bohdziewicz and Wohl. Wohl appointed to replenish equipment for a film making industry. Film Polski formed (November 13). Nationalisation administered by Ford and other film artists. 409 working cinemas.

1945-47: Poland shifts west. Soviets retain Eastern territory. Over four million Poles re-settle into an often lawless West.

1946: First film production house established in a converted sports hall in Lodz. Cartoon film studio established at Katowice, later to move to Wisla, then Bielsko Biala in 1956. First appearance of the periodical *Film*. Brzozowski's short, *Wieliczka*, awarded at Cannes. Formation of the Film Critics Club which becomes a member of the International Federation of the Film Press (FIPRESCI).

1947: L Buczkowski's *Forbidden Songs*, the first post-war feature, holds the box-office record for well over the next decade. The Cracow film course moves to Lodz, still under Bohdziewicz. Cekalski makes *The Cornfields*. Bossak's documentary, *The Flood*, awarded at Cannes.

1948: Hardening of Stalin-influenced government control under Bierut. Deputy Gomulka deposed from office. Wanda Jakubowska's *The Last Stage*. Ford makes *Border Street/That Others May Live*. Wyszomirski and Wohl make *Two Hours*, withheld and re-edited in 1957. National Higher Film School established at Lodz with Jerzy Toeplitz as rector.

1949: Noted comedy, *The Treasure*, by Buczkowski. Wisla Conference spells out "socialist-realism" as applied to the arts. Documentary Film Studio established in Warsaw.

1950: *The Warsaw Robinson Crusoe* by Jerzy Zarzycki, a psychological drama turned into the 'liberation of Warsaw' film, *Unvanquished City*. 1376 cinemas. 4 features and 203 shorts premièred. 'Stakhanovism' (shockworker heroism, seen in *Man of Marble*) introduced in the mines and at Nowa Huta.

1951: Ford's *The Young Chopin*. First foreign post-war film to be dubbed into Polish at Lodz. First show-trial of high officers accused of treason. Gomulka arrested and stripped of his party titles. *The Commune*, directed by Jerzy Kawalerowicz and Kazimierz Sumerski.

1953: Establishment of feature film studio at Wroclaw. Primate of Poland, Cardinal Wyszynski, interned in a monastery. Show-trials continue. Stalin dies (March 6). Andrzej Munk makes documentary, *Kolejarskie Slowo*.

1954: Ford's *Five Boys from Barska Street*. Kawalerowicz's *A Night of Remembrance* and *Under the Phrygian Star*. First award for a Polish cartoon, at the Karlovy Vary Festival, for *Little Billy Goat*. First film projection for television.

1955: Andrzej Wajda's début, *A Generation*. Munk's semi-feature, *Men of the Blue Cross*. The first 'Black documentaries' appear, such as *Look Out, Hooligans!* by Hoffman and Skorzewski. Number of cinemas: 2672. 8 features and 195 shorts premièred.

1956: Kawalerowicz's *The Shadow*, from a story by A Scibor-Rilski. Revolutionary formation of eight 'zespoly' or autonomous production teams. Central Bureau of Cinematography liquidated, replaced by the Main Board of Cinematography under the Ministry of Culture and Arts. Scripts and artistic decisions no longer dictated from above. Twentieth Party Congress of the Soviet Communist Party denounces the crimes of Stalin. Polish chief Bierut dies of shock or suicide. June riots in Poznan. Gomulka recalled, elected Head of State. The Polish 'October'; the dropping of censorship; farm collectivisation shelved.

1957 : Wajda's *Kanal*. Munk's *Man on the Track*. Kawalerowicz's *The Real End of the War*.

1958: Wajda's *Ashes and Diamonds*. Munk's *Eroica*. Tadeusz Konwicki's début, *The Last Day of Summer*. Wojciech Has's double début, *The Noose* and *Farewells*. Chmielewski's *Eve Wants to Sleep*. Studia Miniatur Filmowych, the animation film studio, established in Warsaw. 'Angry' young writer, Marek Hlasko, exiles himself in Berlin. Ford's film of his novel, *The Eighth Day of the Week,* shelved.

1959: Kawalerowicz's *Night Train*. Kazimierz Kutz's *Cross of Valour*.

1960: Munk's *Bad Luck*. Wajda's *Innocent Sorcerers*. Ford's expensive epic, *The Teutonic Knights*.

1961: *Mother Joan of the Angels* from Kawalerowicz. Wajda's *Samson*. Has's *Farewell Youth*. Kutz's *Panic on a Train*. Stanislaw Rozewicz's *Birth Certificate*. Arrest of Henryk Holland (ex-Home Army, father of Agnieszka Holland): he is discovered dead. Andrzej Munk dies in a car crash.

1962: Roman Polanski's first feature, *Knife in the Water. Gangsters and Philanthropists*

from Jerzy Hoffman and Edward Skorzewski.

1963: Munk's *The Passenger*, posthumously finished by colleague Witold Lesiewicz. Wojciech Has's *How To Be Loved*. Kutz's *The Silence*. Bossak's documentary, *Requiem for 500 000*. Daniel Szczechura's cartoon, *The Armchair*.

1964: Has's ambitious adaptation of Count Potocki's *The Saragossa Manuscript*. Ford's *The First Day of Freedom*. Ewa and Czeslaw Petelski's *The Tout*.

1965: Jerzy Skolimowski's début, *Rysopis*, extracted from his film school exercises. Wajda's black-and-white epic, *Ashes*. Konwicki's *Salto*. Skolimowski's *Walkover*. Janusz Morgenstern's *Life Begins Again*.

1966: Kawalerowicz's costly epic, *The Pharaoh*. Skolimowski's *The Barrier*. *Marie and Napoleon*, Buczkowski's last film.

1967: Rozewicz's *Westerplatte*. Henryk Kluba's *The Thin Man and the Others*. Janusz Majewski's *The Sub-Tenant*. Skolimowski's *Hands Up!* shelved until its showing at Gdansk in 1981. Tragic death of Cybulski under a train.

1968: Anti-Semitic (or anti-Zionist) campaigns against the Jewish community results in departure of 20 000 Jews from Poland: symptom of power struggle within the PUWP. Jerzy Toeplitz, Jerzy Bossak and Aleksander Ford lose their administrative posts as part of larger bureaucratic reforms. Ford emigrates. Student manifestations; Gomulka barely retains power. Number of film units now six. Has's *The Doll*. Witold Leszczynski's début, *Life of Matthew*. Wajda's sci-fi comedy, *Roly Poly*, plus his tribute to Cybulski, *Everything for Sale*.

1969: Wajda's *Landscape After Battle*. Zanussi's *The Structure of Crystals*. Hoffman's epic, *Pan Wolodyjowski*. Kutz's *The Salt of the Black Earth*. Death of Bogumil Kobiela in a car accident (July 10).

1970-80: Series of innovative documentaries – predominantly social critiques and screened from the public view – by the 'descendants' of Andrzej Munk: Kieslowski, Lozinski, Wiszniewski, Piwowski and others.

1970: Andrzej Zulawski's *The Third Part of the Night*. Marek Piwowski's *The Cruise*. Andrzej Kondratiuk's *A Hole in the Ground*. December 7: mutual recognition of postwar border between (West) Germany and Poland. December 14-20: a bloody week of workers' riots and strikes in the northern ports in response to stiff food-price increases. Military intervention, many deaths. Edward Gierek replaces Gomulka as Chief of State. Death of Antoni Bohdziewicz (October 20). First national feature film festival at Lagow.

1971: Zanussi's *Family Life*, introducing Maja Komorowska. Zulawski's *The Devil*, never released. Andrzej Trzos-Rastawiecki's *The Leper*. Zanussi's improvised short, *Behind the Wall*.

1972: Wajda's *The Wedding*. Zebrowski's *Salvation*. New cinema reforms - new groups, or 'zespoly'. Gierek promotes a consumer-orientated Poland and begins borrowing large sums from the West.

1973: Has's *The Hourglass*. Zanussi's *Illumination*. Poreba's *Major Hubal*.

1974: Pol-Tel (television body) and Cracow's Animation Film Studio established. Hoffman's blockbuster, *The Deluge*. Trzos-Rawiecki's *Story of a Crime*. Krauze's *The Finger of God*.

Zanussi's *Quarterly Balance*. First Gdansk feature film festival. Death of Wiktor Bieganski.

1975: Wajda's *Land of Promise*. Borowczyk's *The Story of Sin*. Majewski's *Hotel Pacific*. Kieslowski's *Personel*.

1976: Kieslowski's *The Scar*, ushering in the 'Cinema of Moral Anxiety'. Wajda's *The Shadow Line*. Piwowski's *Foul Play*. Strikes at Radom and Ursus (June), followed by arrests and repression. Formation of KOR (Committee for the Defence of Victimised Workers) – first major co-operation of workers with intellectuals.

1977: Wajda's landmark, *Man of Marble*, introducing Krystyna Janda. Zanussi's *Camouflage*. Zulawski's *The Silver Globe*, stopped in the middle of shooting. Majewski's *The Gorgon Affair*, introducing Ewa Dalkowska. Creation of clandestine courses, mushrooming of underground press: *Robotnik* appears, autumn.

1978: Kawalerowicz's *Death of a President*. Wajda's *Without Anaesthesia*. Kijowski's *The Index*, shelved until 1981. Feliks Falk's *Top Dog*. Zaorski's *Room with a Sea View*. Karol Wojtila, archbishop of Cracow, becomes Pope – first non-Italian for many centuries. Formation of independent trade unions (Katowice).

1979: Pope visits Poland (June 2-12) – national euphoria, incalculable impact. Mass commemoration at Gdansk for workers of 1970. Kieslowski's *Camera Buff*, top prize-winner at Moscow Film Festival. Wajda's *The Young Ladies of Wilko*. Filip Bajon's *Aria for an Athlete*. *Two Women* by Bugajski and Dymek. Marczewski's *Nightmares*.

1980: Agnieszka Holland's début, *Provincial Actors*. Kutz's *The Beads of the*

Rosary. Zanussi's double, *The Constant Factor* and *The Contract*. Piotr Szulkin's *Golem*. Barbara Sass's *Without Love*. Summer strikes in response to stiff food-price rises – including strike in Gdansk shipyards. Enter Lech Walesa. Kania replaces Gierek (September 7). Solidarity registered on September 24 by Warsaw tribunal. First legal strike in any Communist bloc country. Inauguration in Gdansk (December 17) of monument to the slain workers of 1970.

1981: Wajda's *Man of Iron* wins Palm D'Or prize at Cannes. Holland's *The Fever*. Documentaries: *Workers 80* and Tomasz Pobog-Malinowski's *100 Days*. Marczewski's *Shivers*. Machulski's comedy début, *Va Bank*. Janusz Morgenstern's *A Smaller Sky*. Gomulka dies (January). Rising tensions; stalemate between authorities and union. Jaruzelski replaces Kania (October). Coup d'état on December 13. Jaruzelski imposes martial law. Arrest and internment of Solidarity activists and others, including its leader, Walesa. Irzykowski Studio founded.

1982: 2nd anniversary of the "Gdansk Accords" – countrywide demonstrations, 4050 arrests, five deaths. Grave economic crisis, food shortages. Kawalerowicz's *Austeria*. Zanussi's *The Unapproachables* (German). Wajda's *Danton* (France). Ryszard Bugajski's *The Interrogation*, a confrontation with the Stalinist years, totally banned. Sylwester Checinksi's *The Great Shar*.

1983: Krauze's fresh comedy, *Weather Forecast* (shelved). Machulski's smash hit, *Sexmission*. Wajda's *A Love in Germany*. Michal Tarkowski's *Koncert*. Waldemar Dziki's *Postcard from a Journey*. Zaorski's *Mother of Kings* (shelved). Nobel Peace Prize to Lech Walesa. Second visit by Pope John Paul II.

1984: 9th Gdansk feature film festival. Zanussi's *The Year of the Quiet Sun*. Roman Wionczek's anti-Solidarity *Dignity*. Brutal abduction and murder of popular Warsaw priest, Father Jerzy Popieluszko.

1985: Radoslaw Piwowarski's Beatle-years comedy, *Yesterday*. Wieslaw Saniewski's *Custody*. Zaorski's farce, *The Baritone*. Szulkin's *O-Bi, O-Ba, The End of Civilization*. Machulski's *Va Bank II*. Trial and sentence of Popieluszko's killers – shades of a Polish Watergate. Death of Stanislaw Wohl.

1986: Wajda's *A History of Romance*. Zaorski's *Lake Boden*. Szulkin's 'contemporary' sci-fi, *Ga Ga*. Addition of new group, *Dom*, headed by Zaorski, to fill gap for younger directors – complementing the work of the Irzykowski Studio. Continual economic problems. Downturn in theatrical features to 30 per annum. 11th Gdansk feature film festival (September).

Bibliography

The following serves as a list of books consulted and as a starting point for further reading.

A History of Poland O Halecki (Routledge and Kegan Paul 1978)

An Outline History of Polish Culture from the Jagiellonian University, Krakow (Interpress, Warsaw 1984)

Jan Lenica, Le Cinéma ed. Jean Loup Passek (Centre Georges Pompidou, Paris 1980)

Twenty Years of Polish Cinema (Art and Film Publishers, Warsaw 1969)

Poland Through the Ages M Golawski (Orbis, London 1971)

Ashes and Diamonds/A Generation/Kanal: The Wajda Trilogy (Lorrimer Publishing, London 1973)

Polish Film special issue (1982)

Eastern Europe, An Illustrated Guide Nina Hibbin (A Zwemmer and Co, London and A S Barnes and Co, New York 1969)

The Road to Gdansk, Poland and the USSR Daniel Singer (Monthly Review Press, New York and London 1981)

W Starym Polskim Kinie Stanislaw Janicki (Krajowa Agencja Wydawnicza, Warsaw 1985)

Starewicz 1882-1965 37th Edinburgh International Film Festival (Filmhouse, Edinburgh 1983)

La Pologne, Un Pays dans la Tête Annie Daubenton (Nouvelle Société des Editions Encre, Paris 1984)

Le Nouveau Cinéma Polonais ed. Jean-Pierre Brossard (33rd International Film Festival at Locarno 1980)

The Polish August Neal Ascherson (Penguin Books/Allen Lane 1981)

Sobieski, King of Poland Otton Laskowski (Polish Library, Glasgow 1944)

Poland: A Handbook (Interpress Publishers, Warsaw 1977)

The Poles Stewart Steven (Collins Harvill, London 1982)

The Black Book of Polish Censorship trans. and ed. Jane Leftwich Curry (Vintage Books/Random House, New York 1984)

O Zbigniewie Cybulskim (Art and Film Publishers/Wydawnictwa Artystyczne i Filmowe Warszawe 1969)

Silex no. 25 "Polonaises" (1983)

Andrzej Wajda Boleslaw Michalek (Tantivy Press, London 1973)

A Change of Tack: Making The Shadow Line Boleslaw Sulik (British Film Institute 1976)

L'Avant Scène du Cinéma no. 317/318 (1983)

Cinéaste no. 3 (1984)

Image et Son nos. 136/137 (1961) and 170/171 (1964)

Polish Cinema Jacek Fuksiewicz (Interpress, Warsaw 1973)

L'Enseignement de la Réalisation (Centre International de Liaison des Ecoles du Cinéma et de la Télévision, Paris 1958)

The Long View Basil Wright (Secker & Warburg, London 1974)

Memoirs of a Star Pola Negri (Doubleday, New York 1970)

Roman Roman Polanski (Pan Books, London 1985)

La Cinématographie en Pologne 1895-1900 Wladyslaw Banaszkiewicz (Centralne Archiwum Filmowe, Warsaw 1956)

Index

Bold type indicates main entry; italic type indicates still.

X

Y

Z